Criminal Justice
Recent Scholarship

Edited by
Nicholas P. Lovrich

A Series from LFB Scholarly

African American Felon Disenfranchisement
Case Studies in Modern Racism and Political Exclusion

John E. Pinkard Sr.

LFB Scholarly Publishing LLC
El Paso 2013

Library of Congress Cataloging-in-Publication Data

Pinkard, John E., 1943-
  African American felon disenfranchisement: case studies in modern racism and political exclusion / John E. Pinkard.
    pages cm. -- (Criminal justice : recent scholarship)
  Includes bibliographical references and index.
  ISBN 978-1-59332-601-2 (hardcover : alk. paper)
  1. Ex-convicts--Suffrage--United States. 2. African American criminals. 3. Political rights, Loss of--United States. 4. Political rights, Loss of--United States--States. 5. Racism--United States. 6. Election law--United States--States. I. Title.
  JK1846.P56 2013
  324.6'20869270973--dc23
                                          2013000007

ISBN 978-1-59332-601-2

Printed on acid-free 250-year-life paper.

Manufactured in the United States of America.

Table of Contents

Preface

I was fortunate to have come into manhood (and political consciousness) during the Civil Rights and Black Protest Movement decades in America. My character and purpose was critically formulated by these decades of struggle. Because of this intimate experience, I am deeply committed to the struggle for social and political justice for marginalized people. This struggle is both a personal commitment and a historical one. I was fourteen years old, standing in my grandmother's living room watching the news report on television as a 'Freedom Rider' bus was shown, on fire, with a bus load of Freedom Riders streaming out of the bus – escaping with their lives. I watched, and I knew that they were engaged in a struggle for my rights. I knew then, that I too had to participate in this struggle. At age 20-21, I remember the burning buildings of a riot-torn city, Newark, New Jersey, and how the National Guard responded to the anomic reaction of an oppressed people that reflected and manifested the anguish and frustration of a voiceless community – and I participated.

Nelson Mandela has said, "Men (and women) are not capable of doing nothing, saying nothing, of not reacting to injustice....It is less prescriptive than (it is) a necessity determined by conscience...." I know the inherent truth of these words. It is my personal commitment to participate in the struggle to make justice possible. This book represents another chapter in this struggle.

Over the past 25 years, I have worked with felon populations and their children. My motivation and commitment to the idea of supporting the right of political minorities and felons to be fairly represented and vote is the result of this life experience, my work, and what I have learned through formal education. It is these combined experiences which have resulted in my deep commitment to social justice, and have helped me translate that commitment into a struggle for political equality for marginalized populations worldwide, and specifically in the U.S. This commitment is, in a very real sense, as described by C. Taylor (1994) is both an "intimate and public (socio-political) one".

I was born during the Second World War, and what I remember most about my youth was my family's extreme poverty. We were poor, African-American, and urban. Our family unit was defined by my mother's socio-economic status (SES): single, female, head-of-household. In the state in which I live and work, the majority of felons fit a similar profile except for their year of birth and their level of education. By 2010, nearly eighty percent of this felon population was African-American or Latino, 96% are male, 75% read on a fifth grade level, most of this felon population would have been listed in a similar SES status (i.e. unemployed, underemployed, poor or low income), and 95% of this population will return to their community, on average, within a 5 year period of their original sentencing.

Professionally, I owned and operated a non-profit corporation that contracted with the state to serve adult, pre-release, resident felons and developed alternatives to conventional incarceration for offenders, encouraging incarcerated persons to rehabilitate and reintegrate into family and community. Since 1991, the program grew from 15 to 130 residential clients and 50 to 90 Day Reporting Center (DRC) clients from Parole. It is the first African American owned and operated program of its type among the twenty-six state RCRP programs, and one of two closely bonded, African American owned Day Reporting Centers of a total fourteen Centers in the State. Our program served between 900-1000 pre-release residents per year. As reported by the NJDOC, our success rates were among the highest in the state, reducing recidivism rates by 16% annually. In addition to this practical service function and political aim, our work provided access to populations who are the subject of this study in a political environment which typically remains closed to field research and data compilation.

The difficulty in gaining access to felon populations in each of the three states of New Jersey, Maryland, and Virginia was a testament to the principle of information control and the closed-door policy inherent in the on-going and essential legitimation and survival process of all institutional bureaucracies. What worked in gaining research access in the various states was not just that the survey met the formal requirements for 'Human Research' as specified by each of the various states but rather, it was knowing or successfully seeking public officials or persons (gatekeepers) who were committed to something greater than "containment" as a social policy in criminal justice. In criminal justice, there are two kinds of people: those who advocate a policy of containment and those who advocate a policy of rehabilitation - 'and never the twain shall meet.' This is the sole reason that it took three years to survey felon populations in three different states.

In New Jersey, it was a matter of contacting the Commissioner of Corrections, an intellectual with a Masters Degree in Social Work and a friend, and asking his permission to survey my program population for the specified purpose. Mutual respect, shared values, familiarity, and trust were enough. As was the case in each state, this could not have been achieved without some combination of these ingredients. We continue to be extremely appreciative of the support and shared values demonstrated by so many individuals.

In Maryland, more time was taken in gaining access than in administering the survey. On March 7, 2007, I submitted my official research application to the Maryland Office of Planning, Policy, Regulations and Statistics, Department of Public Safety and Correctional Services. It was indicated that applicants should allow 60 days after receipt for a formal response. Two months later, on May 7, 2007 I received a letter of response indicating that the Maryland Departmental Research Committee had reviewed my application and the project had been approved subject to the execution of the necessary agreements. Paula Matthews of the Division of Corrections had agreed to mentor my project. My younger son and company V.P. for Institutional Planning and I met with Ms. Matthews within a few weeks of receiving this notice and began to make preparations for survey distribution. Ms. Matthews was a bright committed educator, whose primary commitment was to the learning experience of the Corrections population. She was not a policy maker. She implemented policy as it pertained to her field of responsibilities as Director of Education.

In June, 2007, the Maryland State Legislature changed the law regarding felon disenfranchisement. Effective July 1, 2007, Maryland would change its laws pertaining to felon disenfranchisement to a policy of automatic restoration with certain provisional limitations (as described in Chapter V). On June 4, 2007, I received a letter indicating that "...Your project has been declined due to the recent legislation passed which allows (provisionally) voting for the felon population in Maryland...." By June 14, 2007, I received an email from Ms. Matthews that she decided to continue the research project as an educational project because she believed in its educational value for her felon student population, who deserved access and knowledge of their right to vote. Ms. Matthews had the felon surveys distributed to inmates as they attended the various classes afforded inmates in the Maryland Correctional system, so long as respondents met the survey criteria established for parole eligibility date (PED). It was also one of the survey states in which women were able to be included.

Establishing an initial contact in Virginia was difficult. We tried the informal route first. As the result of conference networking, my older son and V.P. for Development had met several people from Virginia who worked with re-entry initiative programs for felons. We identified two contacts who worked separately with early release felons in Virginia. Each of these women directed programs that had access to re-entry felon populations and each person indicated willingness and genuine interests in participating in efforts to enfranchise the felon population. We sent 100-150 survey questionnaires to both program directors to administer. Both promised to distribute the surveys and return the completed forms to us within a 60 day turn-around period. Both directors maintained apparent enthusiasm and contact with us. Neither administrator returned any of the felon surveys to us. Later, we learned that a local New Jersey based agency also provided Community Corrections programs in Virginia. As friends and colleagues in N.J., we contacted the agency director and asked if he would be interested in administering the felon survey in their facility in Virginia. The facility indicated their support for the project, provided the survey would be approved by the Virginia Research and Management Services Unit. On March 20, 2009, I submitted a research application to the Virginia Department of Corrections. We are still waiting for a response, of any kind. As a 1990s graduate of Hampton University, my son remembered that someone he had graduated with was now Sheriff in Hampton County, Virginia. We contacted Sheriff B.J. Roberts; he reviewed the felon survey, and approved distribution of the survey to the felon population under his direction. In total, we were able to distribute and have 819 completed felon surveys returned from all three states combined.

The Corrections bureaucracy is a rather closed community, understandably protective of its reputation, practices, and image. Membership, no matter how indirect, served me well in gaining access to the felon populations within the various states. These access issues also explain the inability to conduct research samplings as a part of the research methodology included in this project. To many people, correctional institutions are a necessary, yet most undesirable partner in community life. This field survey experience seemed to indicate that the more distant a state was from automatic voter restoration law, the more unwilling they were to participate in the felon voter survey.

Alternative sanction programs such as Community Corrections represents a new paradigm and direction in Corrections reform law and practice and is predicated on an abundance of literature in the criminal justice field.

Research and the implementation of "Best Practices" by practitioners began to change the thinking and practice in Community Corrections; such changes included:

- Diversion of drug offenders to alternative treatment programs;
- Expanding alternatives to incarceration for non-violent offenders;
- Parole and probation reform reducing time served and supervision options;
- Sentencing reform law;
- Broader sentencing reform;
- Changing State disenfranchisement laws.

Not only have I relied on this literature and practical experience for the development of my hypothesis, but resources such as the Bureau of Justice Statistics, The Sentencing Project, Human Rights Watch, U.S. Census data, State Offender Characteristic Reports, The PEW Report, the U.N. Committee on the Elimination of Racial Discrimination, and U.S. Department of Justice Reports provided a foundation for making the study of African American felon disenfranchisement and the problem of permanent political marginalization more comprehensible.

Voting (felon enfranchisement) is both a human and fundamental right within a constitutional democracy: "...When historically marginalized groups are chronically or permanently underrepresented in legislative bodies, citizens who are members of those groups are not fairly represented....".[1] 'Representation' is a primary and fundamental democratic institution. A democratic polity must "...carry out socially necessary tasks on behalf of larger numbers of citizens ... to help individuals and small [interests] groups fulfill personal needs that they are unable to fulfill unaided...."[2] I believe that human and emancipatory needs such as autonomy, identity, recognition, participation, and fulfillment are among the essential interest to which this passage refers. Professor Green adds, "...the vote is properly believed ... to be a necessary condition of democracy. The struggle for political equality has to be a struggle for more than the vote....It has to be a struggle for the right to an unalienated political life...."[3] To the degree that a state does not fulfill these needs and aims, or does so for some but not others, human potential is minimized and we relegate the state to the worst in humankind rather than the best.

I remember being taught by my family how to live in an America that was not ours. My earliest memory was of my grandfather encouraging my brother and me to step aside to allow someone else to walk on the sidewalk because of his color – and ours. Later, I remember **needing** to participate in the Civil Rights movement as a 1960's college student. The Civil Rights Movement and Black Protest Movement changed me. It taught me why I was angry, who I was, and what I needed to do with my life. This movement taught me the importance and inevitability of resistance. I learned firsthand, the politics of identity. It was during my college days and after that I began to understand the dialectic of social and political inequality; each one feeds the other. Felons, too, live with this same anger and sense of unfairness.

At the New School for Social Research I first learned or discovered the significance of my experiences vis-à-vis Critical Race Theory (CRT). CRT emphasizes the importance of resistance, rejecting traditional or prevailing American liberal orthodoxy; engaging in adversarial scholarship; and redefines racial or social justice from the perspective of the oppressed. Critically, the CRT movement is part of a "...long tradition of human resistance and liberation. CRT is both the theory and practice of self-reflection, formal innovation, radical politics, reconstructive experimentation, and vocational anguish. CRT examines the human experience and attempts to reinterpret and remake the world to reveal silenced suffering and to relieve social misery...."[4] CRT echoed everything I had become, and everything to which I had become personally and professionally committed. This research is a reflection of that commitment.

The problem with representation and its consequence, majority rule, is that they 'do not of themselves produce fairness and equality in decision making'. Social inequalities based on race, class, and/or gender creates permanent majorities and permanent minorities. As stated by Professor Green, "...A minority must be nothing more than a random collection of people who lost the last vote..., if that proviso does not generally hold true, then we have not political equality but majority tyranny...."[5] The measure for fair representation therefore is not simply who can vote, but also who sets agenda, who holds office, and ultimately who benefits (i.e., life chances). The underlying question to which this research must respond is – when is it appropriate to treat people differently? Citizens can be treated differently when, and only when, difference in treatment does not result in political or social inequalities.

Finally, it is intended that this study will provide some contribution to my profession, to the academic world of which I am a part, and to those felons who may come across this study and in some way find this study self–validating in their lives.

Acknowledgments

It is impossible to thank all those who have supported me in completing this research. An omission would be almost inevitable. It is best left as a personal note attached to each person's copy. However, I would like to offer my deepest gratitude to my wife Gloria, Dr. David Plotke, Pompey (my Administrative Assistant), family, friends, and colleagues who have been my supporters in spirit or deed.

CHAPTER 1

Introduction and Hypothesis

> "The right to vote freely for the candidate of one's choice is of the essence of a democratic society, and any restriction on that right strikes at the heart of representative government...."[6]
>
> Reynolds v. Sims, 377 U.S., 533 (1964)

Thurgood Marshall's dissent in the 1964 Supreme Court case-Reynolds v. Sims affirms that the right to vote is the essence of a democratic society. Voting is a fundamental right through which constituents are able to voice their needs, choices, and interests. To the extent that the state does not secure this right, or does so for some but not others, human potential is minimized and we relegate the state to the worst in humankind rather than the best. Judith Shklar states that, "...the ballot has always been a certificate of full membership in a society, and its value depends primarily on its capacity to confer a minimum of social dignity..."[7] She further argues that, ...there is no notion more central in politics than citizenship, and none more variable in history, or contested in theory..."[8] The moral and legal contradiction is between principle and practice; quasi-citizen and citizen; recognition and mis/non-recognition; power and powerlessness; advantage and disadvantage; and ultimately between human dignity and denial.

The greater tragedy is when these juxtapositions are internalized and normalized within citizens and the polity. The issue underlying voter participation for felons is citizenship or membership manifested in what Shklar terms social rights. Social rights include principally the right to vote and the right to work. Shklar argues that two rights above all others define public respect (autonomy) and stand as a measure of

1

American citizenship. Shklar concludes, "…the struggle for citizenship in America has, therefore, been overwhelmingly a demand for inclusion in the polity, an effort to break down exclusionary barriers to recognition, rather than an aspiration to civic participation as a deeply involving activity…"[9] Socio-political inequalities based on race, class, and gender defined which citizens would be included or excluded in the polity.

This research focuses on the impact of disparate state felon disenfranchisement laws and their distinctive political and collateral effects on African American felons and their communities. Three related arguments are presented: first, that felon disenfranchisement of persons having paid their debt to society is unfair, unlawful, and inhumane; second, that the variation in state law as it relates to felon disenfranchisement is irrational, inconsistent, and clearly contradicts constitutional democracy in principle; and third, that each of these facts disproportionately impacts African American felons, and consequently disadvantages the African American community.

It is my hypothesis that the loss of the right to vote, equal protection, and fair representation for African American felons dilutes the political interests, efficacy, and representation of African American felons and politically marginalizes the voting strength of the African American community. Race discrimination has a significantly greater political impact within states which permanently disenfranchise all or some African American felons than states which provide for automatic restoration.

Background to the Problem

According to the Advancement Project (Re-Enfranchisement, 2002) in the U.S., eight (8) states (Alabama, Florida, Iowa, Kentucky, Mississippi, Nevada, Virginia, and Wyoming) permanently disenfranchised all felons and ex-felons; and five (5) states (Arizona, Delaware, Maryland, Tennessee, and Washington) permanently disenfranchised some felons, but not all. Thirty-six (36) states allowed persons with felony convictions to have their voting rights restored automatically at some point after they were released from incarceration, while two (2) states (Maine and Vermont) allow persons in prison to vote. A total of thirteen (13) states disenfranchised some or all felons and ex-felons for life. The problem of political marginalization and disenfranchisement is rooted in African American history. This 'crazy quilt' of felon disenfranchisement law was reflective of a nation in conflict with itself with regard to racial equality, citizenship, and the principle of equal representation. The disparate and changing attitudes and political values of the various states vis-à-vis felon disenfranchisement law over the past decade is a testament to my hypothesis.

Racial disparity in state felon disenfranchisement law contradicts the principles of one person, one vote, and equal representation (U.S. constitutional democracy). As a consequence, I examine two questions: What is the political significance and electoral impact of felon disenfranchisement on African American voter participation and representation; and, is there a measurable difference in voter participation and political efficacy between permanently disenfranchised state felon populations and felons in those states that provide for automatic restoration? I will elucidate normative values and patterns which systematically created an African American disenfranchised felon population, and consequently a permanently marginalized African American community.

The U.S. is the only modern democratic country that bars some or all ex-offenders from voting for life, and has a significant percentage of its citizens who cannot vote as a result of felon convictions. The Sentencing Project, Washington, D.C., reports that there are collateral effects and consequences of felon disenfranchisement that disproportionately impact people of color and their communities. While African Americans comprise 13% of the total U.S. population (2010), African Americans represent 37% of the U.S. felon population. Felon disenfranchisement is not only an extra-legal practice and punishment, but also subjects people to these laws by happenstance of geographic location. These laws deny African American felons and African American communities the right to participate fully in the electoral process for no other reasons than punishment and race. Therefore, felon disenfranchisement laws are in conflict with the expressed constitutional commitment to an open, democratic society.

Theoretical Premise

Representation is a primary and fundamental democratic institution. Fair and equal representation of marginalized groups within the American electoral system requires more than the "one person, one vote" principle. Fair representation depends on participation of a whole community that has common interests articulated as an aggregate. It is the way in which marginalized groups can assure their influence will be felt by political majorities in a society suffused with racial projects (i.e., racial bias in specific socio-political categories, such as voter rights). The question is, when is it appropriate to treat people differently? Historically 'difference' treatment has been unfair and occurred around issues of voter registration; equal rights; abortion; compulsory military registration and the draft; felon disenfranchisement; and employment, housing, and educational opportunities. A subsequent question then is, how does 'difference treatment' affect minority groups (i.e., permanent marginalization, adverse life chances, etc.).

It is 'difference treatment' that relegated African American felons and the African American community to second class citizenship. By 2000, there were approximately 36.5 million African Americans in the U.S., almost 17.5 million of whom were male, with some 8.7 million being of adult voting age. By 2007, the approximate number of felons and ex-felons was 7,300,000 people, with one third of that population being African American. Nationally, the total number of African American felons equaled 25% of all African American men. This disproportionate number of disenfranchised African American felons suggests a potential dilution of African American voter influence and representation. In chapters IV, V and VI, I will examine the impact of this racial disparity on a specific class of African Americans in the states of New Jersey, Maryland, and Virginia. I will compare this political impact on African Americans within the counties of Essex, Baltimore City, and Hampton Roads MSA.

Methodology

Methodologically, this study is designed to investigate felon disenfranchisement and its political impact on African American felons' right to vote. This study utilized New Jersey, Maryland, and

Virginia as normative models, focusing on minority interest group representation and voter participation. Practical issues addressed in this text include questions of political efficacy, representation, participation, who can vote, and who would vote if they could (among felons). Theoretical issues include questions concerning political equality and inequality; equal representation; esteem; autonomy; political recognition or non-recognition, and identity. A critical outcome measure for this study is how these standards of political empowerment or disempowerment impact the life chances of African Americans. An underlying principle of this study is that a constitutional democracy functions to equitably secure the rights and freedoms of all its citizens. What happens to a democracy when rights are secured for some citizens, but not others?

Defining the study group was both a problem in law and practice. In this study a distinction has been made between felons as the study group and ex-felons as the group for whom the right to vote has greater political feasibility. A common and practical argument for and against felon disenfranchisement has been the difference between those who "have paid their debt to society," and those who have not. There is a cultural bias in this nation by which all felons, no matter if they are felons by strict definition or ex-felons, are colloquially referred to as 'felons.' As an example, the study of the disenfranchisement of persons who have committed a crime is not referred to as the study of felon and ex-felon disenfranchisement, but rather "felon" disenfranchisement. By definition, ex-felons are persons who have committed a crime, and have completed their sentence inclusive of incarceration, parole or probation. They have therefore paid their debt to society, and according to some, should have the right to vote.

The study groups were violent, non-violent/CDS, or property offenders who were within one year of parole eligibility or max-out. By definition, the "offender" was an incarcerated inmate in a correctional complex, major institution or satellite housing unit under the jurisdiction of the Department of Corrections. Other offenders include state sentenced inmates housed in county jails, halfway houses, Central Medical Units and those assigned to Electronic monitoring/ Home confinement. This population is perceived by some as not having finished paying its debt to society. Most automatic restoration states reinstated the right to vote to ex-felons. This means that by 2007, approximately 5 million persons of a total 7.3 million persons in the criminal justice system could have been enfranchised. References made to ex-felons distinguish ex-felons as those who should have the right to vote, from felons who have not yet completed their sentence. Nationally, 95% of the inmate population will become the ex-felon population.

We can best determine voter attitudes, political efficacy, participation and whether the right to vote matters to this target population by studying felons who are within a year of their parole eligibility or release date. By identifying the study group as felons who were within one year of their parole eligibility or release date I defined the study group as a population that would be ex-felons once having completed their parole stipulation or immediately upon release (omitting that 5% that will never return to society). This defining process effectively incorporated the general and particular meaning of the term 'felon'.

This study begins with an examination of empirical data and state constitutional law as it pertains to felon disenfranchisement. Central to my thesis is a field research survey measuring felon voter attitudes. A Felon Voter Participation Survey was utilized to ascertain felon voter attitudes and also whether felons would vote if universal suffrage included them as a class of citizens entitled to vote. This survey was administered in each of three states with a target population that included three specific urban cluster neighborhoods. After administering and tabulating the results of this survey, I supervised or conducted focus groups and random interviews of felons who participated in the survey. The survey was organized in five sections which addressed four constructs or main ideas plus demographics. The internal consistency for the entire survey and each section was evaluated using Cronbach's Alpha. This model of internal consistency was based on the average inter-item correlation. A high or moderate coefficient indicated that the items in the questionnaire were related to each other and that there was a repeatability or internal consistency of the scale. Testing for reliability was conducted by Cathy Maltbie, Ed.D, Assistant Professor, Department of Education, University of Cincinnati. The results indicated that there was a moderate degree of internal consistency within the survey, and that it was an effective way to measure the ideas related to felon disenfranchisement associated with voter rights. The quantitative analysis in Sections IV, V, and VI was based on the standard for internal consistency established in these test results.

Survey distribution began in June, 2006, and continued through July, 2009. The surveys were administered in New Jersey, Maryland, and Virginia, in that order. The study groups were identified as residents of a community corrections facility (NJ), state corrections institution (MD), and a county corrections facility (VA). The common factor among the groups was that all of the respondents were felons who were one year from parole, probation, or max-out eligibility. Because the administration of the survey began in 2006, this study did not include any questions which could measure the affect the election of the first African American President may have had on the felon survey respondents. A total of 819 surveys were completed and returned of an approximate 1,000 surveys administered in three states. In New Jersey, 409 surveys were completed and returned; in Maryland, 300 surveys were returned; and in Virginia, 110 surveys were returned. In each state, administration of the survey had to contend with different bureaucratic standards of research accessibility, and varying political motivations of "gatekeepers" and of the relevant institutional bureaucracies. Ultimately, none of the formal channels in any of the states resulted in achieving access to the surveyed populations.

It is with much gratitude and appreciation that I thank each of the administrators, officials, and professionals who demonstrated a commitment to this population and this project. This study could not have been completed without their cooperation and efforts. In each case, they only asked to receive a copy of the study when the project was completed. It is a request which has been honored.

The five basic areas covered in the felon survey were: demographics; voter attitude; electoral knowledge; political participation; and political efficacy. Background information includes: gender; citizenship; race/ethnicity; age; educational level; household income; and legal status. Questions concerning electoral knowledge included: felon voter rights; State voter rights; partisanship; and state election law.

Political participation survey questions included: registration to vote; campaign activities; past participation in voting; and willingness to vote. Political efficacy in this study is defined as a belief in one's full membership in the body politic; and "authorship" of the laws, leaders, policies and outcomes of the state. The notion of membership and authorship within the state, as used in this study implies: hearing and being heard; being addressed; recognition; respect; trust; reciprocity; maintaining a sense of "moral contact" between the governed and the governing; and the sense that as a member of the state you can achieve a desired result (collective interest). Survey questions which represent political efficacy includes: voter participation, past and future; political empowerment/ disempowerment indicators; felon voter rights; and felon voter political influence.

A central question in the felon voter survey was: If you were able to vote, would you vote in an election? Yes or no. For analytical purpose, respondents were divided into yes/no groups by state and compared by demographics, legal status, choice responses (i.e. why would you or would you not vote in an election?), and socio-political control scale questions (measuring empowerment and community isolation attitudes among participants [scale 1-6 – Strongly disagree to strongly agree]). Example questions: "People like me are generally well qualified to participate in the political activity and decision making in the U.S." "Most public officials wouldn't listen to me no matter what I did". Critical data will be included such as U.S. Census data on populations by race; literature and data on felon incarceration rates by race; felon disenfranchisement rates by state and race; and felon disenfranchisement laws by state. I will analyze research data in comparison to the literature. This qualitative and quantitative analysis will determine whether felon disenfranchisement disproportionately marginalizes African American felons and dilutes the voting strength and political representation of the African American community.

Hesse-Biber and Leavy (2004) have defined qualitative research as, "...a distinct field of inquiry that...draw(s) on historical, comparative, structural, observational, and interactional ways of knowing...."[10] How and why the subject of African American felon disenfranchisement can be described as a race project will be measured qualitatively. Hesse-Biber and Leavy define quantitative research as research which, "...relies on numbers or percentages in a table or chart to convey meaning...."[11] By contrasting the questions "how" with "how many" African American felons have been disenfranchised by a specific state interweaves meaning and values with numerical or quantifiable comparative data. This combination allows me to understand and describe political conflict (i.e., political recognition or non-recognition, racism, social and political inequalities, and voter participation), and its impact on the life chances of African Americans.

Summary

Critical Race Theory (1995) adds perspective, dimension and significance to current population surveys (CPS), and the role they play in this research paradigm. "... Critical Race Theory (CRT) embraces a movement of...scholars... whose work challenges the ways in which race and racial power are constructed and represented in American society as a whole..."[12] Two CRT axioms reflected in this study are that "ethical aspirations (for knowledge) finds its most obvious concrete expression in the pursuit of engaged, even adversarial, scholarship...."[13] And secondly, that "... scholarship – the formal production, identification, and organization of what (is) called knowledge – is inevitably political. To borrow a phrase from the existentialist tradition, there is no exit – no scholarly perch outside the social dynamics of racial power from which merely to observe and analyze...."[14]

Each chapter of this study develops the case supporting my hypothesis. Chapter II provides a brief history and overview of African American felon disenfranchisement, a theoretical framework using critical race theory, and surveys the pertinent literature in the field of criminal justice research. This chapter develops the case that the "crazy quilt" of felon disenfranchisement by state has no legitimate basis in law, state constitutional history, or variations in restoration requirements. It will be argued in this chapter that the notion of "political impact" is a legal description, able to be measured in empirical terms based on state constitutional law. Chapter III addresses the relationship between felon disenfranchisement, civil rights legislation, judicial review and activism. Chapters IV, V, and VI examine New Jersey, Maryland, and Virginia respectively as cases in automatic restoration, states with some permanent disenfranchisement, and states with permanent disenfranchisement among all felons. In each case we will describe the felon disenfranchisement law pertaining to that state, and the impact of those laws on felon voter participation, interests, and efficacy as measured by the Felon Voter Attitude Survey. I will further illustrate the impact of felon disenfranchisement on a "specific class" of citizens and their community by describing the life chances and political participation of African American felons from the specified counties from each of these states. Chapter VII offers comparative analysis of the impact of these three states' felon disenfranchisement laws and practices. In my conclusion I will demonstrate that the way democratic values of equal representation and political efficacy can be best achieved is by intervention on the felon criminogenic paradigm and the national restoration of ex-felon voter rights.

Conflicting political theories and practices emerge when analysts, leaders and citizens put forth competing world views. In this context, knowledge can be defined as a paradigm or "…world view that defines, for its holder(s) the nature of the world, the individual's place in it, and the range of possible relationships to that world and its parts…."[15] How the African American sees him or herself in the world is contingent upon how and by whom this paradigm is created and defined. As an African American and critical theorist, the response to this challenge contextually must be historical realism, "…a virtual reality shaped by social, political, cultural, economic, ethnic (race), and gender values, crystallized over time….[16] On one level, the content of this study challenges contemporary and historical orthodoxy and authenticity, and on another level it attempts to explicate who can vote, why, and what meaning or significance this has in the democratic state.

The overarching aim of this study is to examine the effects of this crazy quilt of U.S. felon disenfranchisement law on African American voter participation and political efficacy within the states of New Jersey, Maryland, and Virginia. I illustrate these problems by:

- Comparing pertinent state constitutional changes in U.S. felon disenfranchisement laws and electoral practices between Virginia, Maryland, and New Jersey, each respectively representing permanently disenfranchised states, states in which some felons are permanently disenfranchised, and states in which automatic restoration apply.
- In particular, emphasis will be given to high density African American communities as represented respectively by:

Hampton Roads MSA, Virginia; Baltimore City, Maryland; and Essex County, New Jersey. The impact of felon voter disenfranchisement will be compared with respect to issues of voter participation, political representation, political efficacy and African American life chances within these counties.

- Administering a felon voter attitude survey, I will examine the impact of this crazy quilt of U.S. felon disenfranchisement law and practice on African American felon voter participation and political efficacy within these specific states.
- Using this empirical data, I will demonstrate that the disparity in African American felon disenfranchisement, in particular, dilutes the political representation of the African American community and is antithetical to the principle of fair and equal representation.

For fear that the reader might grow anxious anticipating a useful conclusion to the social and political problems presented, I would like to state at the outset some of the lessons learned as a result of my research. The lessons are both general and specific, and therefore applicable to case studies of democratic states in which permanent political majorities and minorities emerge.

- This study in African American Felon Disenfranchisement makes the problem of political marginalization more comprehensible. So long as a 'temporal majority can use power to preserve its view of the social order simply by disenfranchising those with different views (or experiences), no person or minority's rights are guaranteed or secure'.
- The disenfranchisement of felons was not about 'purity at the ballot box' or disqualifying 'bad people' who would corrupt the electoral process, it was about power, privilege, and race.
- The disproportional impact of felon disenfranchisement on African Americans, and equal/fair representation was directly related to disparate life chances, the criminal justice system, and the sociology of race. It matters who participates in, and makes or enforces the law; who gets arrested and incarcerated; the disparities in life chances based on race; and the impact of racism on African American felon disenfranchisement.

- Race discrimination has a significantly greater political impact within states which permanently disenfranchise African American felons than it does in automatic restoration states.
- Politically marginalized African American felons felt both willing and qualified to participate in government, but were denied this constitutional right.

Permanent political marginalization results in the debasement of the human character and the human condition. It also results in the dilution of voter participation and equal representation for African Americans, and the fulfillment of the promise and purpose of the democratic state.

CHAPTER 2

Statement of the Problem

"Tragically, there has been no time within American history
or its institutions in which race has not been a national
dilemma...."[17]

(Lani Guinier, 1994)

"You Fit the Description"

*As I drove down Route 22 nearing my exit off the highway, I
noticed through my rear view mirror a car dart out from the
side of the road and put on its flashing lights. I took the next
exit, followed by a police car, and pulled over. The police
pulled over behind me, jumped out of their car, drew their
guns, and demanded that I get out of my car. I stared. I heard
a second warning. I carefully got out of my car. I was told to
put my hands on my car, and was frisked. I asked, what was
the problem? After asking for, and receiving my driver license,
registration, and insurance card, one officer (while back-up
was arriving) explained that there had been a robbery on
Route 22 several miles back, and I 'fit the description' of the
perpetrator. This was an observation the officer made of me
while I traveled on a highway at 55 miles an hour at 9 P.M. at
night. A second policeman began to yell, "Turn around and
put your hands behind your back." I said, "No." He raised
his gun to my head. I said, "Are you crazy?" "You guys are
always hiding something" was the response. I was ordered to
turn around and put my hands behind my back, once again.*

*Once again, I said "No." The same policeman put his gun to
my head, cocked the hammer, and said, "Do it."*
   *For what seemed like an hour, but was probably only
seconds, nothing and no one moved. I couldn't; he didn't.
Finally, a more rational policeman turned to him and said
"Easy, let's find out what's going on." Then, turning to me, he
said, "Come on, turn around and let me 'cuff' you." I
complied. For what seemed like another hour, we stood on
the fringe of my neighborhood: me in handcuffs, four white
policemen, and two police cars with flashing lights. I felt like
I was standing there with no clothes on, open for ridicule,
accused and found guilty of a crime I knew nothing about. We
stood on the side of the road until the store owner who had
been robbed was picked up by the police and brought to the
site to identify me as the thief. Finally, a police car drove by
very slowly, paused for a moment in front of me, and drove off.*
                                                         (Author)

In an interim report of the State Police Review Team regarding
allegations of racial profiling submitted on April 20, 1999, N.J.
Governor Christine Whitman presented the following position paper to
the media and specific community representatives:
   "The report has determined that to the extent that discretionary
decisions are affected by race there is no question that racial profiling
exist at some level. The problem of disparate treatment is real, not
imagined.... The actual report specifies disparity in stops, searches, and
arrests.... The available data indicates that the overwhelming majority
of searches (77.2%) involved Black or Latino persons...."[18]   A total of
67.5% of the arrests were of Blacks and Latinos. Race, more than any
other factor defines who will be stopped, searched, arrested, and
incarcerated. According to the Sentencing Project, by 1998 African
Americans represented 47% of the New Jersey felon population, 50%
of the Maryland felon population, and 40% of the Virginia felon
population. By comparison, the U.S. Census Bureau (2000) reported
that the African American population in these respective states was:
New Jersey, 14.4%; Maryland 28.8%, and Virginia 20.4%. By the
conclusion of this study (2009) Blacks represented 38.2% of the U.S.
felon population, Latinos 20.7%, and Whites 34.2%. By 2009 Blacks

represented 61% of the felon population of New Jersey, 76% of the Maryland felon population; and 60% of the Virginia felon population. By comparison, the Black population in these respective states was: New Jersey 13.7%, Maryland 29.5%, and Virginia 20%. The total percentage of Blacks in the U.S. in 2009 was 12.6%. There has been an increasing and disproportionate number of African American felons in the U.S. and in each of these states. These numbers become even more dramatic when localized by county. Comparisons of the previously indicated counties (Essex, Baltimore City and Hampton Roads) will be used to illustrate this point.

Michael Omi and Howard Winant argue that the contemporary state is "...the architect of segregation and chief enforcer of racial difference, and have a tendency to reproduce those patterns of inequality in a new guise .... Stereotypes testify to the way a racialized social structure shapes racial experience and conditions meaning...."[19] Evidence which supports this premise within the criminal justice system begins within the law. Many Southern state constitutional conventions following the Civil War codified African American disenfranchisement openly. Over the next century, states – primarily those representing "some" or "all" permanently disenfranchised states – established state constitutional impediments to voter restoration for former felons which, in some cases, were based solely on racial bias.

It is this history which gives credence to the assertion that African American felon disenfranchisement is based on 'modern' racism. More generally, modern racism is characterized in a White (male) dominated society by moralistic racial resentments, animosity, and abstract prejudice (i.e., public opinion polls, affirmative action, social spending, and public or foreign affairs). It is a racism defined by Kinder and Sanders as a "symbolic," "modern," or "subtle" racism. This elusive racism is, "...a blend of anti-black effect and the kind of traditional [inegalitarian] American values embodied in the Protestant ethic...."[20] It is the "...feeling that Blacks are violating cherished values, making illegitimate [unjustified] demands, and gaining too much support from political elites..."[21] Modern racism is an elusive racism which is no longer measured in the hard, defining terms of "red lining," separate and unequal education, segregated bathrooms or seating on buses, poll taxes or white primaries, or segregated drinking fountains. Instead, this 'new' racism is composed of "...three elements:

a defense of traditional values; an exaggeration of cultural – not genetic
– differences; and a denial or absence of positive emotional reactions
[i.e. sympathy or admiration]...."[22] The U.S. criminal justice system is
a microcosm of this modern racism and race ideology. Modem racism
is a racism that is made most manifest in racial profiling
(disproportionate stops, arrests, and sentencing); voter eligibility
criteria; voter information costs; political gerrymandering or
reapportionment issues; political and economic access; public policy
making; and life chance opportunities and outcomes. No matter how
invisible 'modern racism' is, Governor Whitman was correct in saying
that the problem of racism is real and not imagined.

Modern racism, racial disparities and projects within the U.S.
criminal justice system are reflected in New Jersey, Maryland, and
Virginia:

> The United States has the highest prison population rate in the
> world. As reported in PEW (2008), in the United States the
> rate of incarceration in prison and jail in 2008 was 750
> inmates per 100,000 US residents – up from 702 at midyear
> 2002. At midyear 2006, 1 in every 100 U.S. residents was in
> prison or jail. The incarceration rate for African American
> women ages 35-39 was 1 in 100; for African American men
> over 18 years old the rate was 1 in 15; the rate for Hispanic
> women aged 35-39 was 1 in 297; for Hispanic men 18 and
> over the rate was 1 in 36; the rate for White women aged
> 35-39 was 1 in 355; and for White men 18 and over the rate
> was 1 in 106.[23]

The rate of incarceration for African American men is seven times
greater than the rate for all U.S. resident inmates per 100,000. There
was a correlation between this pattern of incarceration and African
American "life chances" as a community of people. According to U.S.
Census Bureau data (2006), the rate at which Black and Latino youth
did not exceed a 9th grade educational level was 5 or 6 times greater
than White youth. The rate at which Blacks and Latinos achieved a
college education or more was 2 to 3 times less than Whites.
Unemployment rate among Blacks and Latinos was more than 2 times

higher than Whites. The poverty rate among all Blacks and Latinos was greater than 2-3 times the rate for Whites.

More than any other social force, what separates members of a polity is the existence of poverty. Hannah Arendt describes poverty as the social question. She makes the point that poverty is not inherent in the human condition. Poverty, as a condition, is critical to understanding the relationship between the haves and have-nots; the powerful and powerless; the enfranchised and the disenfranchised. Arendt states that "...poverty is more than deprivation, it is a state of constant want and acute misery whose ignominy consists in its dehumanizing force..." Poverty is a condition that is not only political but is caused, rather than inherent as a consequence of scarcity in society.[24]

There is a correlation between political empowerment or disempowerment and the life chances of individuals, neighborhoods, and whole communities. Furthermore, there is a direct correlation between 'life chance' indices such as poverty, disparity in educational opportunities and achievement, unemployment and age; and those who are disproportionately arrested, sentenced, and imprisoned. The irony of this consequent and socially debilitating correlation is that each dimension feeds the other. Modern racism minimized the life chances of African Americans; and disproportionately increased the rate of arrests, sentencing, and incarceration, with each feeding the "revolving door" of African American incarceration and reincarceration. As stated by Omi and Winant "...American history reveals that far from being color blind, the U.S. has been an extremely 'color-conscious' society. From the very inception of the Republic to the present moment, race has been a profound determinant of one's political rights, one's location in the labor market, and indeed one's sense of identity...."[25] I argue that a sense of self-worth and issues of identity, recognition or mis-recognition correlate with life choices and 'chances.' In a society complete with race projects, self-deprecating outcomes are intended for marginalized populations.

The US Constitutional Anomaly of African American Felon Disenfranchisement

Historically the struggle for justice and equality has been a human rights struggle that has taken place sometimes in the streets, and sometimes in the courts – but no matter which, it has always been a struggle that began in the hearts of men. It has been a struggle between the haves and have-nots, the privileged and the poor, as well as Blacks and Whites. Theoretically, it has accurately been described as a tension or antagonism between liberty and equality. Where does one's rights end and another's begin? One critical difference between the haves and have-nots argument for and against political equality has been the weapons available to each. For example, the aristocratic and minority view of the legal or judicial resort to the courts by marginalized populations was that it was the last, and perhaps only, lawful weapon they had for addressing violations of their rights and the equal protection clause.

From 1927, when Justice Oliver Wendell Holmes called arguments based on equality the "usual last resort, through 1967 when the Supreme Court suggested that the equal protection clause might provide "the basis for more vigorous judicial review in the service of equality in areas other than [just] race…"[26] what has become known as the 'law of equality' has had a strange history. It has been a history that has protected the rights of individuals as well as the rights of minorities and 'specific classes' of people. The equal protection clause, more than any other amendment, has been used as the arbiter of cases that determined where one's rights ended, and where another began. The right of felons to vote is founded on this idea, or law of equality.

Beginning with Justice Douglas (1939), cases argued on the basis of the 14th Amendment equal protection or due process clause defined equality in law on a presumed rational basis, "…upholding legislation as long as judges could imagine some reason for thinking that the problem posed by one group was different than the problem posed by another. If the court did not think the distinction completely irrational…."[27] By 1942, Justices Douglas, Stone, and Jackson joined to affirm a new definition of the law of equality – strict scrutiny – in the case of Skinner v. Oklahoma. "…When a fundamental right is involved, courts have to give strict scrutiny to laws which treat people unequally. Such laws have to be justified by very strong arguments…"[28] Strict scrutiny is at the heart of the issue concerning felon disenfranchisement – the difference principle, and its impact on one's fundamental rights.

Justice Thurgood Marshall argued in a dissenting opinion (Richardson v. Ramirez – 1974) that "…it is doubtful…whether the state can demonstrate either a compelling or rational policy interest in denying former felons the right to vote…"[29]   Andrew Shapiro, in support of Marshall's dissenting opinion, states that "… scholars widely acknowledge the historically racist motives underlying criminal disenfranchisement in the South. The Supreme Court has also recognized this history…." [30]

In Chapter III, I argue that the disenfranchisement of ex-felons does not meet these strict scrutiny standards and is therefore unconstitutional based on the 14th Amendment, and the 1964 and 1965 Voting Rights Act (as amended through 1980). This argument will be supported by examining disenfranchisement practices within specific states (i.e., New Jersey, Maryland, and Virginia); contemporary statistical data concerning the status of African American felons; and the VRA, 1965 "preclearance requirement" and "triggering formula" within covered state jurisdictions. In contrast to the "automatic restoration" states, this racial formula applies to most permanently disenfranchising states. Felon disenfranchisement practices are a clear and specific departure from the normative democratic participatory standard and, to that extent, is an anomaly.

The Supreme Court has historically contested the right of felons to vote on the basis of strict scrutiny. Examples of this historical progression include "Reynolds v. Sims (1964)", "Richardson v. Ramirez (1974)", and "Hunter v. Underwood (1985)". Shapiro argues that felon disenfranchisement laws are illegal because they deny the vote to a class of individuals who are disproportionately non-White, and that these laws dilute the voting strength of minority communities.

In comparison to 1998, by 2002 eight states permanently disenfranchised felons, five permanently disenfranchised some felons, thirty-six states allowed felons to have their vote automatically restored at some point, and two states (Maine, Vermont) allowed persons in prison to vote. As will be noted, the various states progressively moved toward automatic restoration through 2007 (and has continued to modify onerous elements of disenfranchisement law through 2010). What are the reasons for this continuing disparity in voting rights and the existence of such variation in felon disenfranchisement law?

[TABLE 1]
The "Crazy Quilt" of Felon Disenfranchisement

The "Crazy Quilt" of U.S. Disenfranchisement Law (2002)

Felon Disenfranchisement law by state totals	
No Felon Restrictions	2
Automatic Restoration	36
Some Felon Permanent Disenfranchisement	5
All Felon Permanent Disenfranchisement	8

Note: 2002 data represents 50 states plus the District of Columbia

States that permanently disenfranchised felons combined law and discretionary restoration sanctions to limit the rights of felons. Five of the original thirteen permanently disenfranchising states had been Confederate states which were obliged to redraft their state constitutions in compliance with a Union that had recently adopted the 14th and 15th Amendment. Many state constitutions adopted by ex-confederate states in the post-civil war era included disenfranchising law for the express purpose of racial discrimination. These discriminatory laws were further exacerbated through the use of discretionary restoration sanctions. Criminal voter disqualification laws were changed to affect African Americans as a "specific class". Certain crimes which African Americans were stereotypically presumed to commit (i.e., burglary, theft, obtaining money under false pretenses) were legislated into disenfranchisement law. All thirteen permanently disenfranchising states also used discretionary restoration sanctions such as gubernatorial pardons and mandates, mandatory waiting periods, specific disqualifying felony offense charges, prosecutorial/victim notifications, intrusive procedural requirements, and preferential character tests (i.e., marital history, DNA testing, mental health, CDS history, debts).

As illustrated in the following chart, the average percent of African American men disenfranchised in randomly selected states indicates that in the "all" permanently disenfranchised U.S. states, in the "some" permanently disenfranchised states, and in the automatic restoration states there is a declining rate of disenfranchisement from "all" through "some" to automatic restoration (29.2%, 14.9%, and 11% respectively). Over time, a consequence of the disenfranchisement of felons was the reduction of African American voter participation in the electoral process.

[TABLE 2]
Selected Variations in State Disenfranchisement (1998)

	Total Felons	% Total *	African American Men	% African American Men **
All				
Alabama	241,100	7.5%	105,000	31.5%
Florida	647,100	5.9%	204,600	31.2%
Virginia	269,800	5.3%	110,000	25.0%
Some				
Maryland	135,700	3.6%	67,900	15.4%
Tennessee	97,800	2.4%	38,300	14.5%
Automatic				
New Jersey	138,300	2.3%	65,200	17.7%
No. Carolina	96,700	1.8%	46,900	9.2%
Ohio	46,200	0.6%	23,800	6.2%
U.S. Total	3,892,400	2.0%	1,367,100	13.1%

* Percentage of adult population disenfranchised
** Percentage of African American men disenfranchised
Source: Sentencing Project: Losing the Vote (1998)
When comparing all states within these respective categories the declining rate of disenfranchisement remains constant (as illustrated in the following chart).

[TABLE 3]
Percent of State Felon Disenfranchisement by Group (1998)

	All	Some	Automatic	U.S. Total
% Total Population	4.3%	3.14%	1.13%	2.0%
% African American Men	23.25%	17.2%	8.3%	13.1%

Both groups of permanently disenfranchised African American felons represent a higher rate of disenfranchisement than is the national average for African Americans. It should be noted that while facts presented thus far demonstrate felon disenfranchisement to be a "racial project," these facts have not, as of yet, conclusively proven my hypothesis. Variables such as the percentage of total African Americans by state and county, changing disenfranchisement law and discretionary restoration sanctions by state, and other factors will affect outcomes in this study.

[TABLE 4]
Restoration of Voting Rights for Ex-Felons (2005)
(Selected states)

	Actual Number Felons Disen-franchised	Actual Restoration Numbers		% Resto-ration
All				
Alabama	148,830	1,697		1.1%
Florida	647,100	48,000	(6 yrs)	7.4%
Virginia	269,800	5,043	(6 yrs)	1.8%
Some				
Maryland	78,206	147	(7 yrs)	.18%
Tennessee	28,720	393	(3 yrs)	1.4%
Automatic				
New Jersey	138,300	All ex-felons (100%)		
No.	96,700	All ex-felons (100%)		Full
Carolina	46,200	All Probation-Parole		Full
Ohio	(Imprisoned)	ex-felons ( )		Full

> *Source:* Barred for Life: Voting Rights Restoration in Permanent Disenfranchisement States – Marc Mauer and Tushar Kanis, February 2005
>
> Note: By comparison, in eleven of 14 permanent disenfranchisement states less than 3% of disenfranchised persons have had their rights restored (*Source:* Barred for Life)

As illustrated in the following chart (Table 2-4), I argue that not only has permanently disenfranchising African American felons resulted in greater numbers of disqualified voters, but the rate of restoration of African American felon voting rights has been disproportionately, systematically and effectively thwarted. In eleven of these 13 permanently disenfranchised states less than 3% of disenfranchised persons have had their voting rights restored.

Not only has restoration of voting rights been thwarted in all disenfranchisement states, but restoration has been even more limited in states which permanently disenfranchise felons. Among "some felon disenfranchisement states," while the types of restrictions vary, the common reason for imposing restrictions in the states has been intent. Race discrimination has a significantly greater impact within states which permanently disenfranchise African American felons than states which provide for "automatic restoration." My hypothesis and research is based on categories of state disenfranchisement established in *Losing the Vote* (1998); *Re-enfranchisement*, 2002; and *Sentencing Project Summary Report: Locked Out* 2006. Specific states representing "all" permanently disenfranchised felons and "some" permanently disenfranchised felons are consistent with the *Re-enfranchisement*, 2002 list. By state comparison, felon disenfranchisement law overall has progressed from permanent disenfranchisement toward automatic restoration among most states as illustrated in the following charts.

[TABLE 5]
Categories of Felon Disenfranchisement by States (1998)

	No Disenfranchisement	Prison Only	Prison & Parole	Prison, Parole & Probation	Ex-Felons
Total States	4	* 15	3	14	15

* includes District of Columbia
Source: Losing the Vote (1998)

1. By 1998, a total of 36 states established a policy of automatic restoration of felons' right to vote or had no specific felon disenfranchisement statute.
2. Four of these states had no restrictions on the right to vote; 15 states restricted felons only while serving their prison term; 3 states restricted felons through prison and parole; and 14 states

disenfranchised felons throughout their prison, parole or probation terms.

3. A total of 15 states practiced permanent disenfranchisement of felons (ten of these with varying restoration laws for some felons).

4. New Jersey was one of the 36 automatic restoration states (after Prison, Parole, and Probation); Maryland was one of the states with partial or some permanent disenfranchisement; and Virginia was among the permanent felon disenfranchisement states.

[TABLE 6]

Categories of Felon Disenfranchisement by States (2006)

	No Disenfranchisement	Prison Only	Prison & Parole	Prison, Parole & Probation	Ex-Felons
Total States	2	* 13	5	19	12

* includes District of Columbia
Source: Sentencing Project – Locked Out (2006)

1. By 2006, a total of 39 states established a policy of automatic restoration or no felon disenfranchisement law.

2. Two of these states had no voting restrictions on felons; 13 restricted felons only while serving their prison term; 5 while serving through prison and parole; and 19 states disenfranchised felons throughout their prison, parole or probation terms.

3. A total of 12 states continue to practice permanent disenfranchisement of felons (nine of these with varying restoration laws for some felons).

4. New Jersey remained one of the automatic restoration states (no change); Maryland remained one of the five states with some permanent restrictions; and Virginia continued its status as a permanent felon disenfranchisement state.

The 36 states representing automatic restoration remained constant from 1998 (*Losing the Vote*), to 2002 (*Re-enfranchisement*). The states representing automatic restoration, "all felons permanently disenfranchised, and "some" felons permanently disenfranchised in this study are based on this combined data through 2002. The terms restoration and restriction distinguish between automatic restoration states, and "all" or "some" permanently disenfranchised states. Automatic restoration states established a standard for regaining the right to vote consistent with one of three stages: while completing one's sentence in prison; after completing prison and parole; or prison, parole, and probation. The common factor among automatic restoration states for restoring felon voting rights is the completion of one's sentence. Most permanent felon disenfranchisement states had limited restorative policies and practices available to felons. The few restoration standards these states had included: mandatory gubernatorial pardons; mandatory waiting periods; mandatory notification to prosecutors and/or victims; and intrusive procedural requirements. The express purpose or aim these states shared was the creation of a permanently marginalized and restricted felon population. This was achieved by devising a labyrinth of impediments to regaining the right to vote that would discourage or restrict felons, adding to the list of "collateral effects" of imprisonment for felons, their families, and their communities as described by Marc Mauer and Meda Chesney-Lind (2003).

Social Policy and a Theory of Race Formation
(Racial Disparities in Criminal Justice)

"If you're light, you're alright,
If you're brown, stick around,
If you're Black, stay back."
(Anonymous)

Michael Omi and Howard Winant (1994) assert that the U.S. republic is, and always has been a nation whose governance has been fundamentally based on a theory of race. Racialism pervades the U.S. systemically, as well as socio-psychologically. I contend that no person in the U.S. is exempt from the affects of racism. There is no 'tabula rasa' in modern U.S. society as it pertains to race. We are all, in the U.S., inserted into a comprehensively racialized social structure.

Social policy such as mandatory minimum sentencing, intensified drug laws, and "three strikes you're out" legislation has exacerbated this race dichotomy rather than having modified it. "Mass imprisonment" of people of color has had intended and unintended negative consequences on African American felons, their significant others, and immediate communities. Marc Mauer and Meda Chesney-Lind define this phenomena of collateral effects as, "...invisible punishments which effectively transform or destabilize family and community dynamics, exacerbate racial divisions, and pose fundamental questions of citizenship in a democratic society..."[31]

There is a correlation between the dramatic increase in the rate of arrest and incarceration of African American men and the destabilization of the African American family. If policy-makers and legislators know there is a significant correlation between low educational levels, diminished labor force participation, unemployment, family instability, poverty; and criminogenic behavior and social policy exacerbates these outcomes, then these outcomes are intended.

A report issued by the Human Rights Watch and the Sentencing Project entitled *Losing the Vote, the Impact of Felony Disenfranchisement Laws in the U.S.*, indicated that by 1998 approximately 3.9 million people nationwide were incarcerated, placed on parole, or probation. By 2007, this total number had increased to 7.3 million. By 1998, one-in-fifty adults had permanently lost the right to vote because of a felony conviction. By 2004 this ratio had reached one in thirty-seven. By 2010, an estimated 5.3 million Americans were denied the right to vote because of laws that prohibit voting by people with felony convictions. The likelihood of being imprisoned at some point in their life for Black males born in 1991 was 29%; this is compared to 16% for Latinos and 4% for Whites. Better than one third (38%) of all prison inmates in the U.S. are African American, and 20% are Latino (2009). Not only do offenders serve their ascribed terms, but they are ostracized as citizens even further. Except for two of the fifty states (2009), all felons are disenfranchised in some systemic phase (incarceration, parole or probation).

The increased rate of African American imprisonment from 1980-2009 has been a direct consequence of harsher sentencing policies and the national war on drugs. Harsher sentencing policies have included mandatory minimum sentencing, three strikes laws, truth-in-sentencing laws, and in particular drug sentencing laws, all of which produce a disproportionately higher rate of incarceration for African Americans. African Americans constitute 36% of arrests for drug possession. According to the U.S. Department of Justice, arrestees for drug offenses were almost five times more likely to be sent to prison in 1992 than in 1980. They further indicated that while most current illicit drug users were White (72%), the increasing number of drug offenses accounted for 27% of the total growth among Black inmates, 7% of the total growth among Latino inmates, and 15% of the growth among White inmates. More recently Department of Justice data (2009) reflects that 65% of arrests for drug abuse violations were White and 33.6% were Black. In a *New York Times* article dated May 6, 2008 it was reported that "...large disparities persist in the rate at which Blacks and Whites are arrested and imprisoned for drug offenses even though the two use illegal drugs at roughly equal rates...."[32]

Criminal laws are enforced in a manner that is massively and pervasively biased. The Substance Abuse and Mental Health Services Administration (1999) reported that "...there were an estimated 9.9 million whites (72 percent of all users), 2.0 million blacks (15 percent), and 1.4 million Hispanics (10 percent) who were current illicit drug users in 1998. And yet, Blacks constituted 36.8% of those arrested for drug violations and over 42% of those in federal prisons for drug violations. African Americans comprise almost 58% of those in state prisons for drug felonies; Hispanics account for 20.7%."[33] Whites were less likely then African Americans to be sent to prison among persons convicted of drug felonies in state courts. In the ten-year period from 1999 to 2009, arrests for drug abuse violations for Whites represented almost 61% of the total U.S. drug abuse arrests while Blacks represented 38% among adults 18 years old or older (U.S. Department of Justice, 2009).[34] The Bureau of Justice Statistics (1998) indicated that "...Thirty-three percent (33%) of convicted White defendants received a prison sentence, while 51% of African American defendants received prison sentences. It should also be noted that Hispanic felons are included in both demographic groups rather than being tracked separately so no separate statistic is available."[35] In a May 6, 2008 *New York Times* article it was reported that a Human Rights Watch study stated that racial disparities in drug law enforcement reflected an overwhelming focus on low income urban areas, with arrests and incarceration the main weapons. One result is a devastating impact on the lives of Black men. They are nearly 12 times more likely to be imprisoned for drug convictions as adult White men. The Sentencing Project (2011) reported that more than 60% of the people in prison are now racial ethnic minorities. For Black males in their twenties, 1 in every 8 is in jail or prison on any given day. These trends are intensified by the disproportionate impact of the "war on drugs" in which three-fourths of all persons in prison for drug offenses are people of color.[36]

Racial disparity in drug sentencing is further exacerbated among women. According to the *New England Journal of Medicine*, "...regardless of similar or equal levels of illicit drug use during pregnancy, Black women are 10 times more likely than White women to be reported to child welfare agencies for prenatal drug use."[37] As indicated by the Human Rights Watch (June, 2000): "The racially disproportionate nature of the war on drugs is not just devastating to Black Americans. It contradicts faith in the principles of justice and equal protection of the laws that should be the bedrock of any constitutional democracy; it exposes and deepens the racial fault lines that continue to weaken the country and belies its promise as a land of equal opportunity; and it undermines faith among all races in the fairness and efficacy of the criminal justice system."[38] Again the Sentencing Project 2011 Report indicates that the number of women in prison, one-third of whom are incarcerated for drug offenses, is increasing at nearly double the rate for men. The collateral effects of the increased incarceration rates for women are infectious.

Among the various states, there has been little or no correlation made between the type of crime (i.e. treason, crimes against the state, or election fraud) and disenfranchisement. No other democratic country bars ex-offenders from voting for life, or has such a significant percentage of its citizens who cannot vote as a result of felony convictions. In the U.S., conviction of a felony carries collateral 'civil' consequences apart from penal sanctions such as fines or imprisonment. Among other 'civil disabilities' that may continue long after a criminal sentence has been served, offenders may lose the right to vote, to serve on a jury, or to hold public office. While both state and federal law imposes civil disabilities following criminal conviction, state law governs removal of the right to vote even if the conviction is for a federal rather than state offense. As a consequence, there is an insidious social impact of mass imprisonment on communities of color. Marc Mauer and Meda Chesney-Lind (2005) argue that "...defendants are convicted of felony crimes in a system in which the routine workings of an increasingly massive and punitive criminal justice system have consequences not only for these individuals whose lives are directly touched, but for an extended group of parents, spouses, children, friends, and communities who have committed no crimes....".[39] Nowhere are these effects more dramatic than in the African American community. Three quarters of a million Black men are now behind bars, and over 2 million are under some form of correctional supervision.

State constitutional law, in practice, as it pertains to the disenfranchisement of felons, has had a disproportionately racial impact. Race and the disenfranchisement of felons are irrevocably linked. The advent of harsher sentencing policies regarding specific categories or types of crime has exacerbated this correlation between the disenfranchisement of felons and race. Federal Judge Henry Wingate aptly described the political fate of the disenfranchised: "...The disenfranchised is severed from the body politic and condemned to the lowest form of citizenship, where voiceless at the ballot box ... the disinherited must sit idly by while others elect his (or her) civil leaders and while others choose the fiscal and governmental policies which will govern him and his family...."[40]

As will be illustrated in a felon voter attitude survey, New Jersey, Maryland, and Virginia are normative models in this political and social collateral effects paradigm. By 2006, New Jersey was among the 39 states that automatically restored felon voting rights, Maryland was among the 9 states that permanently disenfranchised some felons, and Virginia was among the 3 states that permanently disenfranchised all felons. These facts represent a real and present challenge to the "right to vote freely for a candidate of one's choice" and, consequently, the "essence" of the modern U.S. democratic state.

The nature, extent, and impact of African American felon disenfranchisement on the modern democratic state present practical and theoretical concerns. To the degree that state law, policy, and practice permanently limits or marginalizes minority group influence on political majorities, the state betrays or negates its founding values.

Thematic Literature Review of Pertinent Criminal Justice Research

Research and literature on felon rehabilitation programs support my argument that felon disenfranchisement, as a collateral effect of imprisonment, presents a fundamental contradiction to the principle of fair and equal representation. It also stands in contradiction to pro-social behavior changes requisite to the successful reintegration of felons into community. In 2005, as quoted by Thompson, 2008, Governor Vilsack passed an Executive order restoring voter eligibility to disenfranchised felon Iowans. Governor Vilsack stated that "...research shows that ex-offenders who vote are less likely to re-offend and the restoration of voting rights is an important aspect of reintegrating offenders in society so that they become law-abiding and productive citizens...."[41] Background literature and research on changing institutional attitudes and direction in sentencing policy; response to prison conditions; offender outcome studies; public safety issues; reform law; and felon disenfranchisement issues dates back to the 1970's. Some of the problems to which the research and practitioners responded were prison overcrowding, staggering increases in the cost of incarceration, high rates of recidivism and the collateral effects of these policies at the expense of the public and public safety. Over the past 30 to 40 years, costs, reform advocates, global or world pressure, alternative sanction program results, academic and social research trends were some of the driving forces that changed the thinking in Criminal Justice policy and practice from "Nothing Works" in the rehabilitation of criminal behaviors; to the "What Works" genre of the 1990's; to "Best Practices" studies that began in the mid-1990's. Leaders in the "What works" genre included the Canada Correctional Service, and persons such as Paul Gendreau, James Bonta, Donald Andrews, James McGuire, Sharon Kennedy, and many others.

From 1980 to 2008, the adult Correctional population in the U.S. more than quadrupled in probation, parole, jail, and prisons. According to the Bureau of Justice Statistics (BJS) 2009 government report, probation numbers increased from 1,118,000 to 4,270,917, the local jail population increased from 184,000 to 785,500, the prison population increased from 319,600 to 1,518,500, and the parole population increased from 220,400 to 828,169 during this 30 year period. This meant that in 1980 the U.S. Correctional population was 1,842,100 and by calendar year 2008 there was a total U.S. Correctional population of 7,308,200, a total that exceeded any other nation in the world. The PEW Center on the States (2009) reported that one in 31 Americans were under some form of correctional control by the end of 2007. This compared to one in 77 a quarter century earlier. Over the last 20 years, state spending on corrections increased by 300 percent. This dramatic growth was the result of political and criminal justice policies that lengthened sentences and incarcerated criminals for minor, non-violent offenses. As indicated in the PEW studies, the average per offender costs for states was $79 a day for inmates, $3.42 a day for probationers, and $7.47 a day for parolees. This increase in the U.S. Corrections population disproportionately impacted on specific cluster neighborhoods and ethnic/racial populations. PEW reported that by 2008, one in 100 persons was behind bars; the ratio for Latinos was one in 36; and the ratio for Blacks was one in 15, with the number of incarcerated Blacks aged 20-34 reaching the ratio of one to nine. As the rate of incarceration increased, so did the costs of incarceration. Studies also indicated that within 3 years of release, 60-62% of all prisoners released were rearrested.

Three issues became important in the literature: how to develop a more equitable, effective, and feasible sentencing policy; how to reduce recidivism rates; and how to measure and reliably determine program success and felon rehabilitative outcome. I argue that what remains to be examined is how to intervene on the human condition common to the criminogenic paradigm. The pragmatic question became, how can states spend less on Corrections without compromising felon outcomes and the public safety? Costs and construction concerns ushered in a re-examination of sentencing policies; ideas or recommendations as to ways to cut facility and per prisoner costs; and maximize efficiency and performance in offender re-entry initiatives and programs.

A host of practitioners and academicians responded to the demand in criminal justice reform. In addition to the work achieved by human rights advocacy groups, researchers systematically developed a science dedicated to a rehabilitative paradigm that would be both measurable and replicable. Researchers such as James McGuire, Paul Gendreau, James Bonta, and Donald Andrews collaborated to codify interventions that could be described and evaluated as programs. The premise was that any intervention carried out with offenders should specify what had taken place; to direct the work being done; to allow evaluation to occur; and to allow others to replicate successful applications. Institutional and community correctional programs were defined as having a common and primary objective: behavioral change in the targeted population. The concept of 'correction' meant "...the adjustment of behavior from a pattern that is criminal or anti-social to one that is more law abiding or pro-social...."[42] This methodology required the application of multiple services designed to respond to the assessed individual needs of the client population. These program response patterns needed to be codified and developed into curriculum. Where possible, standardization became rather common practice. This process required field testing of intervention systems in carefully controlled research trials. Once other practitioners began to emulate the results of these tests, what has become known as "Best Practices" in Corrections intervention was established. As described by McGuire, types and levels of interventions included primary prevention or situational prevention; developmental prevention; secondary prevention; and tertiary prevention. This author's professional work and the emphasis of this study focuses on the tertiary prevention population-adjudicated offenders, those already convicted of a crime. An underlying and program related premise in this work is that (political) participation, or its absence, affects the target populations adjustments to a more law abiding or pro-social behavior.

Human rights agencies and agents as well as institutional and family advocates for fair sentencing practices and equal rights have written and struggled for the rights of felons for as long as the academic and research communities have compiled data. In response to the 1960's political protests, 'cultural reforms' and urban unrest in places like New York there were institutional responses such as "get tough policy" in law and practice that translated into a "lock 'em up" mentality popularized in the Rockefeller Drug laws of the early 1970's. History and research has demonstrated that the "three strikes you're out", mandatory minimum sentencing, and restrictive and racially disproportionate punishment meted out through draconian state drug policies were unsuccessful at mitigating crime. As a result, states began sentencing too many non-violent offenders who were disproportionately poor and non-white, sentencing them for too long and too harshly. The punishment did not fit the crime, it did not reduce crime rates, nor did it achieve public safety. Examples of the collateral effects of this criminal justice system were codified in a range of publications such as: *Invisible Punishment* by Marc Mauer and Meda Chesney-Lind; *Releasing Prisoners, Redeeming Communities (Reentry, Race, and Politics)* by Anthony Thompson; *Race to Incarcerate* by Marc Mauer; *Lock Down America* by Christian Parenti; *The Disenfranchisement of Ex-Felons* by Elizabeth Hull; *When Prisoners Come Home (Parole and Prisoner Reentry)* by Joan Petersilia; *The Right to Vote, The Contested History of Democracy in the United States* by Alexander Keyssar; and *Relief from the Collateral Consequences of a Criminal Conviction: A State by State Resource Guide* by Margaret Colgate Love.

Marc Mauer and Meda Chesney-Lind described the invisible punishments experienced by not only felons, but an extended group of parents, spouses, children, friends, and communities who have committed no crime – primarily living in cluster neighborhoods and predominantly representing people of color. The term invisible punishment describes the effects of policies that have transformed family and community dynamics, exacerbated racial divisions, and "...posed fundamental questions of citizenship in democratic society..."[43] A chapter in Mauer and Lind's book (*Invisible Punishment*), dedicated to "Mass Improvement and the Disappearing Voter" connected the dots between racial disparities in the criminal justice system, disenfranchisement laws, and racial exclusion both politically and socially. Parenti argued that the U.S. is a law and order society aimed at isolating and excluding poor people of color. He states that capitalist societies require the existence of a "surplus population." Mass imprisonment, with 95% of the felon population returning home over a five-year period would serve this purpose well. Overall, the literature illustrated a relationship between the politics of mass imprisonment, race, felon re-entry, community redemption, and felon disenfranchisement. Hannah Arendt (1965) has defined poverty as being a political, rather than a natural phenomenon (the result of violence and violation rather than scarcity).[44] Poverty and its relationship to housing, health, health care, unemployment, the legal system, and the political process, particularly in urban cluster neighborhoods, was a determinative factor in every facet of the criminal justice system from arrests, to incarceration, to re-entry into community. The right to vote is a right that is preservative of all other rights. For this reason, Petersilia described felon disenfranchisement as a 'Civil Death' for felons.

One of the contributions this book makes to the literature is that it illustrates the interrelationship between disproportionate rates of incarceration and felon disenfranchisement, and illustrates how felon disenfranchisement increases the imbalance of power between political majorities and minorities. This racial imbalance of power also resulted in a permanent dichotomy of wealth, influence, and life chances. The felon survey results indicated that the right to vote mattered to this felon population, and most poignantly that this disproportionate balance of power impacted not only the disenfranchised, but the general welfare of the democratic state.

CHAPTER 3

The Right to Participate: A Matter of Law and Moral Certitude

A Matter of U.S. Constitutional Law

We are a nation of laws, and not men. State felon disenfranchisement has its basis in law, state constitutional history, the influence of the 'peculiar institution', values and customs unique to each state. Testing the legitimacy of felon disenfranchisement law rests with this history and a legal interpretation of the terms "political intent" and "impact".

In this chapter, I examine the constitutional grounds, history, and judicial arguments for and against ex-felon disenfranchisement. I will demonstrate that judicial review in felon disenfranchisement cases has been based on changing and sometimes conflicting theoretical beliefs about the nature of man, human need, and perceived notions of human difference.

Three main themes are explored in this chapter: 1) the history of discriminatory state disenfranchisement law; 2) the role, legacy, and effects of the Black Protest Movement and the 1964 and 1965 Civil Rights Acts vis-à-vis felon disenfranchisement law; 3) and the ways judicial review and judicial activism can shape and be shaped by world views regarding the social, political, and racial landscape of the United States. These relationships are contextualized by close readings of the 14th Amendment, the Voting Rights Act (VRA) of 1964 and 1965, and the constitutional guarantee that electoral laws and procedures are the prerogative of the separate states.

The 14th Amendment is the 'due process' and 'equal protection' amendment upon which most Supreme Court opinions regarding individual rights in general, and African American and felon rights in particular, have been based. The Supreme Court cases of Skinner v. Oklahoma; Baker v. Carr; Reynolds v. Sims; and Richardson v. Ramirez are used to demonstrate this point. Using the 14th Amendment, I examine the questions: does the violation of the 'equal protection' clause apply to African Americans and felons as politically marginalized groups? Is there a rational basis or a legitimate and legal justification for the disenfranchisement of felons?

As a consequence of the 'peculiar institution' of slavery and the Civil War, the 15th Amendment was ratified and specifically guaranteed African Americans the right to vote. The combined purpose of the 15th Amendment and the VRA was to eliminate voter discrimination based on race in the U.S. The VRA of 1964 and 1965 was written to address a 100 year history of segregation and racial discrimination in voting which had occurred since the ratification of the 15th Amendment. Using the 14th and 15th Amendment as well as the VRA, I examine whether African American felon disenfranchisement is unconstitutional based on racially disproportionate representation, and selective intent and impact on the African American voter community. The Supreme Court cases of Mobile v. Bolden and Hunter v. Underwood are central to an examination of these questions.

This chapter is an examination of fairness in citizen participation and political practice in the U.S. It is an inquiry into the legal and paradoxical history of suffrage as it pertains to felon disenfranchisement. The U.S. Constitution expressly defines governance, citizenship, and the right of citizen participation. Amendment X affirms that, "...(the) powers not delegated to the U.S. by the constitution, nor prohibited by it, are reserved to the States respectively, or to the people..."[45] Amendment X was the last of the ten amendments ratified in 1791, commonly known as the Bill of Rights and it left the question of citizenship open to interpretation. Thus, from 1791 through 1992, in seven of the twenty-seven amendments to the U.S. Constitution, federal legislators have sought various solutions to the questions posed by Amendment X and have broadly defined and redefined citizenship, citizenship rights, and voter participation.

The debate over citizenship rights first began in 1791, and continued over an 80-year period (1791 to 1870), as legislators found themselves faced with conflicting definitions of citizenship. This was a period when many aristocratic leaders did not trust the 'common' man, and democracy was perceived as being close to anarchy. The 'masses' were seen as too untrustworthy to govern themselves. This is best illustrated in the words of one founding father, John Adams (1776):

> ...The same reasoning which will induce you to admit all men who have no property , to vote, with those who have,... will prove that you ought to admit women and children ; for, generally speaking, women and children have as good judgments, and as independent minds, as those men who are wholly destitute of property; .... Depend upon it, Sir, it is dangerous to open so fruitful a source of controversy and altercation as would be opened by attempting to alter the qualifications of voters; there will be no end to it....[46]

These words describe a nation which, in its first one hundred years of existence, excluded African Americans, Native Americans, all women, and men not of adult age from the right to vote. It was a nation in which the moral standard denied the right to vote to persons based on race, gender, and class. George Washington and John Adams were not elected to the Presidency by a majority of adult citizens, but rather by a majority of a minority of citizens.

Opposition to this aristocratic view emerged over time, and began as a challenge to property and class as criteria for voter exclusion:

> ...It seems to me, sir, that we should not abandon the principle that all men are to have some participancy in the affairs of government, particularly when they may be called upon to contribute to the support of that government. These people... are subject to pay taxes, they are liable to be called on to perform road labor and various other duties; and, sir, they... when the tocsin of war has sounded, rally to the field of battle.
>
> Shall we say that such men shall not exercise the elective process....?

-Mr. Davis of Massac, Illinois State Convention, 1847 [47]

This argument, supporting the right to vote for propertied and non-propertied white males, expanded the number of citizens that could participate in the electoral system for one group, but not for people of color, women, or the 'have-nots.' Without exception, African Americans, Native Americans, women, and men of legal age, have fought in wars beginning with the American Revolution and throughout the history of this nation.

The controversy over the right to vote and the rationale argued by the founding fathers is effectively stated in the following lines by the great compromiser, Benjamin Franklin:

> ... Today a man owns a jackass worth fifty dollars and he is entitled to vote; but before the next election the jackass dies. The man in the meantime has become more experienced, his knowledge of the principles of government, and his acquaintance with mankind, are more extensive, and he is therefore better qualified to make a proper selection of rulers – but the jackass is dead and the man cannot vote. Now..., pray inform me, in who is the right of suffrage? In man or in the jackass...? [48]

U.S. constitutional governance is a matter of law and moral conviction as illustrated through: U.S. constitutional amendments; the history of women's suffrage; the struggle to achieve voting rights for African Americans and to end residency and property requirements, literacy tests, and felon and pauper exclusions. To understand this history, we must understand that all of these events were closely intertwined with one another and could only be understood as part of a single fabric. Defining citizenship and citizen rights became one of the first constitutional prerequisites to determining voter participation and representation. As the result of a civil war and the ratification of the 13th Amendment, slavery was abolished in the U.S. The 14th Amendment, ratified in 1868, defined citizenship and citizenship rights as, "...All persons born or naturalized in the U.S., and subject to the jurisdiction thereof, are citizens of the U.S. and of the State wherein they reside. No State shall make or enforce any law which shall abridge the privileges or immunities of citizens of the U.S....."[49] The Founding Father's aristocratic constraints notwithstanding, no legal exception of persons based on race, gender, class, or legal status was written into the 14th Amendment. The 14th Amendment is the most frequently invoked amendment in judicial cases arguing for the enfranchisement of felons. Two key constitutional phrases were represented in the following words:

> "...(N)or shall any State deprive any person of life, liberty, or property, without due process of law; nor deny any person within its jurisdiction the equal protection of the laws...."[50]

This amendment first defined U.S. citizenship. The guarantee that individual rights of citizens cannot be deprived or violated and that they must be protected in law and practice is expressly stated in the 14th Amendment. It was in the 14th Amendment, Section 2 that 'the right to vote at any election' was ascribed to citizens as a 'right' as opposed to a 'privilege' for the first time. Throughout U.S. history the due process and equal protection clause of the 14th Amendment has been the foundation of arguments protecting the rights of individuals and marginalized groups, including African Americans and felons. The 15th Amendment, ratified in 1870, was written to provide for the right of African American's to vote at a time in history when "...previous conditions of servitude..."[51] would have excluded people of color from representation and political participation.

As illustrated in Mobile v. Bolden, 1980, the 15th Amendment was a specific guarantee of the right of African Americans to vote. This definition allowed for African American voter dilution unless racial 'motivation and purpose' could be proven. In contrast, in Hunter v. Underwood, 1985, the 15th Amendment was utilized as a fundamental argument for the legalization of felon enfranchisement. In Hunter v. Underwood it was noted that felon disenfranchisement had the 'intended effect' of disenfranchising African Americans and consequently led to voter dilution within specified African American communities in Alabama.

Three other amendments relate directly to the historical struggle for voter rights in the U.S. As a result of the women's suffrage movement, in 1920 Congress passed the 19th Amendment affirming that the right to vote "… shall not be denied or abridged by the U.S. or by any State on account of sex…."[52] The 24th Amendment abolished restrictions on the right to vote based on poll taxes or any other tax.[53] This amendment again, was a direct result of a social movement against impediments presented by a White-dominant majority in their attempt to prevent African Americans in particular from exercising their right to vote. This amendment and the passage of the Civil Rights Acts of 1964 and 1965 were important because they further illustrated the historical significance and necessity of federal intervention on state voter restrictions based on race.

It took almost 200 years to assure the right to vote for women and African Americans in the U.S. By 1971, the 26th Amendment was ratified guaranteeing the right of citizens of the U.S., "…who are eighteen years of age or older…"[54] to vote. As a nation then, the U.S. definition of citizenship currently includes women and all persons born or naturalized in the U.S. including people of color. No state has the power to make or enforce any law which would abridge the privileges or immunities of citizens of the U.S. No state has the authority to deprive any person of life, liberty, or property, without due process of law; nor to deny to any person within its jurisdiction the equal protection of the laws. These legal protections are inclusive of the right to vote, and are inalienable.

However, contrary and inconsistent state felon disenfranchisement law has created a crazy quilt of electoral procedures and practices nationwide. Despite the apparent Constitutional wins achieved by women and African Americans, equal protection under the law has not been granted to all citizens within the United States. As previously noted, according to the U.S. Constitution (Article I, Section 4) electoral procedures are prescribed by each separate State legislature. As a consequence, the exercise of the right to vote by felons for national, state, and local representatives is subject to the arbitrary accident of geography. A convicted burglar in Maine may vote in elections while in prison, in Alabama he/she cannot. In 2002, a felon could not vote for twenty years if convicted of a drug violation in the state of Maryland, or ten years for other convictions absent a governor's pardon. In New Jersey, a person convicted of theft automatically regains the right to vote after completing his/her entire sentence (i.e. prison, parole, or probation), while in Virginia such an offender is denied the right to vote for life barring a pardon from the Governor of that state.

The social and political impact of state variations in the right to vote for felons can be illustrated by the 2000 and 2004 Presidential elections. "...In the 2000 presidential election, 4,686,539 Americans – more than two percent of the voting-age population – were barred from the polls...."[55] The right the Supreme Court has called "...the right preservative of all other rights..."[56] was denied most felons in the U.S. More specifically, as of 1998, Florida had the greatest felon population of any state in the nation – 647,100 felons and ex-felons. A total of 436,900 of this population were ex-felons. Approximately 31% or 204,600 of this felon population was African American.[57] Until 2007, Florida disenfranchised felons for life. As determined by the Florida Elections Committee, in election year 2000, G.W. Bush won the State of Florida by 537 votes (and was confirmed by the U.S. Supreme Court). Had Florida's disenfranchisement law (and moral conviction) provided for automatic restitution the outcome of this election may have been dramatically different. If only 25% of the 436,900 ex-felons had voted (consistent with low income voting patterns) and, had 90% of the African American ex-felon voting population voted Democratic (consistent with African American voting patterns in the 2000 election), G.W. Bush would have lost the State of Florida and consequently the Presidential election in 2000.

In the 2000 Presidential Election, at a time when the popular vote margin was .5% (Gore- 48.4% and Bush- 47.9%), 2% of the voting age population was barred from voting because of felon convictions.[58] This same pattern existed in more recent times. "...At the close of 2003 there were roughly 6.9 million people under the control of the American criminal justice system, or roughly 3.2% of the country's adult population....[59] "...By the end of 2004 there were 4,143,792 Americans on probation and 771,852 on parole...."[60] In the 2004 Presidential election, Stanley and Niemi (2006) stated that there was a 2.4% margin of difference in the popular vote between Kerry and Bush (48.3% v. 50.7% respectively)[61], while the rate of disenfranchisement was approximately 1.45% nationally.

The constitutional question that arises is whether disenfranchising felons violates the equal protection guarantees of the 14th Amendment, as well as the principle of "one person, one vote" affirmed in the 1964

Supreme Court case, Reynolds v. Sims. Is it fair and just, or unconstitutional to disenfranchise 3.2% of a citizen population which has paid its debt to society? This question becomes more poignant in a political environment where Presidential elections are won or lost by .5% to 2.4% margins of the popular vote. In the following sections, the questions of felon disenfranchisement in relation to equity, fairness, and constitutionality are more fully explored.

A Matter of State Law

> "...If there is no struggle there is no progress....This struggle may be a moral one, or it may be a physical one, and it may be both moral and physical, but it must be a struggle. Power concedes nothing without a demand. It never did and it never will...."
>
> Frederick Douglass, 1857 [62]

The effort to achieve fairness in citizen participation and political practice in the U.S. has been both an intimate and historical struggle. Democratization in the U.S. has been defined by the powers not delegated to the federal government, but rather reserved to individual states. Kieser (1997) defined democratization as,

> ...much more than holding elections and allowing political parties to form. Democratization means the reduction, and movement along a continuum toward the ultimate elimination of political inequality....Democratization is not a one-time battle but an ongoing clash, in which some groups strive to overcome subordination while other groups may face threats to the political access they have achieved...[63]

Beginning in 1776, for African Americans, women, and felons, "...the struggle for democratization [has been] a struggle to end the second-class political status ...that prevents them from influencing agenda setting, decision making, and other aspects of politics that directly affect their interests...."[64] Individuals and groups that have been permanently marginalized or disenfranchised must be included in the process of democratization if representative governance and political equality is to be achieved.

This struggle for the right to vote has taken place in each of the separate State legislatures as prescribed by their respective State constitutions. Over time, it has been a battle of wills, a battle of moral judgment, and a battle between State Legislators. In many ways this right that is 'preservative of all other rights' has represented the historic class struggle and antagonism of the 'have mores,' 'haves,' and 'have-nots.' In Keyssar's words "...Americans had debated, and fought over, limitations on the right to vote from the revolution to the late twentieth century, and those debates and contests told much about the meaning of democracy in American political life and culture...."[65]

Power concedes nothing without a demand. Voter restrictions had been placed on the poor, immigrants, African Americans, Native Americans, and women for more than two hundred years. Through the spirited élan of people of color, women, and organized resistance movements, politically marginalized groups redefined citizenship as well as who is qualified to vote. Still, disenfranchisement and voter restrictions continued to plague specific groups. These voter constraints were based on conflicting moral and theoretical beliefs about the nature of man, human need, and perceived notions of human difference. It is this 'difference' principle (legislated into State law) that became its own self-fulfilling prophesy. The two fair and equal representation issues of voter dilution and disproportional representation (of the African American community) are a consequence of racial disparities in the social and criminal justice systems and the intertwining of race and felon voter restrictions. For African Americans, conflicting felon state law concerning the right to vote strikes at the heart of essential human needs such as autonomy, both public and private; identity; recognition; and participation.

Historically, voter exclusions have been legislated based on property requirements, citizenship, property tax, age, residency, poverty, mental incompetence, literacy and literacy comprehension, grandfather clauses, poll taxes, the White primary and felony restrictions. Many of these voter restrictions intentionally excluded persons based on their gender, race or class. From 1776 through 1790 voter restrictions based on property or taxpaying, residency, gender, and race were established by the thirteen states. Voting requirements among the various States included: estates worth 40 shillings; 50 acres of land; payment of all yearly taxes; poll tax; 50 pounds proclamation money; 2 years, 1 year, or 6 months residency; males or freemen; and in four of the thirteen States eligible male voters were required by law to be White. In Maryland the requirement was: 50 acres or property above the value of 30 pounds; there was no residency requirement for a property holder and a 1-year residency requirement for a non-propertied resident; the person had to be a 'freemen'; and beyond this requirement, there was no specific reference to race. New Jersey had a similar property requirement: a 1-year county residency requirement, with no written gender or race reference. In Virginia, the property and residency requirements were similar to Maryland's and New Jersey's. However, both gender and race requirements in Virginia were specific: male and White.[66]

By 1855, there were 31 States in the Union and the race requirement in voting among these States had been made clear and specific. Five States had no race requirement; 10 States initially had no race requirement, but by 1855 each had changed their State constitution to specify White only; and the 16 remaining States entered the Union specifying a White only voter requirement. Similar exemptions were made for Native Americans. Maryland began without a race requirement but by 1810 had established a White only requirement. New Jersey had no constitutionally established race requirement until 1844.[67] Virginia established a White only voter requirement in 1762, and did not relinquish this practice until the Civil Rights Act of 1964. By 1835, North Carolina legislated that, "… no free Negro, free mulatto, or free person of mixed blood, descended from Negro ancestors to the fourth generation inclusive…, shall vote for members of the Senate or House of Commons…."[68] Texas stipulated that "…Indians not taxed, Africans, and descendants of Africans were excluded.[69] By 1855, belief that there was (or should have been) a difference in political representation and participation among people based on race was firmly established in law among these states. Nine of the thirteen permanently disenfranchised States were included in the twenty-six States that established race as a voter requirement. Race and criminal conviction became intertwined as part of the single fabric of voter restriction and exclusion.

By 1857 twenty-four States, based on racial or punitive justifications, had established constitutional exclusions for persons convicted of a felony. While the language of exclusion was more similar than dissimilar among the various States, there were distinctions between automatic restoration States and those States which became permanent disenfranchisement States. Common language by which the States excluded felons was: "...those convicted of a felony, persons convicted of any infamous crime, dueling, or bribery...."[70] Maryland, New Jersey, and Virginia were examples of the difference between the States:

[TABLE 7]

State	Date	Constitutional Exclusion
Maryland	1851	Persons convicted of larceny or other infamous crime – unless pardoned by the executive; persons convicted of bribery at elections – forever disqualified from voting.
New Jersey	1844	Those convicted of felonies unless pardoned or restored by law to the right of suffrage.
Virginia	1850	Those convicted of an infamous offense. Those convicted of electoral bribery or an infamous offense.

[71]

Maryland provided voter restoration for persons convicted of larceny or other infamous crimes, and permanent disenfranchisement for persons convicted of bribery at elections. New Jersey stipulated that all persons convicted of felonies could be pardoned or restored by law. Virginia had no provisions for voter restoration. While property and residency requirements remained relatively constant among the various states, voter exclusion by race and felony conviction became more reflective of the moral or theoretical beliefs of the separate states. Each State was able to define 'infamous offenses' differently. Infamous offenses could mean anything from chicken stealing (Oklahoma), to larceny (Maryland), to 'other high crimes or misdemeanors' (Alabama). The intertwining of various voter restrictions had more than one purpose, and did not simply evolve by accident any more than did the variations in State definitions of an 'infamous offense'. Andrew L. Shapiro (1993), in his article in the *Yale Law Journal* entitled: "Challenging Criminal Disenfranchisement Under the Voting Rights Act: A New Strategy", indicates that: "... (A)fter the Civil War, Southern conservatives gathered at state national conventions and codified a growing white backlash against Reconstruction generally and Black suffrage in particular."[72]

The voting barriers that were adopted included literacy and property tests as well as poll taxes among other limits already enumerated. The intent was to disenfranchise as many Blacks as possible without violating the 15th Amendment. In states such as Louisiana and Mississippi the Black voting electorate was reduced from 44% to 1%, and from 70% to 6% respectively as a result of such legislation. Shapiro writes that the effect was clear: "...In the eleven former confederate states, 324 Blacks were elected to state legislatures and Congress in 1872, but only five were elected in 1900."[73]

Shapiro cites further evidence that laws excluding criminals from the electorate provided White supremacists with: "... a critical line of defense in case other parts of the suffrage plan did not withstand attack."[74] Between 1890 and 1910, many Southern states tailored their criminal disenfranchisement laws, "... to increase the effect of these laws on Black citizens."[75] He indicates that the racially discriminatory intent of this legislation was clear, as exemplified by the constitutional convention of 1890 in Mississippi:

> The convention swept the circle of expedients to obstruct the exercise of the franchise by the Negro race. By reason of its previous condition of servitude and dependence, [the negro race is] a patient, docile people, but careless, landless, and migratory within narrow limits, without forethought, and its criminal members given rather to furtive offenses than to the robust crimes of the whites.[76]

The presumed characteristic criminal distinctions between the races included burglary, theft, arson, and obtaining money under false pretenses for African Americans; and robbery, murder, and other violent crimes for Whites. Other states including South Carolina

(1895), Louisiana (1898), Alabama (1901), and Virginia (1901- 02) followed this exclusionary practice. The list of "furtive offenses" expanded to include adultery, arson, wife-beating, housebreaking, and attempted rape. While the purpose and intent of this legislation was made clear immediately upon its passage, the impact of such legislation on African American voter participation, dilution, disproportionate representation and autonomy is still unfolding.

As previously indicated, modern racism began as the tripartite system of White supremist domination ended. While some voter requirements such as property requirements, property tax, and poverty were eliminated over time, other requirements gained greater emphasis such as literacy and literacy comprehension, poll taxes, grandfather clauses and felony convictions. Progressively, voter restrictions were aimed less at poor whites and immigrants, and more at African Americans, Native Americans, and women. Race and gender mattered. By 1855, 24 States established 'White male' as a requirement for voting; 4 others had excluded "Indians" not taxed, Africans and their descendants, and men of color; and the 3 remaining states had no constitutional race requirement. During this same period, 24 States established a felony constitutional exclusion, while seven States did not.[77]

These State constitutional felony exclusions did not change significantly through 1920. The Union was now comprised of 48 States, and 39 of these States excluded felons from the right to vote, while 9 States had no felon exclusion laws. Maryland, New Jersey and Virginia were examples of the felon disenfranchisement laws most States legislated:

In each of these States there was no significant change in felon disenfranchisement restrictions from 1790 through 1920. While there was little or no change in felon voter restrictions within each State, punitive felon laws did change. In comparison to New Jersey and Maryland, the most extreme change was the specification of felon voter law in the State of Virginia. No longer did Virginia law include only electoral bribery and infamous offenses, but the law now included: petty larceny, obtaining money or property under false pretenses, embezzlement, treason, bribery, forgery, or perjury. Felons could now be excluded from the right to vote based on an 'assumed proclivity toward' specific types of crime. These laws applied to felons in

Virginia whether the crime was committed within or outside of the State of Virginia. In Virginia, a felon remained disenfranchised until the disability was removed. Yet there was no written procedure for removing such a disability. By comparison, Maryland's disability lasted until such time as the felon was pardoned by the governor. Still, in Maryland it remained somewhere between difficult and impossible to acquire such a pardon. New Jersey provided two restoration alternatives: a gubernatorial pardon or restoration by law.

[TABLE 8]

State	Felon Disenfranchisement Law (1870-1920)	Duration of Exclusion
Maryland	Those convicted of larceny or other infamous crimes, and those involved in election bribery.	Until pardoned by governor
New Jersey	Those convicted of felonies	Until pardoned or restored by law to suffrage
	Election Bribery	Ten years
Virginia	Persons who, prior to the adoption of this constitution, were disqualified from voting, by conviction of crime, either within or without of this State: persons convicted after the adoption of this constitution, either within or without this State, of treason, or of any felony, bribery, petit Larceny, obtaining money or property under false pretenses, embezzlement, forgery, or perjury.	Until disabilities have been removed

As time has gone by, the inconsistencies between state felon disenfranchisement laws have remained. State franchise law within Maryland, New Jersey, and Virginia established distinct constitutional guidelines concerning felons' right to vote:

- In Maryland, Article I, section 4 of their State constitution reads, "...The General Assembly by law may regulate or prohibit the right to vote of a person convicted of infamous or other serious crime or under care or guardianship for mental disability (ratified in November, 1972 and again in 1978, this section will be changed effective July, 2007 to automatic restoration)...."[79]
- In New Jersey, with a State constitution adopted in 1947 and updated through 2006, Article II, Section I: 7 reads, "...The Legislature may pass laws to deprive persons of the right of suffrage who shall be convicted of such crimes as it may designate. Any person so deprived, when pardoned or otherwise restored by law to the right of suffrage, shall again enjoy that right...."[80]
- In Virginia, Article II, Section I reads, "...In elections by the people, the qualifications of voters shall be as follows: Each voter shall be a citizen of the U.S., shall be 18 years of age, shall fulfill the residence requirements set forth in this section, and shall be registered to vote pursuant to this article. No person who has been convicted of a felony shall be qualified to vote unless his civil rights have been restored by the Governor or other appropriate authority. As prescribed by law, no person adjudicated to be mentally incompetent shall be qualified to vote until his competency has been reestablished...."[81]

Respectively, these state felon franchise laws represent partial (or some) permanent felon disenfranchisement, automatic restoration, and permanent felon disenfranchisement States as defined in this study. The number of states represented in each category, including 'no restrictions' have continued to change over an eight year period.

[TABLE 9]
Total State Felon Disenfranchisement Law

	No Restric- tions	Automatic Restoration	Some Permanent Disenfranchise- ment	All Permanent Disenfranchise- ment
1998	4	32	5	8
2002	2	36	5	8
*2006	3	39	7	4

* includes Virgin Islands, Puerto Rico; and D.C. (Table 1, P. 29, Table 7&8) [82]

Over the last decade there has been a general trend away from strict or permanent felon disenfranchisement. This has been primarily due to the efforts of individuals and organized groups fighting for the rights of felons both in and outside of the courts and prisons such as The Human Rights Watch, The Sentencing Project, and FAMM (Families Against Mandatory Minimum Sentencing); an academic and social (1980's) trend away from punitive policies of containment based on research on 'Best Practices' in reducing criminogenic behaviors and recidivism; and equally as significant, the soaring costs of mass incarceration of increasing numbers of felons on federal, state, and local levels. It was estimated that the average cost of incarcerating a felon in the U.S. was $33,000 to $39,000 a year, as compared to an average cost of $22,000 to $25,000 for residential or community release programs.[83]

In addition, research has shown that the outcome of rehabilitative services for felons significantly reduced recidivism rates as compared to recidivism rates among those released directly from prison. Joan Petersilia (2003) indicated that felons who participated in therapeutic communities, substance abuse programs, cognitive behavioral programs, and vocational educational programs: "... have been shown to reduce recidivism rates by 8-15%...." Petersilia went on to indicate that "... these programs pay for themselves in terms of reducing future justice expenditures...."[84] This disenfranchised felon population was and is called upon to perform road labor and various other duties, and are subject to pay(ing) taxes. The ex-felon population pays taxes just as any other citizen would (for the rest of their working life and then some), and as a specific example, as reported in the Community Corrections Coalition of New Jersey's (CCCPNJ) Newsletter of Fall, 2006, in the State of New Jersey felons completing their sentence in Halfway Houses contributed nearly $550,000 in federal taxes, $61,000 in State taxes, more than $161,000 in child support, more than $300,000 in fines and restitution, and more than $931,000 toward their own stay, offsetting the cost of providing halfway house services in the State of New Jersey during fiscal year 2006. This federal and state revenue was collected from a maximum of 2600 felons, or approximately 10% of the New Jersey felon population.

Costs, more than the political and ethical challenges in felon disenfranchisement law, was more causative of policy changes made in criminal justice practice in the U.S. Increasingly, the cost of constructing new prisons, incarcerating greater numbers of felons, as well as the organized support of the rights of felons altered State felon laws. Clearly, there have been both practical and theoretical explanations for the changes in felon disenfranchisement law.

As previously indicated, by 2007 one in forty-one adults in the U.S. had currently or permanently lost their voting rights as a result of felony convictions; 1.4 million (13%) of all African American men were disenfranchised; more than 2 million Latinos and Whites were disenfranchised; among African American women, one-in-fifty could not vote – a rate four times greater than non-African American women; and 2.1 million disenfranchised persons were ex-offenders who had completed their sentence. These figures make this both a personal and intimate struggle.

Politically marginalized populations have intentionally been severed from the body politic by a dominant majority for self-serving purposes that were in conflict with 'the rule of law', the 'difference principle', and the principles of equal representation and equal rights. Felon disenfranchisement evolved as an extension of the historical questions concerning voter rights, the most basic of which has always been, "who should vote?" We must ask: Why have felons been disenfranchised? Which political institution should be the arbiter charged with validating or invalidating felon disenfranchisement? And, should the court be more alert when a claim discriminates against felons as a 'discrete and insular minority' who might not be able to use the ordinary political process to overcome discrimination?

Civil Rights Act 1964 and 1965 and the Courts

In the twentieth century, social movements and decades of political conflict and change met the challenge of white, male hegemonic domination in the U.S. The Women's Suffrage movement of the 1920s and the Black Protest Movement or Black Liberation Struggle of the 1950s and '60s were two forces which edged the U.S. closer to universal suffrage and fulfillment of the ideal that "all (persons) are created equal." There are those who have argued that the Black Protest Movement did little in the way of achieving sustainable progress for African Americans as measured by quality of life indices. To the contrary, I argue that not only did this movement alter my life chances, but participation in this struggle permanently altered how I saw myself, others, and the world. Not only does this subjective example illustrate how these movements were significant for their constituent groups, but also that the Black Protest Movement became the élan by which the passage of the Civil Rights Act (CRA) of '64 and '65 was achieved.

In August, 1965, Congress passed the Voting Rights Act (VRA) of 1965. As evidence of the significance of the Black Protest Movement, the CRA of '64 and '65 has been used as a basis for almost every court challenge to equal protection and due process cases pertaining to race discrimination and the right to vote for African Americans, minorities, and felons since its inception. From its inception, the contest for felon rights has been associated with African American history and the struggle to gain the right to vote.

The Voting Rights Act of 1965 prohibits race discrimination in voting practice or procedure. The CRA 1965 prohibited literacy tests and poll taxes which had been used to prevent Blacks from voting. In 1975, Congress recognized the need to protect citizens who did not read or speak English well enough to participate in the political process and expanded the protections of the Voting Rights Act to them. According to a report of the Bureau of the Census from 1982, in 1960 there were 22,000 African Americans registered to vote in Mississippi, but in 1966 the number had risen to 175,000. Alabama went from 66,000 African American registered voters in 1960 to 250,000 in 1966. South Carolina's African American registered voters went from 58,000 to 191,000 in the same time period.

The Civil Rights Act of 1964 demonstrated that congress had the power to enforce the law; that social imperatives can be effectuated through political institutions; and that the legislature and judiciary conjointly can resolve political circumstances which threaten to manipulate or distort the democratic process. In the following enactment we see the death toll of the resurgent White Supremacist 'tripartite system of racial dominance' and the movement toward equal rights for women, African Americans, Latinos, and ultimately state felons. The 14th and 15th Amendments and the CRA Act of 1965 were combined in the defense of equal protection and due process court cases.

An Act (VRA-1965)

"To enforce the fifteenth amendment to the Constitution of the United States and for other purposes:

Be it enacted by the Senate and House of Representatives of the United States of America in Congress assembled, that this Act shall be known as the Voting Rights Act of 1965.

Section 2. No voting qualification or prerequisite to voting, or standard, practice, or procedure shall be imposed or applied by any State or political subdivision to deny or abridge the right of any citizen of the United States to vote on account of race or color."[85]

This act has historic and jurisprudential significance for the fact that it lifted discriminatory restrictions on voting that had targeted minorities for over a century. Section 2 prohibited states to "deny or abridge" the right to vote based on race. Section 5 placed the burden of proof on states to prove changes to electoral laws non-discriminatory. Equally as significant, this Act established the Justice Department as having jurisdictional oversight of registration and electoral laws. A series of Supreme Court cases (1960-1995) based on the 14th Amendment and this act, delineated an evolution of voting rights legislation and jurisprudence which established judicial precedent for a more inclusive electoral process. One of the most effective responses to felon disenfranchisement has been the litigation of felon rights in federal and state court.

There are times in history when the legislators and the elected lead, and there are times when they are led by the organized élan' of the masses. The Black Protest Movement or Black Liberation struggle of the 1950s and 1960s was a force which edged the courts and the U.S. closer to universal suffrage and fulfillment of the ideal that 'all persons are created equal'. The Black Protest Movement is a story which began with the political awakening of a nation through characters and events such as Emmett Till; Rosa Parks; Martin Luther King; Little Rock; James Meredith and "Ole Miss"; Sit-ins; SNCC; Freedom Riders; Medgar Evers; Freedom Summer; MFDP; Selma; Montgomery and the 'bridge to freedom'. It was a decade of struggle which culminated in the passage of the Civil Rights Acts and the Voting Rights Act, which have been used as the basis for every court challenge to equal protection and due process cases pertaining to race discrimination and the right to vote for African Americans, minorities, and felons since their inception. Thus, this is a story which cannot go unreported. However, the story and the struggle for equality and equity before the law did not end with the passage of these Acts. As will be shown in the following section, even with the guarantees of these Acts in place, there is no guarantee that their spirit will always be upheld within the U.S. court system.

A Matter of Judicial Review

> "…The most elegant and long lasting changes that humans can effect are ones that involve philosophic restructuring of irrational beliefs…"
>
> (Byron Lewis, 1996)

The problem of felon disenfranchisement is greater and extends further than providing an opportunity for felons to participate in the electoral process. Underlying the problem of felon disenfranchisement is the question, 'Can humankind live by the 'rule of law'? Issacharoff, Karlan, and Pildes frame this question as one of power and power relationships:

...Because democratic politics is not autonomous of existing law and institutions, those who control existing arrangements have the capacity to shape, manipulate, and distort democratic processes.... Democratic politics constantly confronts the prospect of law being used to freeze existing arrangements into place, a phenomenon we call political lockup...[86]

The authors continue on to ask, "... Can institutional arrangements be developed that ... prevent the law from being manipulated by existing office holders for self-interested aims...?"[87] In its authoritative capacity, the Supreme Court utilizes judicial review to assure that the rule of law shapes democracy in the U.S.

An examination of the rule of law and democratic politics begins with the assertion that it is the obligation and "...power of the Supreme Court to determine the constitutionality and ... validity of the acts of other branches of government..."[88] Issachoroff, Karlan, and Pildes argue that, "... any inquiry into institutional arrangements leads inevitably to the question of the relationship between courts, legislatures, executive officials, and voters in overseeing democratic processes...."[89] In Marbury v. Madison it was determined that "...judicial review – the power of the courts to invalidate laws as unconstitutional ... is emphatically the province and duty of the judicial department...."[90] Chief Justice Marshall held in this case that the judiciary has final authority on matters of constitutional interpretation. It is this distinction, with one exception that makes this democracy a 'government of laws and not men':

And be it further enacted, that the Supreme Court shall have exclusive jurisdiction of all controversies of a civil nature where a state is a party, except between a state and its citizens; and except also between a state and citizens of other states, or aliens, in which latter case it shall have original but not exclusive jurisdiction...[91]

Marshall did note that there would not be a judicial remedy for a wrong if the subject matter was political in nature or otherwise committed to the discretion of the executive. Executive or legislative matters of a political nature would be considered nonjusticiable.

However, as illustrated by Justice Rehnquists' majority opinion in Richardson v. Ramirez, 1974, in some Supreme Court decisions judicial review and constitutional interpretation have not been rational, particularly when judges have allowed men rather than the law to rule. If a case was ruled justiciable, but the judges were limited by theoretical, ideological, religious, or situational predilections the democratic process would not be served and fairness, justice, and equality would not prevail.

This point is best demonstrated by a careful reading of the following cases: Skinner v. Oklahoma, 1942; Baker v. Carr, 1962; Reynolds v. Sims, 1964; Richardson v. Ramirez, 1974; Mobile v. Bolden, 1980; and Hunter v. Underwood, 1985. Each of these cases, while not necessarily pertaining directly to felons or felon disenfranchisement, ultimately centered on the 14th Amendment, 15th Amendment, CRA 1965, or the law as it pertains to either equal representation, equal protection, or due process.

Skinner v. Oklahoma

In Skinner v. Oklahoma, in 1942, the 14th Amendment equal protection clause was used to refine the definition of equality under the law from a loosely defined rational basis to a more scrupulous 'strict scrutiny' standard. While this case concerned theft and was not related to felon voter rights in substance, strict scrutiny became the standard for measuring equality in law and compelled clarity in law and practice whenever the courts considered legislation which treated one group differently from another (even if the nature of their crime was similar). A key principle in law which resulted from this case was that the court could be more alert when the claim discriminated against 'discrete and insular minorities' who might not be able to use the ordinary political process to overcome discrimination. Second, it was ruled that when a fundamental right is involved, courts must give strict scrutiny to laws which treat people unequally. Such laws must be justified by very strong arguments, and these arguments had to be "compelling justifications for treating one group differently from another."

The issue in Skinner v. Oklahoma was not voting, yet this illustration is central to the issue of felon disenfranchisement, equal protection, the difference principle and its impact on one's fundamental rights. As will be illustrated, a third similarity between this case and felon disenfranchisement cases was that an underlying issue in each case was fairness, equality, and race discrimination. It is my position that, as stated by Tustinet, while every legal statute treats some people differently, discrimination of discrete and insular minorities and racial discrimination are violations of the 14th Amendment and are therefore unconstitutional. In principle, there will always be majorities and minorities in a representative democracy as it relates to political factions, choices, and electoral outcomes.

The important distinction is that the creation of permanent majority and minority groups in a democracy nullifies the difference principle and equality under the law. Felons are a discrete and insular minority, politically separated and isolated from the body politic, and African Americans are disproportionately represented in that felon population. If felons are permanently disenfranchised, and African Americans are consistently and disproportionately represented in this population, then these circumstances would evidence unequal enforcement of the law based on race, and therefore be in violation of the Equal Protection clause and the VRA '64 and '65. An exception could only be justified if the courts determined a 'compelling reason for treating felons differently than other groups.'

Baker v. Carr

A second legal concern that was addressed by the courts in Baker v. Carr, 1962, was justiciability. Courts are obliged to avoid the 'political thicket' in determining which cases are within their jurisdiction. There cannot be a judicial remedy for a wrong if the subject matter was political in nature, or otherwise committed to the discretion of executive or legislative branches. The question became, how does one distinguish appropriate boundaries which would maintain constitutionally mandated separation of powers? Again, while the substance of Baker v. Carr was reapportionment and not felon disenfranchisement, the standards for determining justiciability in this case was relevant for equal protection cases in general and felon disenfranchisement in particular. Baker argued that his county had not redistricted since 1901. This fact resulted in disproportionate county representation by a ratio of ten to one, causing him to fail to receive the equal protection of the law as required by the 14th Amendment. Justice Frankfurter believed that relief for legislative malapportionment should be attained through the political process and that courts ought not to enter that political thicket. Finally, the Baker case was ruled justiciable and the case concluded with a six part test for determining which questions were political in nature, and it is this same standard of justiciability that felon disenfranchisement cases must meet. Cases which are political in nature are marked by:

1. Political questions such as issues of foreign affairs or executive war powers typically relegated to a separate branch and political department.
2. Issues lacking a judicially discoverable and manageable standard for resolution.
3. The inability to make a judicial decision without an initial political decision.
4. The impossibility of the court to make an independent resolution without expressing a lack of respect for another branch of government.
5. An unusual need for unquestioning adherence to a political decision already made.
6. The potential embarrassment emanating from multifarious pronouncements by various departments or branches of government on one question.

Dissent among members of the court raised concern for history, judicial restraint, and violations of separation of powers. Having declared Baker v. Carr justiciable, the court laid out a new test for reapportionment cases, such as Reynolds v. Sims, 1964.

Reynolds v. Sims

Issacharoff, Karlan, and Pildes' maxim with regard to political elites, "… shaping, manipulating, and distorting democratic processes…"[92] is tested in Reynolds v. Sims, 1964. The question in this case was whether the courts had the authority to prevent the law from being manipulated by existing officeholders for their self-interested aims. Reynolds v. Sims, like Baker v. Carr, was a case which dealt with reapportionment as a central issue. The underlying issue was equal representation and equal protection of the laws. This case added a third and critical building block in the foundation of the legal argument for the right of felons to vote – the principle of one person, one vote. This court test did not proceed without the use of the prior two building blocks- strict scrutiny and justiciability. It went further, challenging the rationality of disproportional voter representation (and its underlying motivations) and asserting an affirmative theoretical argument for equal representation (expressed as an "equal population principle") based on human rights and personal autonomy.

In Reynolds v. Sims, voters in several Alabama counties and other similarly situated counties argued that the Alabama Legislature deprived them of their rights under the Equal Protection Clause of the 14th Amendment. The U.S. constitution mandated that states provide a census of the population every ten years, and that representation in the House of Representatives be reapportioned consistent with any geographic change in population. As Alabama became more urban, one time rural majorities now became minorities. Yet, rural minorities were able to hold on to political power at the state level by refusing to reapportion the state legislatures. Two groups of complainants charged that the State of Alabama was guilty of malapportionment, and consequently brought complaints against representatives of the state. The federal district court found that the two apportionment plans proposed "...would not cure the gross inequality and invidious discrimination of the existing representation which all parties generally conceded violated the Equal Protection Clause, and that the complainants' votes were unconstitutionally debased...."[93]   State officials appealed stating that the District Court erred in holding these proposed corrections to be insufficient.

The Supreme Court, under Chief Justice Earl Warren found that with regard to the two proposed state corrective measures, each "...is so obviously discriminatory, arbitrary and irrational that it becomes unnecessary to pursue a detailed development of each of the relevant factors...."[94]   This case was ruled justiciable, and significantly, it found that the debasement, dilution, or denial of one's right to vote was both irrational and unconstitutional. Chief Justice Warren asserted that "...It has been repeatedly recognized that all qualified voters have a constitutionally protected right to vote...."[95]   This was followed by the

Court opinion that "...the right to vote freely for the candidate of one's choice is of the essence of a democratic society, and any restrictions on that right strikes at the heart of representative government.... (T)he right of suffrage can be denied by a debasement or dilution of the weight of a citizen's vote just as effectively as by wholly prohibiting the free exercise of the franchise...."[96]

Each of these statements address the critical issues felon disenfranchisement faces – felon voter denial and African American voter dilution and debasement. On the strength of arguments held in Gray v. Sanders, Chief Justice Warren argued that the 15th and 19th Amendments prohibit a state from overweighting or diluting votes on the basis of race or sex; and asked, "...how can one person be given twice or ten times the voting power of another person in a statewide election...?"[97]   The court concluded that, "...the conception of political equality from the Declaration of Independence, to Lincoln's Gettysburg Address to the 15th, 17th, and 19th Amendment can mean only one thing – **one person, one vote**...",[98] and further, that "...an apportionment of congressional seats which contracts the value of some votes and expands that of others is unconstitutional..."[99] As a final assertion of this 'equal population principle,' Chief Justice Warren defined an 'invidious discrimination violative of rights' as rights that are "...allegedly impaired [and are] individual and personal in nature.... The right to vote is personal."[100]

> "...Like Skinner v. Oklahoma, such a case [as Reynolds v. Sims] touches a sensitive and important area of human rights,...the right of suffrage is a fundamental matter in a free and democratic society...."[101]   The right to vote is fundamental to democracy, and fundamental rights held in common among all citizens are a measure of personal autonomy and human rights. Justice Warren concluded that "...each and every citizen has an inalienable right to full and effective participation in the political processes of his state's legislative bodies...[102] Denial of constitutionally protected rights demands judicial protection; our oath and our office requires no less of us...."[103]

The argument for the right of felons to vote was strengthened by the findings of Reynolds v. Sims. What emerges from a close examination of the findings is a strong argument for full enfranchisement:

1. The debasement, dilution or denial of one's right to vote is irrational and unconstitutional.
2. The right to vote freely [and fairly] is of the essence of democracy.
3. Political equality in a democracy can mean only one thing – one person, one vote – an 'equal population principle.'

Richardson v. Ramirez

As previously indicated, states must show that a restriction on individual or group rights was necessary to a legitimate and substantial state interest, was narrowly tailored and was the least restrictive means of achieving the state's objective to exempt any group from their voter rights while maintaining those same rights for others. In Richardson v. Ramirez (1974), the U.S. Supreme Court constructed an exemption of criminal disenfranchisement laws from strict scrutiny. The court construed the phrase, "… but when the right to vote at any election… is denied … or in any way abridged, except for participation in rebellion, or other crime…"[104] in Section 2 of the 14th Amendment as granting states an affirmative sanction to disenfranchise those convicted of criminal offenses. Summarizing Justice Rehnquist's argument for the majority and Justice Marshall's dissent best illustrates the opposing arguments concerning felon voter rights. Importantly, the central focus of this case was felon disenfranchisement.

Not only does the 14th Amendment, Section 2, speak to apportionment based on decentenial census data, but it further states that, "…when the right to vote at any election – is denied to any of the … inhabitants of such a state … except for participation in rebellion, or other crime, the basis of representation therein shall be reduced [proportionately]…."[105]   This clause became the central question debated in Richardson v. Ramirez. What were the purpose, background, and meaning of Section 2? Justice Rehnquist delivered the opinion of the court. He argued , "…legislative history indicates that the language [of Section 2] was intended by Congress to mean what it says...."[106] Justice Rehnquist based his opinion largely on the language used by the Committee of Fifteen on Reconstruction (1866), and the Reconstruction Act (1867). He argued that, "...throughout the floor debates in both the House and the Senate, in which numerous changes of language in Section 2 were proposed, the language 'except for participation in rebellion, or other crime' was never altered.... What little comment there was on the phrase in question supports a plain reading of it...."[107]

Justice Rehnquist further maintained that Congressman Bingham of Ohio [a member of the Committee of Fifteen] stated that,

> ...The second section of the amendment simply provides for the equalization of representation among all the States of the Union, North, South, East, and West... New York has a colored population of fifty thousand... if that great State discriminates against her colored population as to the elective franchise (except in cases of crime), she loses to that extent her representative power in Congress...[108]

This statement was supported by Representative Eliot of Massachusetts and Representative Eckley of Ohio. Eckley made specific reference to treason as a high crime which should warrant disenfranchisement, and argued that persons convicted of crime have always been disenfranchised. Senators Johnson of Maryland and Henderson from Missouri contrasted the right to vote of African Americans with the rights of felons, seemingly in support of the formers rights. Each argument left room for interpretation.

Justice Rehnquist further argued that at the time of the adoption of the 14th Amendment, "...29 states had provisions in their constitutions which prohibited, or authorized the legislature to prohibit, exercise of the franchise by persons convicted of felonies or infamous crimes..."[109] Justice Rehnquist's strongest argument rests with the Reconstruction Act (1867), Section 5. This Act established the conditions by which former Confederate States would be readmitted to representation in Congress. It provided, "...That when the people of any one of the said rebel States shall have formed a constitution of government in conformity with the Constitution of the U.S., ...framed by a convention of delegates elected by male citizens...except such as may be disfranchised for participation in the rebellion or for felony of common law...."[110], that state may petition to be readmitted to the Union. In order to avoid military rule of the remaining 10 states not having rejoined the Union, the Blaine amendment was approved limiting military rule until such time as readmission was achieved. This amendment "...provided that when the rebel States should adopt universal suffrage, regardless of color or race, excluding none, white or black, except for treason or such crimes as were felony of common law...."[111] the military law should stop and the states should be readmitted. Justice Rehnquist concluded that, "...This convincing evidence of the historical understanding of the Fourteenth Amendment is confirmed by the decisions of this Court which have discussed the constitutionality of provisions disenfranchising felons..."[112]

Justice Rehnquist recognized that the court had never given plenary consideration to the precise issue of felon disenfranchisement, but also stated that the courts did indicate approval of felon exclusions on more than one occasion. He concluded that the ruling in the Richardson v. Ramirez case should rest with the understanding of those who adopted the 14th Amendment inclusive of Section 2 and the historical and judicial interpretation of the amendments applicability. Rehnquist closed his argument by stating, "...[Section 2] is as much a part of the Amendment as any of the other sections, and how it became a part of the Amendment is less important than what it says and what it means...."[113]

I argue that Justice Rehnquist's judgment was limited by theoretical and ideological predilections which did not serve democratic process or principle. While he recognized that the court had never given plenary consideration to the precise issue of felon disenfranchisement, he summarily determined that the means by which Section 2 became a part of the Amendment was less important than what it says. By determining that the interpretation of Section 2 'supports a plain reading of it,' Justice Rehnquist ignored the fact that he himself relied on an interpretation of 'the historical understanding' of the phrase. His assertion that how it became a part of the Amendment is less important than what it means, is contradicted by the fact that historical reference, the 'Committee of Fifteen on Reconstruction', and the Reconstruction Act were relied upon by both

Justice Rehnquist and Justice Marshall in arguing their respective majority and minority opinions.

What Rehnquist's argument overlooked was that the central issue he presented in this case was the applicability of strict scrutiny, while the underlying issue was race discrimination. How Section 2 became part of the 14th Amendment cannot be argued as less important than 'what it says, and what it means'. The phrase, 'except for participation in rebellion, other crime' was situational in nature and required interpretation. Rehnquist stated in his majority opinion that, "...the Supreme Court of California erred in concluding that California may no longer... exclude from the franchise convicted felons who have completed their sentences and paroles.... Accordingly, we reverse and remand for further proceedings not inconsistent with this opinion...."[114] 'The rule of law' in a democracy enables the State to mediate liberty and equality, justice and fairness. Courts are obliged to utilize judicial review to assure that the rule of law shapes democratic process so as to promote and mediate liberty and equality, fairness and civility. Rehnquist, and his court, distorted the democratic process and failed to fulfill their judicial obligation. The express meaning of Section 2 was inextricably related to circumstances which led to the inclusion of the words "or other crimes". The manner in which Section 2 became part of the 14th Amendment was inextricably connected with what it said and what it meant. By contrast, Justice Marshall's dissent demonstrated this connection, and satisfied the 'difference' principle, 'justice as fairness,' and the constitutional mandate for equal representation.

Justice Marshall began his dissent with a statement of fact in law, that none of the named plaintiffs are residents in Viola Richardson's county. "...In sum, there is no controversy between the parties before this Court.... Petitioner Richardson seeks to use the named plaintiffs' controversy...as a vehicle for this Court to issue an advisory opinion on the issue presented by the suit brought against her by an ex-felon in her own county...."[115] There is a principle in federal law of justiciability, upheld in Flash v. Cohen (1968), "...that federal courts will not give advisory opinions...."[116] Why would conservative Supreme Court Justice Rehnquist, with full knowledge of this principle in law, rule this a justiciable case?

Justice Marshall went further to register his dissent on the merits of the case. The central question was whether or not Section 2 of the 14th

Amendment expressly authorizes states to disenfranchise former felons. Justice Marshall referred to the same Joint Committee of Fifteen on Reconstruction and argued that with reference to the words 'or other crime' in Section 2, "...[that] the proposed Section 2 [had been] sent to a joint committee containing only the phrase 'participation in rebellion' and emerged with 'or other crime' inexplicably tacked on...."[117]   He also argued historical purpose: "...The Republicans who controlled the 39th Congress were concerned that the additional congressional representation of the Southern States which would result from the abolition of slavery might weaken their own political dominance...."[118]

Justice Marshall quoted political commentators of the period (1867) who offered the following: "...It [Section 2] became a part of the 14th Amendment largely through the accident of political exigency...."[119]   He indicated that the purpose of Section 2 was to prevent, or rather cure a particular electoral abuse – the disenfranchisement of African Americans. The special remedy was to reduce representation in states that discounted African Americans. Marshall further argued that, "...constitutional concepts of equal protection are not immutably frozen like insects trapped in Devonian amber.... The Equal Protection clause is not shackled to the political theory of a particular era (Dilenburg v. Kramer, 1972) ....(W)e have never been confined to historic notions of equality any more than we have restricted due process to a fixed catalogue of what was at a given time deemed...the limits of fundamental rights...."[120]

In citing Reynolds v. Sims, Justice Marshall argued that citizens have a constitutionally protected right to participate in elections on an equal basis with other citizens, and that the judicial role was to protect that right when state statutes selectively distribute the franchise: "...If a challenged statute grants the right to vote to some citizens and denies the franchise to others, the Court must determine whether the exclusions are necessary to promote a compelling state interest...."[121] Marshall stated that "...It is doubtful...whether the state can demonstrate either a compelling or rational policy interest in denying former felons the right to vote...."[122]   He suggested that the only compelling interest the state may present is preventing election fraud. Marshall asserted that felon disenfranchisement was not sustainable on that ground because the disenfranchisement provisions were both over-inclusive and under-inclusive. The charge was not limited to those who had committed such fraud, and many who had committed election fraud had been treated as 'misdemeanants' and were not barred from voting. Disenfranchisement law was neither rational nor fair.

Justice Marshall rejected a second argument that if felons were allowed to vote, they would vote to change the existing criminal law. In referencing Carrington v. Rash, he argued that, "...fencing out from the franchise a sector of the population because of the way they may vote is constitutionally impermissible... differences of opinion cannot justify excluding [any] group from ... the franchise...."[123] If we are to live by the 'rule of law', each member of the state is obligated to manage his or her fear or distrust of opinion and human rationality. The history of criminal justice in the U.S. demonstrates that bad laws result from distrusting the collective will. Political elites bound by entrenched comprehensive doctrine can limit representative governance and political equality, ultimately creating permanent majorities and minorities. Justice Marshall summarized his dissent making three cogent points.

1. "...A temporal majority can use...power to preserve inviolate its view of the social order simply by disenfranchising those with different views... if we subscribe to the practice of permanent marginalization of specific populations...."
2. "...The process [and practice] of democracy is one of change. Our laws are not frozen into immutable form, they are constantly in the process of revision in response to the needs of a changing society...." and,
3. "...When this suit was filed, 23 States allowed ex-felons full access to the ballot. Since that time four more states... joined their ranks...."[124]

By 2006, 39 states provided for automatic restoration, and 9 of the remaining 12 states provided varying restoration laws while the remaining 3 of these 12 states continued to practice permanent felon disenfranchisement. Given these facts, there is no practical evidence of a compelling or rational state policy interest in denying former felons the right to vote. In addition, Justice Marshall argued that Richardson v. Ramirez did not meet the requisite legal standards of justiciability.

Mobile v. Bolden and Hunter v. Underwood

Two historic Supreme Court cases that argued the interpenetration of discrimination based on race and felon disenfranchisement were Mobile v. Bolden and Hunter v. Underwood.

Mobile, Alabama was governed by a Commission form government consisting of members who were elected at-large. In Mobile v. Bolden, 1980, it was alleged that at large elections of Commissioners, "...invidiously discriminated against [African Americans] in violation of the Equal Protection clause of the Fourteenth Amendment..."[125] by unfairly diluting the voting strength of African American communities. The case was upheld by the Court of Appeals and the Commission was ordered to be disestablished and replaced by a Mayor/Council form government. The case was appealed to the Supreme Court and the ruling was reversed. The Supreme Court ruled that Mobile's at-large system did not violate the voting rights of African Americans as it related to the Fifteenth Amendment. The Court held that, "...racially discriminatory motivation is a necessary ingredient of a Fifteenth Amendment violation...."[126] Justice Stewart ruled that this amendment prohibits "... only purposeful discriminatory denial or abridgement by government of the freedom to vote on account of race, color, or previous condition of servitude...."[127] The Court also ruled against appellants based on the Fourteenth Amendment. They argued that only "...if there is purposeful discrimination can there be a violation of the Equal Protection Clause, and that disproportionate effects alone are insufficient to establish a claim of unconstitutional racial voter dilution..."[128] The case fell short of demonstrating that the appellants operated purposeful devices to further racial discrimination, "...and [further] that the one person, one vote principle had not been violated in this case..."[129] The Mobile Commission form government had to be accepted as constitutionally permissible "...even though the choice may well be the product of mixed motivation, some of which may be invidious..."[130]

Reynolds v. Sims notwithstanding, Justice Stewart ruled that political dilution and debasement cannot be considered as factors unless racial motivation and purpose could be proven. Adverse impact on a discrete minority, political marginalization, and its effects on equal representation and political equality did not matter in Justice Stewart's ruling. The VRA as amended in 1973 stated that, "... no voting qualification or prerequisite to voting, or standard practice or procedure shall be imposed or applied... to deny or abridge the right of any citizen...to vote on account of race or color...."[131] It is a moral and legal contradiction to sanction a form of representative government which 'may well be the product of mixed motivation, some of which is invidious'. It was not until Mobile v. Bolden and Hunter v. Underwood that the legality of racially disproportionate representation by intent or impact was addressed.

Since 1901, the Alabama constitution had disenfranchised persons convicted of certain felonies and misdemeanors, including moral turpitude. In Hunter v. Underwood, 1985, two appellants, one African American and one White, were convicted of the misdemeanor of presenting a worthless check. These two appellants brought suit against the Federal District Court for relief. They argued that Section 182 of the law was adopted to disenfranchise African Americans and that it had the intended effect. The District Court ruled that the disenfranchisement of African Americans was a major purpose for the Convention at which the Alabama Constitution of 1901 was adopted, although there was no specific evidence that reference to misdemeanors and moral turpitude had been based on racism. They therefore ruled against the plaintiffs. The Court of Appeals reversed the decision holding that under the evidence, discriminatory intent was a motivating factor in adopting 182 (misdemeanants) and that there could be no finding of a permissible intent. The provision for disenfranchising misdemeanants would not have been adopted in the absence of the racially discriminatory motivation, and therefore the section that applied to misdemeanants violated the 14th Amendment. The Court also implicitly found that the evidence of discriminatory impact was indisputable.

The case was appealed to the Supreme Court and it was upheld by the Supreme Court on the same grounds. The standard for this ruling in Hunter v. Underwood was, "...to establish a violation of the 14th Amendment in the face of mixed motives, plaintiffs must prove by a preponderance of evidence that racial discrimination was a substantial or motivating factor in the adoption of 182..."[132] It would then become the responsibility of the registrars to prove that the same decision would have resulted had the permissible purpose not been considered. "...It was found that the crimes selected for inclusion in 182 were believed by the delegates to be more frequently committed by African Americans..."[133] Experts estimated that by January, 1903, section 182 had disenfranchised approximately ten times as many African Americans as Whites. "...These [expert opinions] showed that the Alabama Constitutional convention of 1901 was part of a movement that swept the post-Reconstruction South to disenfranchise [African Americans]..."[134] John B. Knox, president of the Convention stated in his opening address, "...And what is it that we want to do? Why it is within the limits imposed by the Federal Constitution to establish white supremacy in this State..."[135] In Hunter v. Underwood, felon disenfranchisement was ruled discriminatory based on the motivating factors, intent, and disproportionate impact it had on African American felons.

Democratization, the elimination of political inequality in the U.S., has progressed through the courts, legislature, executive officials and activist citizens and voters overseeing the democratic process. In the case of 'discrete and insular minorities' or the struggle to end second class citizenship for African Americans, however, it has been the Supreme Court acting in its authoritative capacity to use judicial review that assured the rule of law. Acquiring the right to vote for ex-felons has been a legal, moral, and extremely intimate struggle not only for felons, but the essence of democracy.

The disproportionate representation of African Americans in the criminal justice system led to the political inequities experienced by African American felons. By January, 2008, according to the PEW Center on the States report, one-in-one-hundred U.S. citizens was behind bars. Among all men ages 18 or older the ratio of incarcerated persons was one-in-fifty-four; among White men 18 and over the ratio was one-in-one hundred and six; among Latinos 18 and over, the ratio was one-in-thirty-six; among Black men 18 and over, the ratio was one-in-fifteen; and among Black men aged 20-34 the ratio was one-in-nine. Among White women ages 35-39 the ratio was one-in-three hundred and fifty-five; among Latina women ages 35-39 the ratio was one-in-two hundred-ninety-seven; among all women ages 35-39 the ratio was one-in-two hundred sixty-five; and among black women ages 35-39 the ratio was one-in-one hundred.[136] In the U.S., the number of incarcerated felons continued to increase, and racial disparities continued to worsen.

The facts have increasingly become an international disgrace. The U.N. Committee on the Elimination of Racial Discrimination in Geneva (February 18 – March 17, 2008) stated that:

> The United Nations' Committee on the Elimination of Racial Discrimination today called on the U.S. to automatically restore voting rights to people with felony convictions upon completion of their criminal sentence, and raised concern that [existing] policies have a disparate racial and ethnic impact and may be in violation of international law.
>
> The Committee remains concerned about the disparate impact that existing felon disenfranchisement laws have on a large number of persons belonging to racial, ethnic and national minorities, in particular African-American persons, who are disproportionately represented at every stage of the criminal justice system".

As of April, 2007, forty-eight (48) states and the District of Columbia prohibited inmates from voting while incarcerated; two states (Maine and Vermont) permitted inmates to vote; thirty-five (35) states prohibited felons from voting while on parole and thirty (30) of these states excluded felony probationers as well; two states (Kentucky and Virginia) continued to deny the right to vote to all ex-offenders who have completed their sentences. Nine others disenfranchised certain categories of ex-offenders and/or permitted the application for restoration of rights for specified offenses after a waiting period.

The U.N. Committee on the Elimination of Racial Discrimination has recommended, among other things, that the U.S. "...review its definition of racial discrimination used in federal and state legislation and in court practice so as to ensure... that it prohibits racial discrimination in all its forms, including practices and legislation that may not be discriminatory in purpose, but in effect...."[137]

Given that African Americans are disproportionately represented at every stage of the U.S. criminal justice system, how can the courts prohibit racial discrimination in form, practice, purpose and intent? What has happened since Hunter v. Underwood? Increasingly states have adopted automatic voter restoration laws and practices with regard to ex-felons, inclusive of various restrictions as determined by each state. To this extent, the response to the question of who should vote has been expanded to include more ex-felons. Still all data indicates that the reasons felons and ex-felons have been disenfranchised have not changed. The historical reasons for felon disenfranchisement have been, and continue to be, voter discrimination based on race   and punitive (and puritanical) justifications.

While there have been many challenges to existing felon disenfranchisement laws, the Supreme Court has taken on this challenge only twice. As indicated by William Walton Liles in his article, "Challenges to Felony Disenfranchisement Laws: Past, Present, and Future", "...the courts holdings have established guidelines for what must be present to successfully challenge a felony disenfranchisement law under the Equal Protection Clause....[138] The five cases presented in this study summarize these guidelines as: strict scrutiny; justiciability; upholding the principle of "one person, one vote," the equal population principle and proportional representation; equal protection with narrow, compelling, and rational exceptions; purposeful discrimination, mixed motivations, and intentional voter dilution; and intentional effect and discriminatory impact on African American felons in particular. Since Richardson v. Ramirez (1974), the challenge has been to test the constitutionality of felon disenfranchisement laws. Legal arguments for and against felon disenfranchisement proceeded through the end of the century based on two principles: to show a pattern of unequal or selective enforcement, or to prove that the law was enacted to intentionally discriminate against African American felons.   Challenging felon disenfranchisement through the court system has been a slow and arduous process; success has been measured in the reduction of felon disenfranchisement law on a state-by-state basis.

Six cases dating from 1974 through 1998, tell the story of this legal battle. Only months after Richardson v. Ramirez, Thiess v. State Administrative Board of Elections, Maryland (1974) attempted to invalidate felon disenfranchisement. In this case the courts ruled that unequal enforcement of the Equal Protection Clause could invalidate felon disenfranchisement law. Still, as a result of insufficient evidence, this decision was not upheld. Seven years later, in Allen v. Ellison (1981), it was argued that intentional race discrimination, once proven, would invalidate felon disenfranchisement based on the 14th Amendment clause. In 1982, Williams v. Taylor held that selective enforcement of the law can invalidate a constitutional felon disenfranchisement law. By 1985, Hunter v. Underwood ruled that both intentional and purposeful racial discrimination in felon disenfranchisement was unlawful. In McLaughlin v. City of Canton, 1995, the court subjected the felon disenfranchisement law to strict scrutiny rather than a rational basis. This heightened level of scrutiny was upheld based on Richardson v. Ramirez.

However, Cotton v. Fordice (1998) proved a setback for invalidating felon disenfranchisement. This case was argued on the basis of intentional race discrimination. The ruling held that although the original Mississippi law was unconstitutional because it was intended to discriminate against African Americans, subsequent amendments broadened the list of crimes for which one could be disenfranchised beyond moral turpitude. In so doing, the felon disenfranchisement law no longer included merely those crimes that African Americans were presumed to commit.

In each of these cases, the central or underlying issue was race discrimination. The questions, arguments, motivation and aims of felon disenfranchisement have not changed from its original purpose dating back to 1776. The aim has been voter discrimination based on race and perceived notions of human difference. The history of felon disenfranchisement is a history of U.S. legal, moral, and ideological predilections which have not served democratic process or principle.

The purpose of this chapter has been to support my hypothesis in theory and law that the loss of the right to vote, equal protection, and fair representation for African American felons dilutes the political interests, efficacy, and representation of African American felons and politically marginalizes the voting strength of the African American community. African American felon voter discrimination has had a direct and deleterious impact on the 'rule of law' and the democratic process. This sentiment is best expressed in the *Harvard Law Review* article, "The Disenfranchisement of Ex-felons: Citizenship, Criminality, and the Purity of the Ballot Box," when the authors state:

> ...When we disenfranchise ex-felons, as when we react in
> other ways to deviance, we are not simply following an

obvious and logical course, but rather we exercise a cultural option...[139]

Chapters IV, V, and VI will illustrate the degree to which African American felon disenfranchisement in state law has had an impact on the political attitudes, motivations, and life chances of this target population in New Jersey, Maryland, and Virginia, as well as on the political efficacy and representation of the African American community.

CHAPTER 4

New Jersey: A Case Study in Automatic Felon Voter Restoration

Introduction

> ...The ballot has always been a certificate of full membership
> in a society, and its value depends primarily on its capacity
> to confer a minimum of social dignity...."
>
> (J. Shklar, 1995)

The right to vote has the capacity to confer a minimum of social dignity
for those who are not 'fenced out', and stands as a badge of ignominy
for those who are. The struggle for felon voter rights is a continuation
of the struggle for equal rights begun in the 1960's. In the second half
of the twentieth century, "Freedom Riders" boarded buses traveling
from Washington, D.C., South to encourage social equality among the
races and an end to the injustice of segregated interstate transportation
facilities. By the mid-1960's, SNCC workers had begun to organize
voter registration drives for African Americans in Mississippi who had
been threatened not to vote at the risk of losing their jobs or being
killed by KKK or WCC members. The importance of having the right
to vote could not have been better demonstrated than during the
contentious and conflict-filled 1960's Protest Movement. The common
thread between the human rights' struggle of the 60's and felon
disenfranchisement was who was being 'fenced out', why they were
fenced out, and by whom.

In preparing this chapter, I have come to realize that the deep, almost forgotten motivation for this research has been to underscore and memorialize the personal and historical importance of assuring an equal voice in governance for all people who have been wrongfully and intentionally excluded from having the right to vote. Shklar's penetrating assertion that 'the ballot has always been a certificate of full membership in society' is incomplete. The vote only has the capacity to confer a minimum of social dignity if all citizen votes have equal weight. As presented in chapters I, II, and III, a political and social challenge for this nation continues to be the elimination of permanent majorities and marginalized minorities based on race, gender, class, or social condition. The following case study in felon disenfranchisement in New Jersey is a study of a special population that was politically marginalized primarily based on race and social condition. In this chapter, I argued that, 'when we disenfranchise ex-felons, we exercise a cultural option'. This study will demonstrate how, where, and why we have built a fence that separates us from felons in one of three states. This study also illustrates the human costs of permanent political marginalization of ex-felons as a special group.

Shklar states that "...[more than] just promoting citizen interests, voting and earning are marks of civic dignity [without which one] feels dishonored, not just powerless and poor ...."[140] Two critical issues for disenfranchised felons were citizenship or full membership in the polity, and felon inclusion in the polity through voter participation and equal representation. Utilizing New Jersey as a model of state automatic voter restoration, Chapter IV examines the impact of state felon disenfranchisement law and its distinctive collateral effect on African American felons and their communities. Three specific questions are answered in this chapter. What are the voting rights and practices of citizens and felons in the State of New Jersey? What is the effect of New Jersey felon disenfranchisement law on felon voter participation, efficacy, knowledge, and attitudes? Does N.J. felon disenfranchisement law and practice have a disproportionate impact on African American felons and the political representation of the African American community?

In this chapter, I review New Jersey state felon disenfranchisement law and illustrate the impact it has had on African American felons and their community. A Felon Voter Participation Survey measured the political effect of felon disenfranchisement on felons, and ascertained felon voter attitudes in New Jersey. This survey addressed practical and theoretical questions pertaining to felon voter rights and equal representation in the polity. Survey questions measured felon voter attitudes regarding political recognition, identity, empowerment or disempowerment. The central survey question was whether New Jersey felons would vote if they had a right to? If so, would the felon vote matter in New Jersey? As illustrated in Chapter II and III, there was an underlying problem of race and racial power in understanding the impact of felon disenfranchisement. This study includes a case study of African American political representation and life chances in Essex County, the largest and second most densely populated urban county in New Jersey. I also examine the impact of African American felon empowerment and disempowerment on local elections as measured by demographics such as income, family units, education, and employment by race.

New Jersey: Voter Rights and Profiles

The State of New Jersey published a Voter Rights Handbook which describes voting requirements for citizens of that state. New Jersey felon disenfranchisement law was clearly delineated in this handbook. In New Jersey, you can vote if you are: a U.S. citizen; at least 18 years old by election day; a New Jersey resident at least 30 days before election day; not in jail, on probation, or parole because of a felony conviction; and registered to vote at least 21 days before the election. Added in the 'Quick Facts' notation was a specific reference for ex-felons. "... In N.J., ex-felons can register to vote. Any person who is no longer in prison, or has completed his or her term of probation or parole, can register to vote. THAT IS THE LAW...." (Emphasis – N.J. Voter Rights Handbook) The handbook lists internet access information for registration forms, steps for completing your voter registration application, where to submit your application, identification requirements, where to vote, and provisional ballot alternatives. With the exception of felons who have not completed their full sentence, N.J. election law is representative of the historical journey toward democratization, and simplifies access to the voting process for all of its citizens inclusive of ex-felons. In N.J. the information costs for qualified voters is extremely low to minimal.

According to the 2000 Census, the U.S. population was 281,998,273 and rose to 308,745,538 by 2010. Of this total population, there was an estimated voting age population of 205, 815, 000, and a registered voter population of 156, 421,311 (76%). In New Jersey, the total population was 8,424,354 (which remained constant in 2010 at 8,414,350), the estimated voting age population was 6,245,000, and the total number of registered voters was 4,710,768 (75.5%). By law, ex-felons are included in the eligible N.J. voting age population. As an example, according to the N.J. Department of Corrections, Bureau of Budget and Fiscal Planning there were 15,332 adult felon releases in calendar year 2000, 12,612 of whom were placed on parole. Therefore, there were a total of 2,720 felon releases that "maxed-out" in calendar year 2000. This population represented the total number of ex-felons released in calendar year 2000 that became immediately eligible to vote in N.J. It must be noted that these figures do not include the cumulative number of ex-felons having completed their parole or maxed-out in prior years, nor the total number felons having completed their probation stipulations of the total 69,559 felons on probation in CY 2000 (as reported by the N.J. Bureau of Budget and fiscal Planning, 12/07/01). The Prison Policy Initiative Atlas lists the total rate of Disenfranchisement of Voting Age Population by state. In N. J., the total estimated disenfranchised voting age population was 2.3% of the N. J. State voting age population (as compared to 3.8% and 5.9%, respectively, for Maryland and Virginia).

Historically, race has been a significant factor in determining who does, or does not have the right to vote in the U.S. Simply stated, the sociology of race in the U.S. has played a role in the politics of each of the separate states. In considering the demographic data defining population characteristics, certainly as it relates to felon disenfranchisement, race is most significant. According to the U.S. Census Bureau, in the year 2000, N.J.'s total population by race was 76.6% white, 13.6% Black or African American, and 13.3% Hispanic or Latino. The 18 years and over population (voter population) was 74.4% white, 12.6% Black or African American, and 12.3% Hispanic or Latino. The proportional distribution of N.J.'s population by race changed significantly from 2000-2010. By 2010 Whites comprised

68.6% (8% decrease) and Latinos, 17.7% (4.4% increase), while the Black population remained constant (13.7%). The 18 year and over population also remained constant (75%).

There is a correlation between arrests, convictions, incarceration rates and urban demographics. Several factors such as education, unemployment rates, family stability, and poverty have a high correlation with rates of incarceration. The fact that African Americans and Latinos are disproportionately represented in the lower rungs of this demographic scale increases the probability that African Americans and Latinos will be disproportionately represented in the corrections system. Both nationally and statewide, the disparity in quality of life indices based on race is significant. High school graduates were 82.1% of the state population as compared to the national total of 80.4%; nearly 30% of N.J. adults possess a bachelor degree as compared to 24.4% of all adults nationally; median household income in N. J. was $57,338 in 2000, and $68,444 in 2010 as compared to the national median income of $44,334 in 2000 and $50,221 in 2010. State per capita income was $27,006 (2000) and $34,566 (2010) as compared to $21,587 in 2000 and $27,041 in 2010 per capita income in the U.S. Black and Latino children complete less than a 9th grade education at a rate 5-6 times greater than whites (23.3%, 27.8%, and 4.5% respectively). Almost 88% of whites complete high school or more while the equivalent rate for Blacks and Latinos was 77% and 56%. Unemployment rates were 3.6% for whites and 9% and 6.7% for Blacks and Latinos. The married couple rate for whites was 82%, and 47% and 68%, respectively, for Blacks and Latinos. Female head of household was 13% for whites and 45% and 23.7% for Blacks and Latinos, poverty among whites was 8.2%, and 26% and 25.6% for Blacks and Latinos. More than one-third of all Black and Latino children live in poverty as compared to one tenth of white children.

The problem of political inequalities by race begins with social disparities based on race. This African American, urban sociology was intimately linked with who was most likely to be arrested and incarcerated, and therefore disenfranchised. African American felony arrests and convictions were disproportionately represented in urban cluster neighborhoods, and this data correlated with the racially disproportionate impact of felon disenfranchisement. In the research project, "Disproportionate Minority Contact in the Juvenile Justice System: A Study of Differential Minority Arrest/Referral to Court in Three Cities", completed by Hulinga, Thornberry, Knight, and Lovegrove (2007), the risk factors for arrest and court referral included: Family SES, Family Structure, Parenting habits/skills, Parent characteristics (age, education, police contacts), Youth characteristics (hyperactivity, repeated grades, CAT reading, language, math scores, poor grades, lack of guilt, weapons use, gang membership), and neighborhood characteristics (organization, disorganization). This study documents a correlation between race and racial power, social disparities, and the disproportionate rate of arrests and convictions of African Americans. Mauer and King (2007) indicate in a separate study that, "...African Americans were incarcerated at nearly six (5.6) times the rate of Whites, and Latinos at nearly double (1.8) the rate of Whites...."[141]

In 2001, the total New Jersey felon population was 28,622, and in 2009 the total population was 25,436 (-11.1%). The N. J. Bureau of Budget and Fiscal Planning and N.J. DOC Offender Characteristics Report (1/20/00) indicated that 18% of the incarcerated population was Latino, 17% was white and 64% was Black in CY 2000. By 2009, the proportions were 18% Latino, 20% White, and 61% Black. The parole proportion was the same, while the probation population was 11% Latino, 53% white, and 33% African American. According to the Urban Institute Justice Policy Center [NJISJ] (2003), the average N.J. inmate functions at a 6.0 grade level in reading and a 5.4 grade level in math. Our data indicated that most inmates either have never been employed or have been consistently or inconsistently under-employed. While the average age of the felon population was 34, 78% of this population was between the ages of 20 and 40. Thirty-eight percent were drug offenders (82% of this population was arrested for selling or distribution). Forty percent of the felon population was committed for violent crimes, and the rest were committed for property or public policy offenses. Eleven percent was identified as having a mental illness, and a total of 32% were identified as having at least one chronic or communicable physical or mental health condition. Ninety–one percent of this felon population was male. The median term for Corrections inmates was 5-6 years. On average, 95% of this population returned to community after completing their sentence. By 2009, the only changes in this data was that 29% of the corrections population was in for drug offenses, 50% were committed for violent crimes, and 96% were male. The rest of the social characteristics of the population remained constant.

The New Jersey voter profile included: three-quarters of a voter population that was registered to vote; ex-felons that represented 2.3% of the over-all voter population; among the 18 and over population three-quarters were White, and the balance were evenly divided between Blacks and Latinos. Nationwide, Blacks and Latinos were five times more likely not to finish the 9th grade than Whites. White students had a significantly greater probability of completing high school than Black or Latino students. Unemployment rates for Blacks and Latinos were almost 2-3 times greater than whites. Female head of household rates for Blacks and Latinos were 2-3 times greater than for whites; married couple rates for whites were almost twice the rate of Blacks and one-third greater than Latinos; poverty among Blacks and Latinos was three times greater than for whites; median household income for N. J. was significantly higher than the national average at 64.5 (thousand), in comparison to the median income for Newark of 34.5 (thousand).

It is significant that the demographics of the felon population mirror the sociology of African American and urban populations. This voter profile describes majority and minority populations that have divergent needs, and dramatically different life chances and consequences. Mauer and King (2007) indicate that there has been, "...a 500% rise in the number of people incarcerated [since 1970] in the nation's prisons and jails, representing a total of 2.2 million people behind bars...."[142]   African Americans "...now constitute 900,000 (41%) of the total 2.2 million incarcerated ...."[143] This exponential growth has disproportionately impacted the African American community. "...Statistics document that one in six Black men had been incarcerated as of 2001. If current trends continue, one in three Black males born today can expect to spend time in prison during his lifetime...."[144]

If we view the social dichotomy between majority and minority populations in Rawlsian terms, existing inequalities should be adjusted to contribute in the most effective way to benefit the least advantaged first. African American ex-felon interests are not represented in mandatory minimum sentencing, expanded drug sentencing, or "3 strikes you're out" legislation. Legislation emphasizing education, health, employment training and placement, substance abuse awareness, and parenting skills best reflect African American felon interest group needs. The only way to achieve fair representation for ex-felons is to assure their voice at the ballot box. In New Jersey, the total estimated ex-felon voter population is 143,635. How significant are these numbers? If this ex-felon population could vote, would they? And, if ex-felons voted, would it make a difference in public policy, ex-felon life chances, and the African American community?

New Jersey Felon Voter Attitude Survey: A Matter of Choice?

Automatic voter restoration in New Jersey assures ex-felons the right to vote. This is common practice among the 39 automatic restoration states (CY 2006). A felon voter survey was administered to this New Jersey population to measure voter attitudes among this special class of voters. This survey sample was not a random sampling, but rather a sample determined by the accessibility to a pre-release population residing at the Center for Urban Education, Inc., Newark New Jersey. Through the cooperation of the New Jersey Department of Corrections, this writer was allowed to survey incoming pre-release felons who were within one year of their parole eligibility date. I am grateful for the assistance and support of N.J. Commissioner George Hayman in allowing this survey to be administered to this N.J. felon population. This survey was administered to 409 New Jersey felons in CY 2007, and the central question asked was: "... If you were able to vote, would you vote in an election?" The range of responses included:

> "...I would vote because I feel something better needs to be done...."
> "...I would vote because everyone has the right to voice their choices...."
> "...I would not vote because I feel its set anyway...."
> "...Felons should be able to vote because we do change...."

"...I would vote because I feel my vote would make a difference...."

Seventy-six percent (76%) of the respondents said yes they would vote if they could, and twenty-four percent (24%) said no, they wouldn't. By contrast, voter turnout in Presidential election year 2000 was 54.2%, and 60.3% in 2004.[145] In 2008, the voter turnout rate was 61.6%, the highest vote turnout rate since 1964. There was a significant contrast between voter participation in the 2000, 2004, and 2008 Presidential elections and self-reported felon voter participatory interest. This distinction in voter participation is more poignant when compared over the past forty year Presidential electoral period, from 1964-2008. During this time voter turnout reached a low of 50.8% in 1996, and a high of 63.3% in 1964. Voter turnout continued a steady decline during this period, with the exception of 1992 (56.8%), and did not begin to turn upward (to 61.6%) until 2008. These facts make it all the more significant that a population of felons who have experienced political marginalization, would indicate a higher rate of voter interest than the general population.

The racial and ethnic composition of the survey population was 75.1% Black, 12.7% Latino, and 8.3% white. Twenty percent of this population was committed for violent offenses, 66% were committed for drug offenses and the remaining 14% were committed for property or public policy offenses. Eighty-three percent of this population was between 22 and 40 years of age. The surveyed population self- reported that 45% of the respondents were high school graduates or that they had received their G.E.D. Another 16.6% indicated that they had completed some college or Vocational Education. Fifty-one percent of the respondents classified themselves as low income. Forty percent classified themselves as middle income.

Approximately two-thirds of the state felon population was Black, and three quarters of the survey population was Black. One third of the state felon population was incarcerated for drug offenses and two thirds of the survey population had been incarcerated for drug offenses. In proportion to the state felon population, fewer violent offenders were included in the survey population. The survey population self-reported a higher level of education than the state felon population. In both the state felon population and survey population 70-80% of the population was 20-40 years of age. Among felons that indicated they would vote in an election, race and age indices were consistent with the total felon survey participants. Among the felon population that said they would not vote, the survey population had a higher percentage of younger respondents (56% age 22-29, as compared to 36% for yes respondents, and 40% for all respondents).

Forty-nine percent of the yes respondents self-reported themselves as low income, and approximately 60% of the no respondents reported themselves as low income. The corresponding percentages reported as middle income were 43% and 31.6%. Among the yes respondents the proportion of violent offenders was similar to the total survey population, while the no respondents had a higher percentage of violent offenders (25.5%). This percentage was still lower than the state felon percentage of violent offenders (40%). Among the yes respondents, the percentage of drug offenders (68%) was similar to the total survey population, while the no respondents had a lower percentage of drug offenders (59%). Both were higher than the state felon percentage (34%). One question this data raises is whether there is a correlation between voter attitude and types of crime. For example, violent offenders typically serve longer sentences than drug offenders. Further studies could determine whether longer sentences might have an adverse effect on felon voter attitude. Not unlike the general voter population, the felon surveyed population had a higher percentage of younger respondents that said they would not vote.

An important measure of felon voter attitude is voter participation. The felon voter survey included questions concerning registration, prior voting practices, and campaign activities as indices of felon voter participation. Survey respondents were asked the question: "Have you ever registered to vote?" Thirty-five percent of the respondents said that they had registered, while 64% said they had not. By comparison, 41% of the yes respondents said they had registered to vote while 58% said they had not. Fifteen percent of the no respondents indicated that they had registered to vote, while 84% said they had not. A second question asked: "Have you ever voted in an election?" Twenty-four percent of the surveyed population had voted in an election. Seventy-five percent had never voted in an election before. Twenty-eight percent of the yes respondents had voted prior to being incarcerated, and seventy-two percent had not.

Ten percent of the no respondents had voted in the past, while almost 90% had not. Prior felon voter practices had a significant effect on felon voter attitudes, political efficacy, and participation. A third political participation question was: "Have you ever participated in campaign activities?" Seventeen percent of the surveyed population had participated in campaign activities and eighty-one percent had not. By comparison with the survey population, nineteen percent of the yes respondents had participated in political campaigns, eighty percent had not. Among the no respondents, 12% had participated in political campaigns while 86% had not. Participation in campaign activities was the lowest participatory level of engagement for both respondent groups. The highest level of voter participation among this felon population was voter registration and voting. This, once again, was consistent with general electoral population practices.

The literature on voter participation in American politics supports these results. As reported by Verba, Schlozman, and Brady (1998), about 14% of U.S. citizens participated in political campaigns. They indicated that, "...Voting stands out clearly as the more commonly reported activity....Fewer than one in four respondents reported making a campaign contribution,...and fewer than one in ten indicated having worked as a volunteer in an electoral campaign....[146] They indicated that while 71% of their survey population stated that they voted in the 1988 General Election, in fact only about 50% actually did. Verba, Schlozman and Brady stated that self-reports of voting are exaggerated and that over-reporting of turnout is common.[147] While 76% of the N.J. survey respondents may have a 'felt need' to vote in an election, it is more probable that 76% of this felon population would not vote if they could.

These facts are supported by voter turnout rates reported by the 2012 U.S. Census (CPS) and *Vital Statistics* (2009-2010). Almost 131 million people reportedly voted in 2008, an increase of 5 million voters over 2004. This increase included 2 million more Black voters, 2 million more Latinos, and 600,000 more Asians. The age group 18-24 years of age also showed a statistically significant increase from 47% to 49% from 2004 to 2008. Black voter turnout increased to 13% (from 11% in 2004), Latino vote to 9% while White voter turnout reduced by 1% to 66%. Overall, demographic voting patterns were the same: women voted at a higher rate than men (53% to 47%); lower income levels participated at a lower rate than higher income levels (i.e. $15,000 or below - 6%, 30,000-49,000 – 19%, 50,000-79,000 – 21%).

Educationally, voter turnout for the "no high school" population was lowest at 4%, High School graduate voter turnout was 20%, some college was 31%, college graduates was 28%, and post graduates was 17%. Voter turnout increased with age. The critical difference in voter turnout in 2008 over 2004 was among Blacks, Latinos, Asians, and the younger aged voters (18-24).

There is a social group phenomenon in voter attitudes and participation. Abramson, Aldrich, and Rohde (1999) stated that while, "...voting is an individual act, group memberships influence voting choices because people who share social characteristics may share political interests. Group similarities in voting behavior also may reflect past political conditions...."[148] These authors further illustrated that social characteristics such as race/ethnicity, gender, age, class, income, and especially education are social group variables which are predictors (if not causes) of who will vote. Ex-felon voter practices would more likely replicate the voting interests of similar SES populations. The PEW Hispanic Center and PEW Research Center (2009) reported that the electorate in the 2008 Presidential Election was the most racially and ethnically diverse in U.S. history with almost one-in-four votes cast by non-Whites. Voter turnout for Blacks reached 65.3% (compared to 66.1% for Whites). Latino participation increased to 49.9% and Asian voter participation increased to 47% in 2008.

Pomper (2001) stated that in the Presidential Election of 2000 there was a turnout of 17% among persons aged 18-29, and 33% among persons aged 30-44. The turnout among persons earning $15,000 or less was 7%, among persons earning $15,000-29,999 the turnout was16%, and among persons earning $30,000-$49,999 the turnout was 24%. In the 2000 General Election, Blacks represented 10% of voter turnout, and Latinos represented 4%. Educationally, voter turnout was 5% for persons with a 12th grade education or less, and 21% for persons having completed a high school education.[149] As illustrated, these demographic patterns slightly increased in 2008. It is reasonable therefore, to project that between 17% and 24% of this felon population would vote if they could, based on self-reported registration, prior voting practices and race, age, income, and educational indices. As reported in this survey, the majority of felons would vote if they could. In 2008, 3,144,831 felons were ineligible to vote in the U.S.; 98,246 in N.J.; 78,114 in Maryland; and 62,319 in Virginia. These figures included persons in prison, on parole or probation.[150]

In the open-ended responses, residents were asked to explain why they would or would not vote if they could, and one response read: "I would not because I feel its set anyway." This is an example of the response one felon had who decided he would rather not vote. The word 'set' means fixed, not only as a foregone conclusion, but also as policy and practice which this felon sees as a disservice. These policy decisions and efficacious consequences were in the interest of the advantaged, at the expense of the disadvantaged. Further evidence of this divide is illustrated in comparing 'yes' responders to 'no' responders to the question of voter participation. With regard to registration, campaign participation, and prior voting participation, 'no' responders had a significantly lower rate of participation than did 'yes' responders. These 'no' responses are at once, a resignation of one's political rights and an indication of a lack of self-esteem, identity, and dignity. To further illustrate this point, question no. 31 read: "If you answered yes or no to question number 14, please explain why you would or would not vote in an election."

[TABLE 10]

	Yes–Respondents		No–Respondents	
My vote would not matter.	7.1%	(22)	40.8%	(40)
My vote could add political recognition and public consideration to felon issues.	19.9%	(62)	7.1%	(07)
It is too much time and trouble to vote, so I would not vote.	2.9%	(09)	14.3%	(14)
I would vote because it is my right to do so once I have paid my "debt" to society.	69.5%	(216)	37.8%	(37)
No response	.6%	(02)	0	
Total =		(311)		(98)

Fifty-five percent of the 'no' responders, as compared to 10% of the 'yes' responders said: "My vote would not matter", and "It's too much time and trouble to vote, so I would not vote". Almost 41% of 'no' responses were: "My vote would not matter." This voter attitude represents a lack of trust or faith in electoral participation among the majority of 'no' responders. This political resignation, described by Abrams, Aldrich, and Rohde as a 'decline in external political efficacy' is a learned, mental attitude which perpetuates advantage and permanently marginalizes the disadvantaged.

Almost 90% of the 'yes' responders stated positive reasons for wanting to vote. Their responses affirmed the importance of voter participation for the felon population. Approximately 70% of the 'yes' responder group said: "I would vote because it is my right to do so once I have paid my debt to society." Another 20% of the 'yes' responder group felt that: "My vote could add political recognition and public consideration to felon issues." The respondents saw felon voter participation as empowering. In response to the question, "Should felons be given the right to vote?" Eighty-seven percent of the total respondent group said that felons should be given the right to vote. Voter rights, political recognition and representation matters to the majority of the New Jersey felon population. Seventy percent of this population felt that felons should regain the right to vote upon completion of prison, probation, and parole. Future studies can examine why, in the face of intended and unintended declines in felon external political efficacy, the majority of felons continue to see voting as their right and a way of having their voice heard. This study shows that the majority of felons do recognize voting as their right and as a way of having their voice heard.

In addition to felon voter participation, felon voter attitudes are measured by political knowledge and political efficacy. It was noted by Abramson, Aldrich, and Rohde that there is a strong relationship between formal education and voter turnout. "...Better educated Americans have skills that reduce the information costs of voting and can acquire information about how to vote more easily than less educated Americans; they are more likely to develop attitudes that contribute to political participation, especially that citizens have a duty to vote and that they can influence the political process...."[151] Knowledge that contributes to political participation and the belief that citizens and voters can influence the political process enhances voter attitudes and political efficacy. The felon voter survey measured specific knowledge as it related to felon voter rights, N.J. citizen voter rights, registration, and political ideology or party preference.

Did New Jersey felons know if, or when, they would regain the right to vote? Fully 65% of the respondents knew that citizens who had been convicted of a felon crime would be able to vote once they had completed prison, parole, and probation. Better than 14% of the respondents thought that they lost their right to vote for life, and 17.6% of the respondents thought that they lost their right to vote until they completed prison, or parole, or probation; approximately one-third of the felon population did not know their political rights. There was no significant difference in these responses when examined separately as 'yes' responders and 'no' responders. Fourteen percent of the 'yes' responders, and 15% of the 'no' responders thought that they lost their right to vote for life. Sixty-seven percent of the 'yes' responders, and 60% of the 'no' responders knew they would regain their right to vote once they completed their entire sentence. Voter education as part of felon discharge planning would increase felon awareness of their rights.

Almost 66% of the felon respondents said that New Jersey citizens could vote if they met all of the following requirements: U.S. citizenship; at least 18 years of age by the time of the next election; having resided at their present address for at least 30 days; and that they were not in prison, on parole, or on probation. An equivalent percentage of respondents indicated that only persons having completed prison, parole, and probation could vote. This consistency in survey responses demonstrated that the majority of the survey population understood their rights. Again, the remaining one third of this population did not know their rights or the rights of N.J. citizens. As in the previous question, there was no significant difference in the survey populations responses when examined separately as 'yes' respondents and 'no' respondents. Between 16-17% of the survey population thought that you only needed to be a U.S. citizen to vote.

New Jersey felon respondent knowledge was limited. In response to the question, "Politically, would you consider yourself a Democrat, Republican, Independent, Third party preference, or Undecided?" Felon survey responses to this question suggested an inability to distinguish party preference. Focus group discussion suggested that party preference was not a clearly understood concept. Political ideology was equally as difficult to interpret. In response to the question, "Do you consider yourself a political liberal or conservative? One-third of the respondents were undecided, 20% were moderates, almost 12% said they were conservative, and approximately 10% indicated that they were liberal. By comparison, SES groups similar to felon populations predominantly voted Democratic. Pomper illustrated that in the 2000 General Election 90% of Blacks voted Democratic, 54% of whites voted Republican, and 67% of Latinos voted Democratic. Fifty-nine percent of those with less than a high school education voted Democratic, and those having a high school education were evenly divided on party or candidate preference. Fifty-seven percent of those earning less than $15,000 a year voted Democratic, 54% of those earning $15-29,999 voted Democratic, while the vote was evenly split between Democrats and Republicans or their candidates among persons earning $30,000-49.999. Nationally, in the General Election of 2008 95% of Blacks voted Democratic, 55% of Whites voted Republican, and 67% of Latinos voted Democratic. Sixty-three percent of those with no high school voted Democratic, 52% of those that had a high school education, 51% with some college, 50% of college graduates, and 58% of those having postgraduate study voted Democratic in 2008. Low income persons and persons up to $99,999 per year voted Democratic; and again persons earning $200,000 or more voted Democratic.

In 2000, liberal, moderate and conservative Republicans voted heavily for the Republican candidate (67%, 88%, and 95% respectively); liberal, moderate, and conservative Democrats voted heavily for the Democratic candidate (91%, 86%, and 73% respectively). Moderate independent votes were evenly split between Democrats and Republicans, while liberal independent votes favored the Democratic candidate. Conservative independents favored the Republican candidate (68%, and 79% respectively). Finally in 2000, Republicans received 35% of the total vote, Independents 26%, and Democrats received 38% of the total vote. In 2008, 89% of self-reported liberals voted Democrat, 60% of moderates voted Democrat, and 78% of conservatives voted Republican. Eighty-nine percent of Democrats voted Democratic, 52% of Independents voted Democratic, and 90% of the Republicans voted Republican. Moderates and liberals represented 66% of the vote. Felon political ideology was mostly undecided, secondly moderate, and third evenly divided between conservatives and liberals. Pomper indicated that moderate Republicans, Democrats, and Independents represented 59% of the total vote in the 2000 General Elections.[152] Combined, the undecided and moderate felon respondents equaled 51% of the surveyed population. These survey results indicate that the assumption that felons would vote heavily Democratic are not necessarily true. What is more probable, however, is that felons will vote more consistently as marginalized groups do that share common social characteristics and demonstrate common political interests.

Political efficacy is the most effective measure of voter attitude, political participation, and constitutional democratization for marginalized populations. Pomper states that George I. Balch defined feelings of external political efficacy as: "… the belief that …political authorities respond to attempts to influence them…."[153] Political efficacy implies that one can trust that one will be heard and responded to. Mutual reciprocity and a dialogical relationship between representative and the represented are integral to one feeling a sense of membership, social dignity, and empowerment in the polity. Felon disenfranchisement, by definition and intent, silences the voice of a specific minority and relegates communication to a politically elite monologue. Political efficacy is a loud, affirmative response to the question as to whether the right to vote matters. Two final survey questions demonstrate this social imperative for felons.

The question was asked, "To what degree do you feel your vote would matter?" Overall, 64% of the respondents felt that it would matter to some, good, or great degree; while 32% felt that it would not matter. Among 'yes' responders 73.1% said that the vote mattered to varying degrees, while 23.4% of 'yes' responders said it would not matter. Among 'no' responders 37.8% of the responders said that their vote would matter, while 59.2% said it would not matter. While 32.5% of the 'yes' group said it would matter to a great degree, 35.7% of the 'no' responders said it did not matter to any degree. The majority of survey responders affirm that the felon vote would matter, and almost three-quarters of the 'yes' responders affirm that the felon vote would matter. Almost one-third of the total survey responders felt that the felon vote would matter very little or no degree, and almost 60% of the 'no' responders felt that the felon vote would matter very little or no degree.

An abbreviated Sociopolitical Control Scale developed by Marc Zimmerman and James Zahniser was used in the felon survey to measure the degree to which both groups felt a sense of social dignity, or empowered or disempowered. According to this Scale, external political efficacy was an effective measure of felon autonomy, empowerment or disempowerment, community isolation, leadership competence and policy control. Zimmerman and Zahniser utilized a scale of (1-6) from Disagree to Agree to measure these social values.

For purposes of analysis, scales (1-3) have been collapsed into Disagree, and scales (4-6) have been collapsed into Agree.

This Socio-Political Control Scale measured feelings of empowerment, leadership, community isolation, and policy control for the 311 'yes' respondents and 98 'no' respondents. In all six questions, 'yes' respondents indicated definitive, positive answers. By a ratio of almost 3-1 'yes' responders said that it mattered to them that they participate in local issues and organizations; by a ratio of 3-1 they felt that local elections are important enough to bother with; two-thirds of 'yes' responders (2-1) did not feel that politics and government was too complicated for a person like them to understand; by a ratio of 2-1 they felt that people like them were generally qualified to participate in political activity and decision-making in the U.S.; by a ratio of almost 2-1 they felt that they would enjoy political participation because they want to have as much say in running government as possible; and by a 20% margin, they felt that most public officials would listen to them. 'Yes' respondents have a strong belief in their right to participate; their knowledge and competence to influence or make policy; and a relative trust that they will be heard and responded to. 'Yes' respondents not only felt that their vote would matter, but that exercising their right to vote would be empowering.

[TABLE 11]

Yes – Respondents Collapsed:	Disagree (1-3)		Agree (4-6)		No Response	
People like me are generally well qualified to participate in the political activity and decision-making in the U.S.	30.9%	(96)	65.2%	(203)	3.9%	(12)
I enjoy political participation because I want to have as much say in running government as possible.	34.7%	(108)	61.1%	(190)	4.2%	(13)
A good many local elections aren't important enough to bother with.	73.3%	(228)	21.9%	(68)	4.8%	(15)
So many other people are active in local issues and organizations that it doesn't matter much to me whether I participate or not.	76.2%	(237)	19.3%	(60)	4.5%	(14)
Most public officials wouldn't listen to me no matter what I did.	57.5%	(179)	38.6%	(120)	3.9%	(12)
Sometimes politics and government seem so complicated that a person like me can't really understand what's going on.	66.3%	(206)	29.2%	(91)	4.5%	(14)

Total = (311)

[TABLE 12]

No – Respondents Collapsed:	Disagree (1-3)		Agree (4-6)		No Response	
People like me are generally well qualified to participate in the political activity and decision-making in the U.S.	46.9%	(46)	48.0%	(47)	5.1%	(05)
I enjoy political participation because I want to have as much say in running government as possible.	63.3%	(62)	32.6%	(32)	4.1%	(04)
A good many local elections aren't important enough to bother with.	52.0%	(51)	41.9%	(41)	6.1%	(6)
So many other people are active in local issues and organizations that it doesn't matter much to me whether I participate or not.	52.0%	(51)	43.9%	(43)	4.1%	(04)
Most public officials wouldn't listen to me no matter what I did.	50.0%	(49)	46.9%	(46)	3.1%	(03)
Sometimes politics and government seem so complicated that a person like me can't really understand what's going on.	67.3%	(66)	29.6%	(29)	3.1%	(03)

Total = (98)

To what degree do these choices represent feelings of empowerment, leadership, community isolation, and policy control for the 'no' respondents? 'No' responders said by an 8% margin, that it matters that felons participate in local issues and organizations; by a margin of 10% they felt that local elections are important enough to bother with; by a ratio of 2-1 they did not feel that politics and government were too complicated for a person like themselves to understand; they were evenly divided on the question of whether they were well qualified to participate in political activities and decision-making; by a little less than 2-1 they indicated that they did not enjoy political participation and did not want to have much to say in running government; and they were evenly divided on whether public officials would listen to them.

'No' responders felt that, as individuals, they were capable of understanding what's going on but that, as a group, felons were disempowered and that their opinions would not matter; that felons were locked into a type of community isolation; slightly more respondents felt that local elections were not important enough to bother with than those who did; and that their opinions would not matter to public officials. More 'no' responders had a belief in their right to participate and their competence to make decisions than those who did not; but they did not trust that they would be heard or listened to. They did not enjoy political participation and they did not feel that their vote would matter. As a politically alienated population, this attitude had the potential to become an intended or unintended self-fulfilling prophesy.

Do Ex-felon Voter Rights Matter in Essex County?

"The mood and temper of the public in regard to the treatment of crime and criminals is one of the most unfailing tests of the civilization of any country"

(Winston Churchill, 1910)

In New Jersey (2006), the total estimated ex-felon voter population was 143,635. How significant was this number? The majority of felon respondents said they would vote if they could, and that they should regain their right to vote when they have completed their sentence. The question is, if ex-felons voted would it make a difference in public policy, ex-felon and felon life chances, and the African American community? In Chapter III, it was demonstrated that the 2000 Presidential Election was so polarized that 570 votes in the state of Florida ultimately determined 'who would be President'. In Florida felons had been permanently disenfranchised, but had ex-felons been given the right to vote George W. Bush would very likely not have become President of the U.S. Based on this probability, the ex-felon vote in 2000 could have altered U.S. political leadership and made a difference in history. Fair representation for felons is measured not only by who can vote, but also who would vote and who benefits first. This section of chapter IV focuses on who can vote in Essex County, who should benefit first, and the potential effects of African American felon empowerment or disempowerment.

Essex County is the second most densely populated urban county in New Jersey. By 1999, Essex County had the highest proportion of African Americans (37.1%) of all the 21 counties in New Jersey. When combined with Latinos (14.2%) people of color are the majority population and greatest potential voting coalition of any county in the state. Essex County also represented (and continues to represent) the largest population of incarcerated felons of any county in the state of New Jersey (21% in 1999, and 16% in 2009). Combined, African Americans and Latinos equaled 82% of the New Jersey felon population (64% and 18% respectively, and 61% and 18% in 2009).

Prisoner reentry was not an equal opportunity phenomenon in any of the counties. Prisoners did not return to their respective counties. Prisoners returned disproportionately to 'cluster neighborhoods' within their respective urban counties. Of the 21 New Jersey counties, ten accounted for 84% of the total felon population. They returned to high density localities more commonly defined by race, ethnicity, class and its accompanying SES. As stated by Nancy LaVigne, "...(Prisoner reentry) affects some communities much more than others. In fact, every study conducted on where released prisoners reside shows heavy patterns of concentrations, with released prisoners residing in major cities and, within those same cities, clustering in a handful of neighborhoods...."[154] Ex-felons living in these cluster neighborhoods are characterized as disadvantaged, with high levels of unemployment and poverty. Nancy LaVigne indicated that, "...these communities also lack strong social mechanisms that reinforce pro-social behavior, with low levels of social cohesion among residents and norms that are too weak to be effective at eliciting positive behavior. These are communities without strong norms, social trust, informal social control mechanisms, or support (systems)...."[155] Three politically significant points were reflected in felon reentry cluster neighborhoods. First, political alienation and disempowerment may be one of the collateral effects of this reentry phenomenon. Second that political mobilization in local politics (as opposed to state or national politics) may be a more effective strategy of felon voter intervention and participation. And finally, cluster neighborhoods represent a more effective geographic, apportionment-based, rather than race-based 14th Amendment, equal protection argument for felon enfranchisement.

Essex County represents this reentry phenomenon. While there are 79.6 persons per square mile in the U.S., in New Jersey there are 1,134.5 persons per square mile. In Essex County there are 6,285.4 persons per square mile. By contrast, specific localities within Essex County have dramatically different population densities. The suburban, urban communities of Belleville, Bloomfield, Irvington, and Newark represent the range from average New Jersey density to high density levels respectively. Proportionately the populations residing in these cities, including the reentry population, manifests the 'sink behavior' described by LaVigne. These four cities also represent a Congressional District that is the subject of this chapter. The *Star-Ledger* of August 29, 2007 reported updated SES trends recorded in the 2006 Census: in CY 1999 median household income (in thousands) was 42.0 in the U.S., in New Jersey 55.1, and in Newark 26.9. By 2006, the respective H/H median incomes were 48.5, 64.5, and 34.5. When compared by race, the contrast was even more dramatic, with Blacks having lower than the median income on every geographical level. The number of persons below the poverty line was also significant. In 1999, the percent of persons below the poverty line was 12.4% in the U.S., for New Jersey 8.5%, and for Newark it was 28.4%. In 2006, comparable percentages were 13.3%, 8.7%, and 24.4%

High density, underemployment, unemployment, economic disadvantages, and poverty fed, and was fed by communities that lacked strong social mechanisms that reinforced pro-social behavior, low levels of social cohesion and norms that were too weak to be effective at eliciting positive behavior. Research and literature in 'Best Practices' criminal rehabilitation studies illustrated that these community characteristics also correlate with felon criminogenic behaviors and high risk indices for recidivism among the ex-felon population. Felon life chances as well as voter attitudes were affected by where one resided. It mattered where one lived.

"...In the U.S., more than 656,000 people were released from state and federal prisons in 2003 alone..., a four-fold increase over the past two decades...."[156] More people are being released each year and are typically returning to a select number of neighborhoods. Recidivism, the rate by which persons released from prison are returned to prison within a three-year period, is a testimony to the impact social conditions have on prisoner reentry. Nationally, 60-65% of released prisoners are returned to prison within a three year period. Of those felons that were released in New Jersey (143,635), between 26,000 and 30,000 returned to Essex County. If we assume that 17-24% of this population would vote is a reasonable estimate, then there were 4,420-7,200 potential ex-felon voters in Essex County, minus those that may recidivate. Given these estimated numbers, what was the possible impact of ex-felon voter participation?

One Essex County election by which to test this question was the New Jersey State Senatorial election (Legislative District #28). The primary election was held in June, 2001 and the general election in November, 2001. There were 100,901 total registered voters in the primary election. There was a turnout of 13% of Democratic voters and 3% of Republican voters. The Republican candidate ran unopposed, while Willie Brown, Chief Aide to Mayor Sharpe James ran against incumbent Ron Rice in the Democratic primary. In the primary election Ron Rice received 6,224 votes and Willie Brown received 5,238, a margin of 986 votes.

Ex-felon voter participation could have potentially altered the Democratic primary election. This potential outcome notwithstanding, it is more likely that the candidate of choice among ex-felons would have been Ron Rice. Ron Rice had a history of support for alternative sanctions for felons inclusive of GED programs, identification cards, and deregulation of driver license sanctions. Mayor Sharpe James' administration had taken no affirmative positions in relationship to felon reentry initiatives.

In the General Election, 43.5% of the registered voter population voted in November, 2001 in District #28. With 69% of the votes (26,319), Ron Rice won by a significant margin over a well established name, Marion Crecco, who gained 30% (11,323) of the vote, and an unknown independent, Brian Coleman with 1% or 389 votes.

[TABLE 13]

Primary	Ron Rice	Willie Brown	Marion Crecco	Total Registered Voters	
Belleville	331	522	526	16,636	D. 6%, R. 5%
Bloomfield	337	975	1,227	26,232	D. 6%, R. 7%
Irvington	2.044	1,773	77	24,241	D. 17%, R. 7%
Newark	3,512	1,968	74	33,797	D. 18%, R. 5%
Total County	6,224	5,238	1,904	100,901	D. 13%, R. 3%

Election Results, 2001

[TABLE 14]

General	Ron Rice	Marion Crecco	Brian Coleman	Total Registered Voters	% of Voters
Belleville	2,865	3,675	105	16,662	43%
Bloomfield	4,504	6,595	132	26,545	45%
Irvington	8,494	676	79	24,598	39%
Newark	11,431	700	87	34,274	39%
Total County	27,294	11,646	403	102,079	41%

Election Results, 2001

Marion Crecco won the wards of Belleville and Bloomfield by 57% and 59%, respectively; and Ron Rice won the wards of Irvington and Newark by 93% and 94%, respectively. A candidate could not win Legislative District #28 without some combination of Newark or Irvington along with significant votes in the other two districts. While Marion Crecco had an established name in Belleville and Bloomfield, Ron Rice was well established in Irvington and Newark.

Although the margin of victory precluded any possible ex-felon voter significant impact in the general election, felons and ex-felons did participate in the State Senators campaign as volunteers. These volunteers passed out literature and cleaned up after campaign activities. This participation also provided access to the State Senator and his staff. These felons were able to be seen and heard, as well as hear the views of their representative. This felon participation inspired feelings of recognition, and membership. Felons were also able to observe the political process in action. Some of the political dynamics of this election included: Legislative District #28 being redistricted to include the blue collar, predominantly white wards of Belleville and Bloomfield and exclude the predominantly African American Central ward of Newark, as well as South Orange, and Maplewood. This is particularly significant because three specific 'cluster neighborhoods' in Essex County are in the Central Ward, West Ward, and South Ward of Newark. Each of these wards is 90-100% African American, and predominant sites of felon reentry.

The felon population that participated in campaign activities was able to observe political party infighting firsthand. Intra-racial and Democratic infighting left Ron Rice off the party line ticket in the primary election with opposition from the leader of the Democratic political machine, Mayor Sharpe James, supporting the party line. The party line included Democratic Chairperson Tom Giblin, North Ward Democratic leader Steve Adubato, U.S. Representative Donald Payne, and Democratic Gubernatorial candidate Jim McGreevy. Local political infighting underscored the potential importance of felon voter participation. The 986 margin of victory by State Senator Rice had been achieved against great odds. A difference of 500 votes in Belleville and Bloomfield could have changed the outcome of the election. Ex-felon voter participation could have solidified the election outcome for the State Senator.

Do ex-felon voter rights matter? Seventy-six per cent of the felon survey respondents said they would vote if they could, and sixty- four percent felt that their vote would matter. There is also a human cost. Anthony Thompson, in his study "Releasing Prisoners, Redeeming Communities", reports an intimate story of attempted redemption. "...Voter registration card in hand, Jesse Miller stood in line for twenty minutes in November to cast her vote for governor. But fear turned her away before she got the chance. Convicted of a drug charge more than a decade previously, Miller feared the stigma of her felony would cause her problems, because even though she had served her time, paid the court-ordered fines, she never received an official certificate of discharge restoring her rights. 'When I went to get in line I had so much fear in me because I knew I hadn't done the whole process, I was scared to vote'...."[157] Redemption is very personal. How one feels on the inside, affects one's actions. Negative institutional encounters easily discourage the next attempt. One reason the felon vote matters is because the human cost of not voting is so great. Felon disenfranchisement can become its own self-fulfilling prophesy. As an alternative, automatic felon voter restoration can reduce the personal barrier to re-entry and civic participation.

There are other reasons that the felon vote matters. The campaign and election of State Senator Ron Rice teaches that mutual reciprocity and a dialogical relationship between representative and the represented are integral to one feeling a sense of membership, social dignity, a sense of self, and empowerment in the polity. Even if the felon vote did not make the numerical difference as to who won the election, felons in New Jersey affected criminal justice policy, public policy, and potentially affected the life chances of felons living in cluster neighborhoods that were 90-100% African American by their presence, participation, and demeanor in the 28th Legislative District political campaign. Senator Rice has advocated for felon educational and employment opportunities over the years he has interfaced with them.

Maximizing the inclusion of citizens in having, and exercising the right to vote is fundamental in a constitutional democracy. If the ballot is to be a measure of full membership in a society, and if the vote is to have the capacity to confer a minimum of social dignity, then all citizen votes must have equal weight.

CHAPTER 5

Maryland: A Case Study of a State Mandating 'Some' Permanent Disenfranchisement

Introduction

> "Control of a society's memory largely conditions the hierarchy of power."
>
> Paul Connerton
> "Let Your Motto be Resistance" (1983)

Distinctions made in political access and participation, between potential voters within a specific group, illustrates the importance of controlling the right to vote. Power and control by political elites have always been centered in the urban core. Modern racism and interest group conflict has largely been conditioned by this hierarchy of power. Baltimore City, having separated from Baltimore County, Maryland in 1851, ranked fourth in total population in comparison to the 23 counties of Maryland. By 2007, Baltimore City had a total population of 637,455 (down from 651,154 in 2000). With a population density of 8,058 persons per square mile, Baltimore City exceeded the population density of all counties in Maryland.[158] This population density is more than four times greater than each of the four larger counties of Montgomery, Prince George, Baltimore and Anne Arundel.

In five Maryland Counties, African Americans account for 25% or more of the total population. In Prince George's County and Baltimore City, African Americans account for over 50 percent of the total population (with African Americans representing 64.8% of Baltimore City's population by 2006).[159] There is a direct correlation between the demographics of Baltimore City and arrests, convictions and the incarceration of felons in the cities and counties of Maryland. According to the Maryland Division of Corrections Annual Report (2004), 67.5% of the Maryland Corrections population was committed from Baltimore City, and 76.5% of those committed were Black.[160]

Felon disenfranchisement has historically been a method of disqualifying African Americans from voting based on race. By comparison to New Jersey, Maryland felon disenfranchisement law represented a second and more restrictive limit on the right to vote for felons. Maryland represents a political culture in which 'some' permanent felon disenfranchisement, combined with discretionary felon voter laws restricted African American voter participation based on race. As stated in Chapter IV, there are human costs to permanently excluding segments of a society from the right to vote. Ultimately, what is at stake is an equal voice in governance for felons; equal representation for the African American community; and recognition, autonomy, and social dignity for a special class of citizens.

This Maryland study further illustrates the complex problem of political marginalization based on race; it demonstrates that permanent political marginalization is a cultural option and addresses the question of why the U.S. has constructed fences that separate us from felons in a second of three states. I will use Maryland as a model of 'some' permanent state felon disenfranchisement law. Just as in Chapter IV, there are three specific questions answered in this chapter. What are the voting rights and practices of citizens and felons in the State of Maryland? What is the affect of Maryland felon disenfranchisement law on felon voter participation, efficacy, knowledge, and attitudes? Does Maryland felon disenfranchisement law and practice have a disproportionate impact on African American felons and the political representation of the African American community?

In this chapter, I define felon disenfranchisement according to Maryland State law. A Felon Voter Participation Survey has been used to measure the political impact of felon disenfranchisement on felons, and to ascertain felon voter attitudes in Maryland. This survey examines felon voter rights, equal representation, felon voter attitudes, political recognition, identity, empowerment or disempowerment. The central question was whether Maryland felons would vote if they had a right to? If so, would the felon vote matter in Maryland? Control of a community's memory largely conditions (and determines) the hierarchy of power. I will elucidate an underlying problem of race and racial power exacerbated by 'some' permanent disenfranchisement law. This study includes a case study of African American political representation and life chances in Baltimore City, the fourth largest, and most densely populated urban political unit in Maryland.

Maryland: Voter Rights and Profiles

"Felons who have completed their sentences will be able to register to vote in Maryland under a new law signed by Governor Martin O'Malley yesterday."

Baltimoresun.com
5/22/07

This Baltimore.com article begins to explain why Maryland best represents current trends in state disenfranchisement law, and more particularly the five original states that established 'some' permanent felon disenfranchisement law (Arizona, Delaware, Maryland, Tennessee, and Washington). Trends in state felon disenfranchisement law, since 1998, have progressively moved from permanent felon disenfranchisement to automatic restoration (see Table 3-3). In addition, discretionary restrictions established in the thirteen 'some' permanent felon disenfranchisement states and permanent felon disenfranchisement states altered political thought, law, and policy from an emphasis on restrictive disenfranchisement laws to restorative legislation. While this progression was intensified in this last ten-year period, discretionary felon voter restrictions continued to reflect the racial and political values of the various states beginning as early as the 1850's.

Maryland was among the states which had established racial and discretionary restrictions and practices for felons and African Americans historically. By 1851, the Maryland Constitution stated that persons convicted of larceny or other infamous crimes, including persons convicted of bribery at elections were permanently disqualified from voting. The term "infamous crimes" was common language among states that practiced discretionary restrictions for the purpose of disqualifying some or all felons from the right to vote. The only distinction between these states was the degree and specificity of infamous crimes. As has been illustrated, many of these distinctions were based on an assumed proclivity of African Americans to commit certain types of crimes.

In Maryland, Article I, Section 4 of the State constitution reads "... The General Assembly by law may regulate or prohibit the right to vote of a person convicted of infamous or other serious crime or under care or guardianship for mental disability (ratified in November, 1972 and again in 1978). Maryland's eligibility standards for voter registration through July, 2007 was:

- Be a U.S. citizen
- Be a Maryland resident
- Be at least 18 years old
- Not be under guardianship for mental disability
- Not have been convicted of buying or selling votes
- Not have been convicted more than once of a crime of violence
- Not have been convicted of an infamous crime (any felony or crime involving an element of deceit, fraud, or corruption) unless: (1) you have been pardoned, or (2) you have completed the court imposed sentence (1st conviction), or (3) at least 3 years has passed since you completed the court imposed sentence (2nd or later conviction).

Note: The court imposed sentence includes probation, parole, community service, restitution and fines."[161]

Felon voter restoration guidelines for Maryland, as described in N. Taifa's "Re-enfranchisement" (2002), included requirements such as: Governor's approval; mandatory waiting period of **20 years for drug violation** and **10 years for other violations**; permanent disqualification for election offenses; a review or approval of marital history, religious preferences, and social activities. Three points can be made given these restorative guidelines. They are not restorative guidelines, but rather restrictive standards. Intrusive guidelines such as marital status, religion, and social activities suggest presumed values or social standings of particular populations. Compounding the cost of voting for the felon population by mandating full payment of restitution and fines as a prerequisite to voter restoration is the equivalent of a poll tax on a population that can least afford it.

Maryland State disenfranchisement law effectively changed July 1, 2007. Passage of Maryland Senate Bill #488 extended voting rights to felons who completed their sentences, including parole and probation. More than 50,000 Marylanders became eligible to vote July 1, 2007. State Senator Gwendolyn Britt, a Prince George's Democrat and one of the sponsors of the legislation underscored the significance of this achievement, saying: "...It certainly doesn't mean the floodgates are going to open, but this underscores the full meaning of citizenship. When you have paid your debt to society... you should be free to vote."[162]

Chapter 159 of the Maryland Constitution specifies that standard citizenship and resident voter requirements inclusive of age and registration remain constant. The specific changes in Maryland disenfranchisement law (2007) were that an individual is not qualified to be a registered voter if the individual:

1) has been convicted of a felony unless he/she has been pardoned; or in connection with a first conviction, has completed the court ordered sentence including conviction, probation, parole, community service, restitutions, and fines; or

2) in connection with a subsequent conviction, has completed the court ordered sentence imposed for the conviction, including the same requirements as a 1st conviction and that at least three years have elapsed since the completion of the court ordered sentence as described for 1st conviction felons.[163]

Although Senate Bill #488 passed in the State Legislature and was signed by the Governor, Maryland's new felon law does not meet the full measure of automatic restoration. The extraordinary cost of voting for felons (i.e. restitution and fines) remains a part of the Maryland disenfranchisement law. The three-year waiting period for 2nd time offenders contradicts the principle of felons regaining the right to vote once they have paid their debt to society. Prior to passage of Bill #488, Maryland's disenfranchisement law was intentionally restrictive. Passage of Bill #488 changed Maryland disenfranchisement law to provide for felon voter restoration (with specific exceptions).

This review of the law reveals who has the right to vote in Maryland. Of those that have the right to vote, how many registered to do so? Would the inclusion of the ex-felon vote matter in Maryland, or more particularly in Baltimore City? In the 2008 Presidential election, there were an estimated 208,323,000 eligible (registered) voters, and an estimated voter turnout rate of 63% or 131.2 million people.[164] This was the highest turnout rate in the U.S. since 1964. The 2006 U.S. Census Bureau population estimate for Maryland was 5,615,727, with a voting age population of 4,211,795 (75.8%). The estimated number of registered voters in Maryland was 3,157,495 (75%). The population estimate for Baltimore City was 631,366, with a voting age population of 473,524 (75%) and a registered voter population of 333,876 (70%).[165]

Baltimoresun.com estimated that effective July 1, 2007, 50,000 ex-felons became eligible to vote in Maryland. At least 67.5% of this population or 33,750 ex-felons reside in Baltimore City (of whom 76.5% are African American). This ex-felon population represents an estimated 1.2% of the Maryland State voter population, and 7.12% of the Baltimore City voter population. Giving ex-felons the right to vote would significantly increase the potential political influence of African Americans in Baltimore City and the ex-felon voter age population in the State of Maryland. As indicated in Chapter IV, ex-felon voter participation can have a more direct effect on local elections than state elections. Based on the numbers of persons committed to Corrections from Baltimore City, the political effect of ex-felons gaining the right to vote could be significantly greater in Baltimore City than in the State of Maryland. Prior to July 1, 2007, Baltimore City and African Americans in particular may have been underrepresented or disproportionately represented both locally and statewide.

Gerald Pomper (2001), indicated that "…in addition to geographical and party differences, the American electorate was polarized along social lines (in the 2000 Presidential election)…"[166].

This polarization remained constant in 2004 and 2008. The cleavage in 2000, 2004 and 2008 was between the rich and poor, Whites and other ethnic and racial groups, gender, age, religion, and income groups. The importance of who can vote is not only measured by law and total numbers, but also by social group interests. As an example, with regard to the 2008 Presidential Election, the NYT (Nov. 6, 2008) wrote, "... Senator Barack Obama, the first Democratic presidential candidate to receive more than 50 percent of the popular vote since Lyndon B. Johnson in 1964, made large gains for his party ... among young voters and Hispanics....The contours of the electorate have changed remarkably since 2004. In a striking measure of potential political realignment, the gap between self-described Democrats and Republicans has grown. In 2004, each party accounted for 37 percent of the electorate, but this year (2008), 39% of the voters said they were Democrats and 32% said they were Republicans...."[167] Obama won over groups which had typically been aligned with Republicans, such as suburban voters and parents. Significantly, Obama also strengthened Democratic support among traditional Democratic voters by increasing the turnout among other groups. In 2008, while 48% of males voted Republican, 56% of women voted Democratic. Black voters comprised 11% of the electorate in 2004, and 13% in 2008. Blacks also voted more heavily Democratic in 2008 (95% in comparison to 88% in 2004). Better than 66% of persons aged 18-29 voted Democratic. The social profile of the electorate matters.[168]

By 2006, Maryland's total population had increased by 6% (from 2000) to 5,615,727. Of this total population, 6.6% were persons under 5 years old, 24.2% were persons under 18 years old, 75.8% were of voting age, and 11.6% persons were 65 years or over. Women represented 51.6% of the general population. Whites represented 63.6%, Blacks 29.5%, Asians .9%, and Hispanics or Latinos 6.0% of the general population; there were no significant changes demographically by 2010. High school graduates represented 83.8% of persons aged 25 and over and 31.4% of this population possessed a bachelor's degree or better. Median annual household income was $57,019, and 9.2% of the population lived below the poverty line. In terms of population density, there were 541.9 persons per square mile.[169]

By comparison, Baltimore City's total population decreased by 3% from 651,154 in 2000 to 631, 356 in 2006. Of this total population, 7.1% were persons under 5 years old, 24.8% were persons under 18 years old, 75.2% were of voting age, and 12.1% persons were 65 years or over. Women represented 53.4% of the City's population. Whites represented 31.7%, Blacks represented 64.8%, Asians 1.9%, and Hispanics or Latinos 2.4% of the City's population. High school graduates represented 68.4% of persons aged 25 and over and 19.1% of this population possessed a bachelor's degree or better. Median annual household income was $29, 792, and 21.5% of the population lived below the poverty line. Population density in Baltimore City was 8038.9 persons per square mile.[170]

There were significant and divergent group interests between the general population of Maryland and Baltimore City residents. The potential interest group conflict between state and local constituents was defined by urban demographics such as: population growth, education, household income, poverty, density and race. While Maryland's population increased by 6% over a six year period to 2006, Baltimore City's population decreased by 3% during that same period. While whites were approximately two-thirds of the Maryland population, they were less than one-third of the Baltimore City population. Conversely, Blacks were less than one-third of the Maryland general population and almost two-thirds of the Baltimore City population. Better than 80% of the Maryland population had a high school education, and less than 70% of the Baltimore City population had a high school education; more than 30% of the state population possessed a bachelor degree or better and less than 20% of the Baltimore City population possessed a bachelor degree or better. Household income within the State was almost double that of Baltimore City. The total number of persons living below the poverty line was almost two and one half times greater in Baltimore City than in the State of Maryland. Population density was almost fifteen times greater in Baltimore City than Maryland.

The needs of Baltimore City's population were dramatically different than the general population of Maryland. The problem of political inequalities by race begins with social disparities based on population density, income, poverty and race. Given the density in Baltimore City, Baltimore City can be defined as an urban cluster neighborhood. African American felony arrests and convictions are disproportionately represented in urban cluster neighborhoods. Additionally, the risk factors for arrest and incarceration include contrasting demographics such as those illustrated by Maryland and Baltimore City. For this same reason, 67.5% of the Maryland Corrections population was committed from Baltimore City and 76.5% of those committed were Black. The social group needs and profile of the Maryland felon population was more similar to the population of Baltimore City than the general population of Maryland.

In 2004, the total Maryland felon population was 22,662, and in 2007 the population increased by 3.2% to 23,397. The <u>Maryland Division of Corrections Annual Report 2004</u> and <u>Maryland Department of Public Safety and Correctional Services 2007 Database</u> indicated that 76.5% of the felon population was Black, and 21.8% were White in 2004, and 73.4% were Black, and 22.4% were White in 2007.[171] In 2004, 94.9% of this population was male and 5.1% was female. In 2007, the ratio remained relatively constant with 5.2% of the population female and 94.8% male. Approximately 98.8% of the felon population was 18 years old or older. At least 9.6% of this population is serving a life sentence and therefore would not qualify as part of the Maryland voting age population. Approximately 90% of this population will return to community. By age, 20,672 felons could, at some point as ex-felons, qualify to vote in the State of Maryland if they chose to reside in Maryland after completing their sentence. Approximately 35% of the felon population was aged 18-30; 34% was aged 31-40; 21% aged 41-50; and 7.3% was aged 51 and over. The length of sentence in Maryland by comparison to New Jersey is excessive. The average length of sentence in Maryland is approximately 13.5 years, with an actual average length of stay of less than 5 years.[172] This average length of stay is more in keeping with average State length of sentence norms. The types of crimes identified in three categories are: violence- 46.2%; CDS- 22.9%; and property offenses- 26.6%. The three most common violations were: murder-19.9%; drug offenses- 22.9%; and robbery- 14.5%.[173] Almost 80% of the felon population was committed from Baltimore City (67.5%), Baltimore County (8.5%), and Prince George's (3.6%).[174]

As indicated, the felon profile corresponds with the social profile of the Baltimore City population. The Maryland and Baltimore City voter profiles contrasts majority and minority populations that have divergent needs, and dramatically different life chances and consequences. Given these facts the question is, would ex-felon voter participation assist the Baltimore City population achieve political access and fair and equal representation.

Maryland Felon Voter Attitude Survey: A Matter of Choice?

"I've served this country in a war to protect the democratic right of its citizens to vote, in so doing I've earn(ed) the right (to vote) regardless of mistakes I've made".

(Maryland felon survey respondent, 2007)

Maryland best represents current trends in 'some' permanent felon disenfranchisement law, and reflects standards shared with the five original 'some' permanent felon states. Variations in the definition of 'infamous crime' and discretionary restrictions allowed each of these states to determine which felons would be allowed to vote, and those that would be disqualified for life. In each case, eligibility standards were based on punitive values, race, and values reflective of a particular history and region. The fact that distinctions were made in felon voter qualifications in the same state illustrates the importance of controlling the right to vote. As will be illustrated, variations in felon voter restrictions also affected felon voter attitudes.

A felon voter survey was administered to the Maryland Department of Public Safety and Correctional Service population to measure felon voter attitudes. This survey was administered to 300 Maryland felons over a four-month period beginning in June, 2007. This survey sample was not a random sampling, but rather a sample determined by the degree of accessibility to the Maryland Corrections population provided by the Maryland Department of Public Safety and Correctional Service. Therefore, conclusions drawn from this survey were limited by the sampling methodology and population to which there was access. I am grateful for the assistance of Ms. Paula Matthews, Educational Liaison, Maryland Division of Corrections, who assumed responsibility for administering the survey for her commitment and support of this project.

The central question asked in this survey was: "If you were able to vote, would you vote in an election?" As illustrated in the opening quotation from an older, African American felon, the comments of respondents to this question was as adamant and assertive of their rights as was their overwhelming collective declaration that they would vote if they could. In comparing New Jersey and Maryland felon reasons for voting, the intensity and commitment to the right to vote and indignity of disenfranchisement law was greater among Maryland respondents. The expressed need to vote was greater among Maryland felon respondents than New Jersey respondents either because of, or in spite of the fact that Maryland disenfranchisement law was more restrictive. The following quotations and survey results from Maryland respondents support this conclusion.

- "I am 22 years old, African American. Through the history … I have studied, I have been mislead and miseducated about myself…and… life events. Yes, I would vote."
- "The government has the power over the people, and if the ratio was (candidate) C over (candidate) D, D would get in anyhow because of its power. For instance "Bush"."
- "What does it matter because the tallying of votes always gets messed up some kind of way."
- "I would vote because there are a lot of issues with prison and the treatment of prisoners that needs to be fixed and the judicial system needs to be changed".
- "I would not want to vote because I am considered a felon and will always be marked as a felon. I don't have the same opportunities of most Americans. Jobs, homes, etc., so why should I vote?"
- "I have made a mistake in my life. My vote may be the one to help change things in my children's life."

These are not dispassionate, apathetic responses. These responses were reflective of history, the politics of institutional racism, the human need for recognition, dignity and autonomy.

Of the 300 Maryland respondents, 89.3% said they would vote if they could, and 10.7% said they would not vote even if they were given the opportunity. Almost nine-out-of-ten respondents said they would vote (13% higher than the New Jersey felon response). The response was even higher among female respondents. The Maryland female respondents represented 20% of the respondent population (60), and 93.3% of this population responded indicating they would vote if they could. As previously noted, self-reported voter participation is often exaggerated and, additionally, people vote more consistent with their demographic profile and other political variables. By comparison, in 2008, the national voter turnout was 63% of the electorate, in New Jersey and Maryland it was 62% and 62.4%, respectively. The demographic profile common to the felon population was low income, with an average fifth grade reading level. Voter participation for low income populations was typically lower than the norm, and commonly in the range of 14-25 %. It was significant that most of the respondents felt that they should vote.

In Maryland, 79.3% of the respondents were male, and 20% were female (.7% did not respond to this question). Approximately 75.3% were African American or Black, 6% were Latino or Hispanic, and 13.7% were White. A total of 51.3% of this population was committed for violent offenses, 42.7% for drug offenses, and 3.7% for property offenses. Better than 99% of this population was age 18 or more, 8% were age 18-21, 70% were age 22-40, 18% were age 41-50, and 2.7% were age 51 and over. The population self-reported that 36% of the respondents were high school graduates or that they had received their GED. Another 14.6% indicated that they had completed some college or Vocational Education. More than half of the respondents reported that they had not completed high school. More than 52% of the population reported themselves as low income and better than 40% reported themselves as middle income. Only five percent reported themselves as upper income.

In Maryland, another significant measure of who could vote was the number of times a person had been convicted of a crime. Forty percent of the respondents reported that they had been convicted of a felony one time, 33% had been convicted twice, and 22% had been convicted three or more times, with the balance not having responded to this question. Consistent with national reports on incarcerated women, the demographics on the Maryland female population was significantly different than men. Two thirds of the female population was African American or Black, 10% Latino, and 21.6% White. Approximately 31.7% of female felons were convicted of violent crimes, 66.6% were convicted for drug offenses, and 1.7% for property offenses. Ninety percent of the female population was between the ages 22-40, with 8% percent between ages 41-50, and 1.7% between ages 18-21. Fifty percent of the female population had completed high school or their GED, and 5% had completed some college or Vocational Education. Seventy percent of the female population reported that they were low income, and 28.3% reported that they were middle income. Sixty percent of the women had been convicted once, 36.7% had been convicted two times, and 3.3% had been convicted three times or more.

It was significant that for both groups the added punitive restrictions on repeat offenders did not serve as deterrent to criminal offenses given the fact that one third, to more than half, of the offender population repeated the offense. It also means that prior to 2007, under Maryland felon disenfranchisement law, more than half the felon population would have been disenfranchised. Under the new law (post 2007), more than half of this felon population would have to wait at least three years after completing their court-ordered sentence before qualifying to register to vote. These added disincentives increased the probability that an already marginalized population would not participate in voting.

By comparison, better than seven-in-ten African American respondents, two-in-three Latino, and almost all White respondents indicated that they would vote if they could. Age distribution among 'yes' respondents were equal to the age distribution of the total respondent group. Not unlike the general voter population and total respondent population, 'yes' respondents had a higher percentage of younger respondents that said they would not vote. The 'yes' respondent group self-reported a slightly higher educational level than the total respondent group had. Better than 50% of the total group reported that they had less than a high school education, and 45% of the 'yes' respondents indicated that they completed less than a high school education. There was no difference in the number of total and 'yes' group respondents completing their high school education or GED. Sixteen percent of the 'yes' respondent population reported that they completed some college or Vocational Education, exceeding the total respondent population by almost 2%.

The legal status of the 'yes' population was equivalent to the self-reported status of the total respondent population. The 'yes' respondents self-reported that their household income was equal to the total respondent population's income. Forty percent of the 'yes' respondents reported that they had been convicted of a felony one time, less than 33% of this population reported that they had been convicted twice, 15% reported having been convicted three times, 8% indicated that they had been convicted four or more times, and 4% had no response. Again, these self-reports on repeated offenses was further evidence that added punitive restrictions did not serve as a deterrent to continued criminal offending even among the 'yes' respondents.

As in Chapter IV, the Maryland felon voter survey included questions concerning registration, prior voting practices, and campaign activities as indices of voter participation. Thirty-two percent of the total respondent population said that they had registered to vote at some point in their lives prior to having been incarcerated, while 68% had not. Thirty-four percent of the 'yes' respondents reported that they had registered to vote prior to having been incarcerated while 65.7% had not. Twelve percent of the 'no' respondents had registered to vote at some point prior to having been incarcerated, while 87.5% of this population had not. Approximately one-third of the total population and 'yes' population had registered to vote at some point in their lives prior to having been incarcerated.

Almost nine out of ten 'no' respondents had never registered to vote prior to having been incarcerated. Between nineteen and twenty percent of the total respondents and 'yes' respondents, said that they had voted in an election prior to having been incarcerated. Six percent of the 'no' respondent population indicated that they had voted in an election prior to incarceration, with better than 87% of this population stating that they had never voted in an election prior to incarceration. Eighty percent of the total population and 'yes' population said that they had never voted in an election. Slightly less than 11% of the total population and 'yes' population indicated that they had participated in campaign activities prior to their incarceration. More than 9% of the 'no' population reported they had participated in campaign activities prior to incarceration. Approximately 90% of all groups indicated that they had not participated in campaign activities at any time prior to their incarceration. In rank order, voter registration, voting, and campaign activities were the participatory activities of a minority of this felon population. This rank order of participatory activities was consistent with the literature on voter participation in American politics.

A second measure of voter attitude was the degree of knowledge felons had about voting requirements and the political process. One question respondents answered was: if you had only one prior conviction, what were the qualifications you would have to meet in order to register to vote. Better than 64% of the total respondent population, and 66% of the 'yes' respondents new that they had to complete prison, probation, parole, community service, restitution, and fines prior to qualifying to vote. By comparison, 50% of the 'no' respondents knew their voting requirements.

Another question was: if you had been convicted more than once, what qualifications would you have to have in order to vote. Approximately one-third of all respondents knew that, in addition to the previously stated qualifications, persons who had committed two or more offenses also needed to complete a three-year waiting period. Seventy-seven percent of the total respondent group, and 79% of the 'yes' group indicated that they knew Maryland law concerning felon disenfranchisement changed in July, 2007. Less than 60% of the 'no' respondents knew that the law had changed in July, 2007. Approximately 68% of all respondent groups knew that the new felon law specified that felon voter restoration would now occur when felons completed prison, probation, and parole. Approximately 27-28% of all respondents knew that in Maryland, citizens have the right to vote if you are a U.S. citizen, a resident of Maryland, at least 18 years of age, not under guardianship or mental disability, not convicted of buying or selling votes, not been convicted more than once of a violent crime, and not been convicted of an infamous crime unless three years have passed since having completed their sentence.

One-out-of-five total respondents and 'yes' respondents, and one-out-of-four 'no' respondents thought that you only had to be a U.S.

citizen to be eligible to vote. Almost one in five of all groups thought that one only had to be 18 years of age in order to vote. And, approximately one in five total respondents and 'yes' respondents thought that one qualified to vote if you are a U.S. citizen, a Maryland resident, 18 years of age, and not under guardianship for mental disability. This wide range of responses indicated significant confusion, inconsistency and lack of knowledge of citizen voting rights among the felon respondent population.

Approximately one in four total and 'yes' respondents knew that in order to cast a vote in Maryland, one had to register at least 30 days before election day. Only 12.5% of the 'no' respondents knew the registration requirement in Maryland. Almost 58% of the total and 'yes' respondent groups did not know Maryland voter registration requirements. Better than 65% of the 'no' respondents did not know this voter registration requirement. In four-out-of-seven questions, 'no' respondents had less political or electoral knowledge than did 'yes' respondents.

Voter preference (or ideology) was another measure of voter knowledge. Forty percent of the total respondents and 42% of the 'yes' respondents in Maryland classified themselves as moderates. Fifteen percent of the 'no' resident population classified themselves as moderates. Almost 20% of the 'yes' population, and 23% of the total respondent population were undecided; and 50% of the 'no' respondents said they were undecided. Twenty-one percent of the total and 'yes' respondents said they were conservative; and 15.6% of the 'no' respondents said they were conservative. Better than 13% of the total and 'yes' populations classified themselves as liberal, and 6.3% of the 'no' group classified themselves as liberal. Proportionately, more than twice as many 'no' respondents were undecided as were 'yes' and total respondents. It is also significant that total and 'yes' respondent groups non-response rate was 2.7% and 1.5% respectively, the 'no' respondents rate was 12.5%. A total of 62.5%, or two-thirds of the 'no' respondents either indicated that they were undecided as to voter preference or offered no response. Approximately 75-80% of the total or 'yes' respondents indicated a partisan preference or ideology.

To measure the degree to which the respondents understood voter preference or ideology, they were asked two questions. In response to the question of increasing childcare funds for the poor, approximately

90% of the total and 'yes' respondent groups felt that childcare funds should be increased to some or a significant degree. Three quarters of the 'no' respondent group were of the same opinion. On Foreign policy, in response to the question of approval or disapproval of U.S. involvement in the U.N., 48% of the total respondents approved and 34% had no opinion. Among 'yes' respondents, 51% approved and 31% had no opinion. Among 'no' respondents 19% approved and 56% had no opinion. The majority of these respondent groups indicated that they were ideologically or politically moderate to liberal.

When asked about partisan preference, 44.3% of the total respondent group, and 48.1% of the 'yes' respondent group said that they were best represented by the Democratic party, while 12.5% of the 'no' respondent group said they were. Only 6.3% and 6.7% of the total and 'yes' group respondents, respectively, indicated that their party preference was Republican, and 3.1% of the 'no' respondent group preferred the Republican party. Again, there was a distinction between total and 'yes' groups as it applied to Independent political preference. Both total and 'yes' respondent groups indicated that about 18% of these groups were best classified as political Independents. Six percent of the 'no' respondents indicated that they were best classified as Independents. Interestingly, while only 2% of the total and 'yes' groups indicated that they had a third party preference, better than 6% of the 'no' respondent group indicated they had such a preference. A total of 65.5% of the 'no' population indicated that they were undecided as to partisan preference as compared to 26.7% of the total group and 22.1% of the 'yes' group. Non-responses of each group to this question were 6.3% for 'no' respondents, 2.7% for total respondents, and 2.2% for 'yes' respondents.

Based on these indices, the 'no' respondents were more apathetic, least trusting of mutual reciprocity and the political process than the other two groups. The contrast in voter attitude between 'no' respondents and 'yes' respondents was significant. Feelings of membership or non-membership, social dignity, and empowerment or disempowerment can be measured by these contrasting responses. 'Yes' respondents had a greater sense of empowerment and commitment to voter participation than did 'no' respondents. Respondent answers to the question as to why they would or would not vote in an election offers further explanation as to the human cost of felon disenfranchisement. In response to the question regarding voter participation, 50% of the 'no' respondents said they would not vote because their vote "would not matter", while only 10% of the total group and 5.6% of the 'yes' group felt that way. Almost 62% of the 'yes' respondent group and 55% of the total group felt that they should vote because " it was their right to do so once they had paid their debt to society." Another twenty percent of these two groups felt that they should vote because their vote could add political recognition and public consideration to felon issues. Seventy-five to eighty percent of these two groups offered these two reasons as to why they would vote.

Respondents indicated contrasting felon voter attitudes when asked to respond to issues concerning felon voter rights. Almost 94% of the respondents felt that felons should be given the right to vote. Ninety-five percent of the 'yes' respondents and 81% of the 'no' respondents felt that felons should be given the right to vote. Seventy percent of the total respondent population felt that their vote would matter to varying degrees in the overall electoral system. Seventy-six percent of the 'yes' group and 25% of the 'no' group felt that their vote would matter. Sixty-eight percent of the respondents felt that they should be given the right to vote once they completed their sentence of prison, parole or probation. Almost 70% of the 'yes' respondents and 53% of the 'no' respondents felt the same. Twenty percent of the total respondent and 'yes' groups, and 25% of the 'no' group said that felons should be given the right to vote once they have completed their prison sentence.

When asked reasons why felons should not be given the right to vote, 75% of the respondents said that they did not feel any of the proposed reasons were justifiable. Seventy-eight percent of the 'yes' group agreed that no reason listed justified felon disenfranchisement. Forty-four percent of the 'no' respondents agreed that there was no justifiable reason listed. Twenty-five percent of the 'no' respondents felt that the reason felons should not be given the right to vote was because the views of felons would not be respected. Another 12% of the 'no' respondents felt that once you committed a felony, you should not be given this privilege again. Eight percent of the total group, and 6% of the 'yes' population agreed that the views of felons would not be respected. 'Yes' respondents generally felt that there was no justifiable reason for disenfranchising felons.

Political efficacy, the belief that political authorities respond to attempts to influence them, implies that one can trust that one will be heard and responded to. As suggested previously, political efficacy is one of the most effective measures of voter attitude. As in Chapter IV, an abbreviated Sociopolitical Control Scale developed by Marc Zimmerman and James Zahniser was used to measure the degree to which the respondents felt membership, social dignity, empowerment or disempowerment. For purposes of analysis, scales (1-3) have been collapsed into Disagree, and scales (4-6) have been collapsed into Agree. This scale measured feelings of leadership, empowerment, community isolation, and policy control for the respondent population. Because the survey results between total respondents and 'yes' respondents were essentially the same in the Sociopolitical Control Scale, comparative analysis is made between 'yes' respondents and 'no' respondents.

As in Chapter IV, 'yes' respondents indicated definitive, positive answers to all six questions. Seven in ten 'yes' respondents felt that people like themselves were generally well qualified to participate in political activity and decision-making in the U.S. Almost three in five 'yes' respondents said that they enjoy political participation because they want to have as much say in running government as possible. Four out of five respondents felt that many local elections were important. Four out of five 'yes' respondents indicated that it mattered to them as to whether they participated in local issues or not. Three out of five respondents said that most public officials would listen to them, and seven out of ten respondents felt that politics and government was not too complicated for a person like them to understand. Again 'yes' respondents had a strong belief in their right to participate; their knowledge and competence to influence or make policy; and that their vote would matter. 'Yes' respondents trusted or believed that they could make themselves heard and that they would be responded to.

The 'no' respondents had an opposite opinion; more than 50% of the 'no' respondents did not feel that people like them were qualified to participate in political activity and decision-making. More than three out of four respondents did not enjoy political participation or want to have much say in running government. More 'no' respondents than not, felt that local elections were not important (by 48% to 38%).

TABLE 15

Yes Respondents Collapsed:	Disagree (1-3)		Agree (4-6)		No Response	
People like me are generally well qualified to participate in the political activity and decision-making in the U.S.	26.5%	(71)	71.6%	(192)	1.9%	(05)
I enjoy political participation because I want to have as much say in running government as possible.	38.8%	(104)	57.8%	(155)	3.4%	(09)
A good many local elections aren't important enough to bother with.	79.9%	(214)	17.1%	(46)	3.0%	(08)
So many other people are active in local issues and organizations that it doesn't matter much to me whether I participate or not.	82.5%	(221)	14.9%	(40)	2.6%	(07)
Most public officials wouldn't listen to me no matter what I did.	60.4%	(162)	37.0%	(99)	2.6%	(07)
Sometimes politics and government seem so complicated that a person like me can't really understand what's going on.	72.0%	(193)	25.4%	(68)	2.6%	(07)

Total (268)

TABLE 16

No Respondents Collapsed:	Disagree (1-3)		Agree (4-6)		No Response	
People like me are generally well qualified to participate in the political activity and decision-making in the U.S.	53.1%	(17)	34.4%	(11)	12.5%	(04)
I enjoy political participation because I want to have as much say in running government as possible.	78.1%	(25)	9.4%	(03)	12.5%	(04)
A good many local elections aren't important enough to bother with.	37.5%	(12)	43.7%	(14)	18.8%	(06)
So many other people are active in local issues and organizations that it doesn't matter much to me whether I participate or not.	25.0%	(08)	59.4%	(19)	15.6%	(05)
Most public officials wouldn't listen to me no matter what I did.	34.4%	(11)	53.1%	(17)	12.5%	(04)
Sometimes politics and government seem so complicated that a person like me can't really understand what's going on.	37.5%	(12)	46.9%	(15)	15.6%	(05)

Total   (32)

Almost three out of five 'no' residents felt other people were active in local issues and organizations and it didn't matter whether they participated or not. More than 50% of the 'no' respondents said that most public officials wouldn't listen to them. By a margin of 10% (47% to 37%), 'no' respondents felt that politics and government seemed too complicated and that a person like them could not really understand what was going on. 'No' respondents had little belief that political authorities would respond to attempts to influence them nor trusted that they would be heard. They were not convinced that the right to vote would matter, and fewer 'no' respondents felt like they qualified to participate in political activity and decision-making than those that did. Most did not enjoy political participation or want to have much say in running government. 'No' respondents did not feel that public officials would listen to them. More 'no' respondents felt that they did not understand politics than those that did. Again, 'no' respondents felt locked into a type of community isolation and, as a politically alienated population, this attitude had the potential to become an unintended or intended self-fulfilling prophecy.

Do Ex-felon Voter Rights Matter in Baltimore City?

> "A society is most vigorous and appealing, when both [majority and minority] critics are legitimate voices in the permanent dialogue that is the testing of ideas and experience."
>
> Daniel Bell (1961) [175]

The right to vote mattered to the surveyed felon population. It was a right the surveyed population took personally. Felon responses indicated that: as a veteran, the surveyed felon had earned the right to vote regardless of mistakes he had made; the felon vote could be the vote that changed things in their child's life; and that their vote could change the judicial system. Ninety percent of the surveyed respondents said they would vote if they could, and 70% of this population said they should regain their right to vote when they completed their sentence. By 1999, the total ex-felon population of Maryland was 59,700 with an additional 20,672 felons eligible to leave prison within a five-year period beginning in 2004. Would this population have the capacity to help elect a candidate? Could this voting bloc not only make a difference as to who got elected, but also affect public policy with respect to ex-felon and felon life chances and the interests of the African American Community?

Baltimore City, with a population of 637,400, was more densely populated than any of the 23 counties of Maryland. With a population density of 8,058 persons per square mile, its population density was fifteen times greater than the average density per square mile of Maryland, and was four to six times greater than any of the four largest counties of Maryland. Almost 65% of Baltimore City's population was African American, 67.5% of Maryland's Correction population was committed from Baltimore City, and 76.5% of Maryland's total Correction population was African American or Black. Prisoner re-entry was not an equal opportunity phenomenon in Maryland anymore than it had been in New Jersey. Felons were disproportionately committed to prison from Baltimore City and they returned to 'cluster' in Baltimore City at that same rate.

Felons returned to a high density city more commonly defined by race, ethnicity, class, and the accompanying socio-economic standards. Median income in Maryland was almost twice that of Baltimore City, while Baltimore City's population living below the poverty level was more than double that of Maryland's. High density, underemployment, unemployment, economic disadvantage, and poverty characterized life chances in Baltimore City. Populations living in Baltimore City manifested the sink behavior described by LaVigne. They lacked strong social mechanisms that would reinforce pro-social behavior and social cohesion. Again, if we assume that 17-24% of this felon population would vote, there were between 12,400 and 17,500 additional potential votes in Maryland, with two-thirds of this population residing in Baltimore City.

There was no quantifiable evidence that the felon or ex-felon population of Maryland or Baltimore City could alter the outcome of the 2008 Presidential election or the 2002 gubernatorial election. However, as with State Senator Gwendolyn Britt, there was evidence that their presence and participation (along with that of their families and significant others) could affect public policy; ex-felon and felon life chances; and the interests of the African American community. In

2008, 62% of Maryland voters supported President Obama, while 36.5% voted for McCain. In Baltimore City, 87.2% of the voters went Democratic while 11.7% voted Republican. The Baltimore City voter profile and felon demographic profile were so compatible that it is reasonable to assume that the Baltimore ex-felon voter preference would be similar to voters in that city. They were comparable by party affiliation, ideology, race, income, education, and age. While felons would not have wanted to alter the 2008 election outcome, nor could they have, their inclusion could have impacted public policy. Barack Obama had included a strong position favoring Corrections reform and criminal justice reform in his campaign platform.[176]

In the 2002 Maryland Gubernatorial race, 55% of the Maryland voters were registered Democratic and 29% were registered as Republicans. Almost 80% were registered as Democrats in Baltimore City, and 9.5% were registered as Republicans. With 100% of the precincts reporting, the Republican (Ehrlich) won the gubernatorial seat over the Democratic candidate (Townsend) by 51% (842,252) to 48% (785,575). The margin of victory was 56,677 votes. In Baltimore City, Townsend won the gubernatorial election by 75% (116,892) to 24% (37,165). The estimated 17,500 additional felon votes could not have made a difference in the election outcome. Had the full potential of felon voter participation been realized, and 75% of a possible 79,000 ex-felons registered and voted, Townsend would have won the gubernatorial seat by approximately 3,000 votes. This assessment underscores the necessity of maximizing felon inclusion and the importance of voter turnout. [177]

Baltimore City was a microcosm of all that was both challenging and possible in urban politics. The political culture of Baltimore City classically mirrored the urban politics of late 20th and early 21st century America. From 1972 through 2006, only three men served as Mayor of Baltimore City- Mayor Schaefer (1972-86), Mayor Schmoke (1987-2000), and Mayor O'Malley (2000-2006), who relinquished his seat in his successful bid for Governor of Maryland in 2007. Structurally, Baltimore City was a strong Mayor-Council form government, with a 19-member council and a five-member Board of Estimates. Any mayor that controlled ten members of the Council and three members of the Board ran City Hall. This occurred in all three administrations. The first two administrations were described as 'museums of unsuccessful urban policies and government initiatives'. This phrase described a government that relied on state-sponsored capitalism in the form of state and federal subsidies (i.e., HUD, state and federal grant money) as opposed to market investments to promote economic growth for the city.

The predominant number of African Americans living in Baltimore City notwithstanding, Kurt Schmoke was the first African American ever elected to the office of Mayor in Baltimore City. Among claims of being soft on crime, questionable drug policies, and charges of corruption within his administration, Mayor Schmoke was replaced in 2000 by Martin O'Malley who was well known to be a member of one of the states most powerful political dynasties. Mayor O'Malley ascended to office (from his City Council chair) with three mandates: to reform the city's economy; to slash the crime rate; and to break with Baltimore's corrupt political culture. A second significant fact of O'Malley's ascendancy was that he did so by garnering 53% of the total vote and 30% of the Black vote while running against two front-running African American City Council members (Schmoke did not seek a fourth term).

Not unlike many urban cities, Baltimore City was essentially a one-party (Democratic), partisan community. Democrats outnumbered Republicans 9-1, assuring that whichever Democrat won the primary election would most likely become the local officeholder. Again, this was true for each of these respective Mayors. Secondly, crime and punishment remained a major campaign and policy issue throughout each administration. Clearly, the felon population was a central character in local politics by default, if by no other means. The question: Could felon voter participation change the role felons played in urban politics from being a political issue, to becoming political constituents?

In 1999, Martin O'Malley won the Mayoralty of Baltimore City by 53%, garnering 10,068 more votes than his two strongest opponents combined. The fact that O'Malley's opponents were unable or unwilling to unify their efforts to elect one African American candidate resulted in each dividing the remaining 70% of the African American vote, assuring that neither would be victorious. In Baltimore City, the estimated potential felon vote was 12,500 persons. If the African

American community had coalesced behind one candidate that continued to support 'policing as social work theory', the combined votes of the remaining African American voters and the felon vote could have altered this election outcome.[178] These examples further support the assertion that felon voter inclusion, along with increased voter participation and voter turnout, could have its most immediate affect on local politics as compared to state and federal. What could not be ignored was the human cost of political exclusion and marginalization. How one felt on the inside was conditioned and controlled by the policies and practices sanctioned, defined, and implemented through political elites, the power of the state and its representatives. Permanent political marginalization of any group serves as an effective disincentive for the effected group, and as a warning to the enfranchised. No one is assured fair and equal representation until everyone is.

CHAPTER 6

Virginia: A Case Study of a State Mandating Permanent Felon Disenfranchisement

Introduction

"...When we disenfranchise ex-felons, as when we react in other ways to deviance, we are not simply following an obvious and legal course, but rather a cultural option...."[179]

There are compelling human needs to which the democratic state is obliged to respond. Failing to do so, does not obviate human need or the states obligation, but rather creates intended and unintended social and political effects. As indicated by respondents in this study, one of the effects of increasingly more stringent state disenfranchisement law has been an increasing demand for the right to vote. In each of the surveyed states, the question was asked: If you were able to vote, would you vote in an election? In New Jersey, 76% of the respondents said they would; in Maryland, 89% of the respondents said they would; and in this chapter, 96.2% of the Virginia respondent group said they would vote if they had the right. These States, respectively, represent increasingly more stringent state felon disenfranchisement law.

The democratic state is obligated to assure constituent human and emancipatory needs such as autonomy, identity, recognition, belongingness, participation, and fulfillment. In disenfranchising ex-felons, the state stands in direct contradiction with this obligation. Respondents in this study demonstrated that permanent political marginalization frustrates human potential and intensifies anomic response; and that 'the historic struggle for political equality is more than a struggle for the right to vote, it is a struggle for an unalienated political life' (Green, P., 1985).

Virginia represents those states that have permanently disenfranchised felons for life. Through 2003, there were eight states in this category. By 2007 (through 2012), there were only two remaining states practicing such draconian law – Kentucky and Virginia. This chapter focuses on Virginia, and more particularly its southeastern geographic area – Hampton Roads (including Norfolk, Newport News, and Virginia Beach). There are two facts that will be effectively illustrated in this study. Felon disenfranchisement law has reflected the history and sociology of race in the United States and, in particular, the racial and political values and interests of specific states within this nation. I have argued that political inequality and disparities in life chances began with social disparities based on race. Virginia reflected a history of colonialism, slavery, statehood, Civil War, and modern times which contrasted democratic principle with an ideology of racial dominance culminating in social disparities based on race. Virginia was the birthplace of eight U.S. Presidents including the authors of the Declaration of Independence, the Virginia Plan, the Bill of Rights - as well as the Three-fifths Compromise, the capital of the Confederacy, 'Black codes' and "Jim Crow" law. These historical contradictions reflected a political culture in which an enduring and permanent felon disenfranchisement practice became law.

While it is recognized that the first people to arrive in Virginia did so about five thousand years ago (Native Americans), recorded history begins with the history of colonialism. As such, Virginia is recorded as one of the original states of the Union, sharing contributions from Native American, European, and African cultures. Established as a colony in 1607, African workers were enslaved in this colony beginning in 1619. Slavery was codified in Virginia by 1661. The distinction between imported Europeans and Africans in law was made clear by classifying Africans as slaves (durante vita) and Europeans as indentured servants for a specified period of up to seven years. These same colonists proceeded to appropriate land from Native Americans by both force and treaty. One hundred years later, spokesman from this colony began protesting the distresses of "taxation without representation" and sent representatives to the Continental Congress. By 1776, Virginia, along with the other colonies, had declared their independence from the British Empire. Virginians were instrumental in drafting the U.S. Constitution, and ratified it in 1788. The first draft of the U.S. Constitution counted every slave as 3/5's of a person, which would have allowed Virginia the largest bloc of votes in the House. By 1860, one third of Virginia's population was slaves.

Based on an assertion of their right to maintain slavery as an institution, Virginia seceded from the Union in 1861, with Richmond becoming the capital of the Confederacy. In 1870, having been defeated in the Civil War (by 1865), Virginia was restored to the Union after writing a new (racially inclusive) state constitution. By 1883 the politically conservative White Democratic Party gained power and passed segregationist "Jim Crow" laws, and by 1902 rewrote the state constitution to include poll taxes and other voter registration restrictions intended to disenfranchise African Americans. Felon disenfranchisement is a legacy of this history. In modern times, the struggle for the right to vote was made manifest through the 1960's Civil Rights Movement. In Virginia, the Davis v. County School Board of Prince Edward County was made part of the Brown v. Board of Education Supreme Court decision, affirming the right to equal education for African Americans.[180] This achievement led to other civil rights gains such as protection of suffrage for African Americans, absent felon disenfranchisement. Historic Virginia represented the politics and sociology of race in the United States and the racial and political values and interests of states that permanently disenfranchised felons.

Virginia is divided into independent cities and counties which function in the same manner. Thirty-nine of the forty-two independent cities in the United States are in Virginia. Incorporated towns are recognized as part of the ninety-five counties in Virginia, but are not independent. The contrasting demographic profiles by city and county in the commonwealth of Virginia distinguished disparities in life chances within the various counties and municipalities in Virginia. Virginia has eleven Metropolitan Statistical areas: Northern Virginia, Hampton Roads, and Richmond-Petersburg are the three most highly populated. As of 2006, Virginia Beach was the most populous city in the commonwealth, with Norfolk and Chesapeake second and third. Norfolk forms the urban core of this metropolitan area, which is home to the world's largest naval base. By 2006, Virginia had a population of 7,642,884. Almost 74% of this population was White, and 20% were Black. No significant change took place in population by race in Virginia by 2010. In 2010, Virginia's population totaled 8,001,024 with 68.6% White, 19.4% Black, and 7.9% Latinos. Population density in Virginia was 178.8 persons per square mile.[181] By comparison Hampton Roads had a total population of 1,795,015 and population density of 2,647 persons per square mile.

The largest cities in Hampton Roads included Virginia Beach, Norfolk, Chesapeake, and Newport News.[182] In Norfolk there was an estimated population of 235,747 with a population density of 4,362.8 persons per square mile. Norfolk was 48.36% White and 44.11% Black.[183] Newport News had a population of 180,150, and population density of 2,637.9 persons per square mile. Newport News was 53.5% White, and 39.07% Black.[184] Virginia Beach had an estimated population (2008) of 440,415, and a population density of 1,712.7 persons per square mile. Virginia Beach was 73% White and 21% Black.[185] **Density in Hampton Roads and its accompanying major cities were 14.7, 24.2, 14.2, and 9.5 times greater than the density in the state of Virginia.** The proportion of Blacks in two of three of these cities was greater than in the State of Virginia. Blacks represented at least two out of five of the Norfolk and Newport News population. As previously indicated, density and race are significant measures in estimating quality of life factors in urban communities, as well as rates of arrests, convictions and incarceration. In 2004, Whites were estimated to be approximately 1/3 of the felon population (31.5%), and Blacks were almost 2/3 of the felon population (60%). The total incarcerated population was 34,784 inmates.[186] Approximately 32% of this population returned to six of 130 sending communities upon their release. Approximately 90% of this population was male, with 94% of this population able to return home after completing their sentence. Seventeen percent of this population would return to Norfolk, Newport News, or Virginia Beach.[187] Norfolk, Newport News, and Virginia Beach were urban cluster neighborhoods.

In comparison to New Jersey and Maryland, Virginia had the most restrictive felon disenfranchisement law. I will use Virginia as a model of permanent felon disenfranchisement, and examine the human cost to the felon population and specific communities. Just as in Chapters IV and V, there are three specific questions answered in this chapter. What are the voting rights and practices of citizens and felons in the State of Virginia? What is the effect of Virginia felon disenfranchisement law on felon voter participation, efficacy, knowledge, and attitudes? Does Virginia felon disenfranchisement law have a disproportionate impact on the African American community? In this chapter, I will define felon disenfranchisement according to Virginia State law. A Felon Voter Participation Survey will be used to measure the political impact of felon disenfranchisement on felons, and to ascertain felon voter attitudes in Virginia. This survey will examine felon voter rights, equal representation, felon voter attitudes, political recognition, identity, empowerment or disempowerment. The central question is whether Virginia felons would vote if they had a right to? If so, would the felon vote matter? I will include a case study of elections in Hampton Roads.

Virginia: Voter Rights and Profiles

> "Everyone wants a seat at the table because no one wants to be the meal".
>
> (Author unknown)

> "In elections by the people, the qualifications of voters shall be as follows: Each voter shall be a citizen of the U.S., shall be eighteen years of age, shall fulfill the residence requirements set forth in this section, and shall be registered to vote pursuant to this article. No person who has been convicted of a felony shall be qualified to vote unless his civil rights have been restored by the Governor or other appropriate authority. As prescribed by law, no person adjudicated to be mentally incompetent shall be qualified to vote until his competency has been re-established."[188]
>
> Virginia State Constitution, 1971
> (Article II, Section I)

Felon disenfranchisement law in Virginia contrasts the compelling human need for recognition and participation with the deep rooted values and political convictions of an antebellum southern regional political culture. It is for this reason that Virginia represents not only states which permanently disenfranchise felons, but it also illustrates why 'everyone wants a seat at the (voting) table'. No one wants to be the meal.

The Constitution of the Commonwealth of Virginia was the legal document that was used as a model to both define and limit the powers of the state. Virginia enacted its first constitution in 1776 and, in addition to numerous amendments, there have been six major subsequent revisions of the constitution in 1830, 1851, 1864, 1870, 1902, and the current Virginia Constitution ratified in 1971. These new constitutions have been part of, and a reaction to, periods of major racial and social upheavals in specific regions of Virginia.[189] The Virginia constitution codified the 'founding moment' of constituent democracy for both the Commonwealth of Virginia and the United States in 1776. Among those who drafted the 1776 Virginia Constitution were James Madison, Thomas Jefferson, and George Mason. While declaring dissolution of the rule of Great Britain for 'detestable and insupportable tyranny' these Founding Fathers, as well as the subsequent State Constitutions, wove into the fabric of State law principles of race domination and racial hierarchy.

By the 1820's Virginia was one of only two states that limited voting to landowners while other residents (poor whites of what would become West Virginia in 1863) became increasingly discontented with their lack of representation in the state legislature. A Constitutional Convention was convened in 1829-1830. The issues surrounding this new constitution were equal representation, suffrage, and class division (landowners v. less affluent residents). While this new constitution limited the requirements for voting, it did not receive broad base support from the various regions of Virginia, with western Virginia dissenting in particular. From 1840 to 1851, western Virginia continued to make several attempts to win electoral reform in the state legislature, but was defeated on each attempt.

The abolition of slavery and secession from Virginia were primary concerns leading to the constitutional convention of 1851. The primary change adopted at this convention was the elimination of the property requirement for voting. From that period forward, all white male residents would be eligible to vote. Again, as the result of Virginia seceding from the Union and joining the Confederacy in 1861, Virginia set up a new constitutional convention in 1863-4 with that convention approving the separation of West Virginia into a separate state. The 1864 Virginia constitution also abolished slavery in Virginia and disenfranchised anyone who served in the Confederate government.

The postwar Virginia Constitutions underscored the dichotomy between racial domination and hierarchy, and the principles of constituent democracy. The 1870 Virginia Constitution was written in response to federal Reconstruction legislative mandates. In protest of Black suffrage, many White Virginia conservatives did not participate in the voting for delegates to the new constitutional convention. Therefore, Radical Republicans led by Judge John Underwood dominated the convention. Historically, this constitution became known as the 'Underwood Constitution' or derisively, the 'Negro Constitution' by its opponents. Significant provisions included in the constitution were: extending the right to vote to all men over the age of 21 (therefore including African American men); establishing a state school system with mandatory funding and attendance; and providing that judges would be elected by the General Assembly rather than by popular election. Not including the clause that disenfranchised ex-Confederate soldiers, the 1870 Constitution was ratified by a popular vote of 210,585 to 9,136.

By the twentieth century (1902), Jim Crow law was a fixture in southern state governance and had already disenfranchised African Americans in six Southern states. The 1902 Virginia constitutional convention was called together expressly for the purpose of eliminating the African American vote while avoiding any violation of the Fifteenth Amendment. Senator Carter Glass led the convention in achieving this goal by creating new requirements for voting. All voters would have to pay a poll tax and pass a literacy test. An exemption was granted for military veterans and sons of veterans. Combined, these requirements effectively excluded African Americans, with a more limited effect on poor white males. This new law effectively reduced the Virginia electorate by one-half. Other significant provisions of the 1902 Constitution included: racial segregation in public schools; the abolition of the county court system; and the creation of the State Corporation Commission. To prevent the possibility of African American opposition, the convention refused to fulfill its pledge to put the proposed constitution to popular vote. The constitution was adopted without ratification by the electorate. The 1902 constitution remained in effect longer than any previous Virginia constitution.

The current Virginia constitution was drafted by the Commission on Constitutional Revision established by Governor Godwin and the General Assembly in 1968, and was ratified by popular vote on July 1, 1971. The impetus for this revision was the Civil Rights Act of 1964 and the series of Supreme Court cases beginning with Brown v. the Board of Education. These legislative and judicial acts struck down most of the draconian law codified by the 1902 constitution such as the restrictions on African American voting and segregated education. Virginia history was a history of racial projects intended to, among other things, permanently disenfranchise African Americans. It is this history which best explains why Virginia is one of the last two remaining states that by statutory law mandates permanent felon disenfranchisement.[190]

The Virginia State Constitution, Article II, Section I states that 'No person who has been convicted of a felony shall be qualified to vote unless his civil rights have been restored by the Governor or other appropriate authority.' As reported by Nicki Tafia in "Re-enfranchisement", Virginia law specified that the governors approval was mandatory, and that even then there was a three-year mandatory waiting period for non-violent offenders and a five-year mandatory waiting period for violent offenders, as well as a requirement that the applicant present three letters from reputable persons along with their application, and finally that they demonstrate civic responsibility. These requirements were restrictive impediments by intent, not restorative guidelines. As illustrated in [table 2-4], in actual numbers this meant that Virginia restored 5,043 felon's their right to vote out of a total of 269,800 disenfranchised felons over a six-year period ending in 2005; this represented a 1.8% restoration rate and 98.2% restrictive rate over this six-year period.

The contradiction between principle and practice in Virginia constitutional law was further compounded by its written Bill of Rights which stated "…That all men are by nature equally free and independent and have certain inherent rights…" which includes, "…life, liberty, the means of acquiring and possessing property, pursuing and obtaining happiness and safety…." The antithesis of this principle was that in practice Virginia systematically and quite intentionally disenfranchised African Americans; established English as the required standard language for the Commonwealth for all persons; and its definition of marriage was that "…only a union between one man and one woman (was seen as a) valid marriage or recognized by this Commonwealth and its political divisions…."[191] The Virginia Bill of Rights stated that no other union could be considered legitimate or be considered for any of the benefits of a marital union. These human rights violations defied essential human and emancipatory needs, fenced specific groups out of society and the equal protection of the law, and epitomized the xenophobic and moralistic resentments, animosities, and abstract prejudices of an antebellum southern political culture.

Based on the eligibility standards established in the current Virginia State constitution, of the 7,642,884 estimated 2006 population, 5,800,949 residents met the age, residency, and citizenship requirements to vote in Virginia. Of these 5,800,949 Virginia residents, at least 31,106 Corrections inmates and 47,899 parole and probation felons were not eligible to vote. In 2004, minimally 79,000 felons were disqualified from voting in Virginia for the rest of their lives. Could this population make an electoral difference once given the opportunity to vote in Virginia or Hampton Roads? From 2005 through 2007 the registered voter population of Virginia remained relatively constant (5500 variation) with the 2006 voter registration population reported to be 4,554,583. Approximately 78.5% of the eligible voter population in Virginia registered to vote in 2006. By comparison, the Hampton Roads region had a population estimated at 1,795,015 (2008) and a voter registration rate of 77.5%.

As reported in Wikipedia.org, "… In the last century Virginia shifted from a largely rural, politically Southern conservative state to a more urbanized, pluralistic, and politically moderate environment. Since the 1970's, Virginia has moved away from a racially divided single-party state. African Americans were effectively disenfranchised until after the passage of the civil rights legislation of the 1960's…

Regional differences played a large part in Virginia politics. Rural southern and western areas supported the Republican Party in response to their "southern strategy" while politically moderate urban and growing suburban areas, including Northern Virginia became the Democratic Party base...."[192] Political party strength in Virginia has also been in flux. While Virginia's Governor Tim Kaine was a Democrat, lieutenant Governor Bill Bolling was a Republican, and Republican Robert McDonnell became Attorney General by 360 votes following a legally mandated recount of ballots for that race in 2005. In the 2007 state elections, the Democrats regained control of the State Senate, and narrowed the Republican majority in the House of Delegates to eight votes. Even if 20% of the felon population had been able to participate in the electoral process (approximately 16,000 citizens), they could have altered the outcome for Attorney General.

The upset election victory of Democrat Jim Webb as one of Virginia's two U.S. Senators in 2006 demonstrated disaffection with the incumbent administrations performance. Democrat Mark Warner replaced retiring Senator John Warner in the 111th Congress. Following this trend, in 2008, President Obama became the first Democratic Presidential candidate to win Virginia since 1964. No Democratic Presidential candidate had won in Virginia in the ten prior Presidential elections. It was an election that marked the demise of the Republican 'southern strategy' with Obama winning every region of the country by double digits except the South, as well as winning such key southern states as Maryland, North Carolina, Florida, and Virginia. Obama won Virginia by a 6% margin, 52.6% to 46.3%. The actual popular voter count was 1,959,532 to 1,725,005.[193] Of the state's eleven seats in the U.S. House of Representatives, Democrats held six seats and Republicans five. By 2010 Virginia U.S. Senators were both Democrats, with eight (8) Republican and three (3) Democratic Representatives. Based on 2006 population statistics, the felon population represented 1.36% of the potential voting population of Virginia. It is important to determine the political level at which this margin may make a difference.

In part, voter preference can be measured by social group interests. How a potential voter might vote within a state, county, or municipality may be compared by demographic profile. By 2006, Virginia's population was 7,642,884. Of this total population 6.8% were under the age of five, 24.1% were under the age of 18 years old, 75.9% were of voting age, and 11.4% were over age 65. Women represented 50.8% of the general population. Whites represented 73.6%, Blacks represented almost 20%, Asians represented 4.6%, and Latinos represented 6% of the general population. High school graduates represented 81.5% of persons aged 25 and over and 29.5% of this general population possessed a bachelor's degree or better. Median annual household income was $51,103, and 9.5% of the population lived below the poverty line. Add to this profile the contrasting population density reports on the state, county, and municipal levels and one can distinguish social group needs or interests by location.[194]

In Norfolk, the total population in 2000 was 234,403 with an estimated 235,747 by 2007, and 242,803 by 2010. As previously indicated, density in Norfolk was the highest in the state at 4,362.8 people per square mile. Approximately 24% of the population was under the age of 18 in 2000, and 20.8% by 2010, 76% were of voting age by 2000, and 79.2% by 2010, and 10.9% were at least 65 years old. Fifty-four percent of the population was male and 48% female. A total of 47.1% of the city was White, 43.7% were Black, 2.81% were Asian, and 3.8% were Latino. The median household income was $31,815 and by 2010, increased to $42,677. At 19.4%, the population below the poverty line in Norfolk was more than double that of the state of Virginia. Population below the poverty line decreased to 16.5% by 2010.

In 2000, the Newport News population total was 180,150 people. This number remained relatively constant to 2010 with 180,719 people. Population density was 2,637.9 people per square mile. More than 27% of the Newport News population was under the age of 18 years, 72.5% were of voting age, and 10.1% were 65 years old or older. Fifty-six percent of this population was female, and 44% was male. Fifty-three percent of the population was White, 39% was Black, 2.3% were Asian, and 4.22% were Latino. The median household income was $36,597. Median household income increased to $49,562 by 2010. About 11.3% of the Newport population lived below the poverty line.

In 2000, the estimated population of Virginia Beach was 425,257 and 437,994 in 2010. Population density in Virginia Beach was 653.6 persons per square mile. Better than 27% of the Virginia Beach population was under the age of 18 in 2000, and declined to 24% in

2010, 72.5% were of voting age in 2000, and rose to 76% in 2010, and 8.4% were 65 years old or older. Fifty-four percent of this population was female and 46% was male, fifty-one percent was female by 2010. About 71.4% of this population was White, 19% Black, 5% Asian, and 4% Latino. The median household income was $48,705. About 6.5% of the population was below the poverty line.[195]

Divergent group interests and needs between the general population of Virginia and these municipalities are marked by demographic indices such as density, race/ethnicity, household income, and populations living below the poverty line. Population density for the state of Virginia was 178.8 persons per square mile as compared to 4,362.8 for Norfolk, 2637.9 for Newport News, and 653.6 for Virginia Beach. Norfolk's annual household income was 62% of the average state household income, Newport News' household income equaled 70% of the state average household income, and Virginia Beach's household income equaled 95% of Virginia states household income. While African Americans represented 20% of Virginia's population, African Americans represented 44.1% of Norfolk, almost 40% of Newport News, and almost 20% of Virginia Beach's populations. In Virginia, 9.5% of the population was living below the poverty line. In Norfolk, Newport News, and Virginia Beach those living below the poverty line were 19.4%, 11.3%, and 6.5%, respectively. In comparison to the quality of life members of the Commonwealth at-large experienced, social disparities within these three municipalities minimized the life chances of its members.

The basic social needs of members of these municipalities were significantly greater than those within the entire state. Because these same demographic indices reflect who is more likely to be arrested, and convicted of a felony, it helps explain why 17% of the Virginia Corrections population came from these three municipalities. As will be illustrated, the social group needs and profile of the Virginia felon population was similar to the citizens of these municipalities.

In 2004, the total Virginia felon population was 34,784 with 32 of these inmates listed as out of state offenders. During this same period, there were 4,640 parolees and 43,259 probationers for a total caseload of 47,899. By 2007, the total Virginia felon population was 38,495 (37,410 in 2010) with 45 of these inmates listed as out of state offenders. During this same period, there were 7,189 parolees and

49,775 probationers for a total caseload of 56,964. In December, 2007 there were a total of 12,563 releases. Almost 12% of this returning population was female, and 88.1% of the returning population was male. In Virginia, as is the norm for most state Correctional institutions, approximately one-third of the inmate felon population returned home to their sending communities every year. Of the 38,495 inmates, 92.4% or 35,557 were male and 7.6% or 2,938 were female. Among the male population, 58.3% (22,445) were Black and 32.1% (12,362) were White with the remaining inmates (1.9%) listed as other. Among the female felon population, approximately half, 1,418 were Black, and 1,498 were White.

The race/ethnicity of the returning population was consistent with the inmate population. More than 99% of the inmate population was 18 years old or older. Approximately 5.6% or 2,167 persons had received a life sentence, with another 18 persons having received a death sentence. Approximately 94% of the current inmate population will return home to their sending communities, with the average length of stay having been 41.6 months or three and a half years. In Virginia, more than 87% of the released population received supervised probation following incarceration. Another 11.5% are placed on parole. By age, approximately 36,143 inmates and 56,964 parolees and probationers currently could be eligible to vote if Virginia provided for the automatic restoration of the ex-felon vote. Approximately 31.7% of the felon population was aged 18-29, 30.1% was aged 30-39, 26% was aged 40-49, and 12.2% was aged 50+. Type of crimes or legal status for this population is listed in three categories: 56.3% or 21,657 were listed as violent offenders; 28.2% or 10,869 were listed as non-violent offenders; and 15.5% or 5,963 were listed as drug offenders. The three most common violations were: larceny/fraud (15.1%), robbery (15%), and assault (11.4%). Seventeen percent of this population was committed from Norfolk, Newport News, and Virginia Beach.[196]

This Virginia felon profile is comparable to the respondent felon population in this study. Additionally, this felon population profile is more consistent with the population profile of the respective communities in Hampton Roads than the Commonwealth of Virginia. How could voter participation of this felon population affect the electoral process in Virginia and the Hampton Roads municipalities?

Virginia Felon Voter Attitude Survey: A Matter of Choice

Permanent felon disenfranchisement law in Virginia assures that felons lose their right to vote for life. A felon voter survey was administered to this Virginia felon population. The focus of the felon survey was to determine the degree to which voting mattered to them, and whether they would vote if they were enfranchised. This survey sample was not a random sampling, but rather a sample determined by the accessibility to a felon population incarcerated in Hampton County, Virginia. Through the cooperation of the Hampton County Sheriff's Office, this writer was allowed to survey felons who were within one year of their parole, probation, or release eligibility date. I am grateful to Sheriff B.J. Roberts and Executive Director Dawn Smith and their staff for administering this survey to this Virginia felon population. This survey was administered to 110 Virginia felons beginning in December, 2008 through July, 2009, and the central question was: "… If you were allowed to vote, would you vote in an election?" The range of responses was:

"… The only way for change is a heard voice and a stated opinion…"
"… I don't feel that one single vote makes a difference…"
"… People risked their lives to give me the right to vote…"
"… It's a constitutional right that I may have lost forever…"
"… If I've paid my debt than let it go…"
"… I feel by losing my right to vote, it's a life sentence…"
"…We have a Black President now because people took advantage of the opportunity to vote…"
"… I'm a U.S. citizen. You get punished for your crime. Voting is a right. That means I get punished for my rights too…"
"… Taking (my right to vote) from me is like stripping me of my citizenship…"
"… I do my time, I get out, get a job, obey the laws, pay my taxes- but can't vote. How American is that…."

It is significant that the most stringently restricted felons offered the most vociferous and highly passionate responses to felon disenfranchisement. Not only did these respondents offer, by far, the greater number of self-reported reasons for voting, but the responses were also the most vehement. Collectively, these voices underscore Shklar's assertion of the importance of voting and citizenship; Keiser's definition of democratization; the essence of constituent democracy; and an awareness of African American history and the struggle for justice, equality and the right to vote.

More than 96% of the respondents said that they would vote if they could, and 3.8% said they would not. As previously indicated, voter turnout in 2004 was 60.3%. The Presidential Election results of 2008 was the highest voter turnout since 1964 at 61.1%. The distinction between voter turnout among registered voters and felon respondent interest in voting was dramatic.

The demographics of the surveyed population communicates their political interests and needs. Approximately 93.6% of the respondent population was male. African Americans made up 70% of this population; 22.7% were White; and 1% was Latino. More than 9% of this population was 18-21 years of age; 58.2% was 22-40 years of age; 21.8 % was aged 41-50; and 10.9% was 51 years old or older. The legal status of the respondent population was: 14.5% violent offenses; 66.4% CDS or drug offenses; and 13.6% were property offenses. Almost 31% of the survey population had been convicted one time; 25.5% of this population had been convicted of a crime twice; 22.7% had been convicted three times; 10.9% had been convicted four times; and 9.1% had been convicted five or more times. The respondent group self-reported that: 15.5% had completed the 9th or 10th grade; 8.2% had completed the 11th or 12th grade; 20% completed High School; 31.8% achieved their GED; with 24.5% indicating some college or Vocational Educational experience. Again, the respondents self-reported that: 51.8% were low income; 44.6% were middle income; and 2.7% were upper income.

More than 92% of the state felon population was male, and 95% of the respondent population was male. Approximately two thirds of the state felon population was Black, and almost three quarters of the respondent population was Black. More than 99% of both the state felon population and the respondent population were 18 years old or older. Although this study did not measure legal status as a factor in determining voter attitude, there was significant variation in legal status between the state felon population and the respondent population. In comparison to the state felon population, the respondent population had fewer violent offenders (56.3% to 14.5%), more drug offenders (15.5% to 66.4%), and fewer property offenders (28.2% to 13.6%).

Equal representation requires full participation of the members of a polity. In practical terms, this principle is made manifest only if and when both majority and minority populations in a society are fairly represented. Profiles of the general population and felon population in Virginia describe majority and minority populations respectively. Political participation, knowledge and political efficacy are measures of voter attitudes and fair representation for majority and minority populations in this study. The Virginia felon voter survey included questions concerning voter registration, prior voting practices, and campaign activities as indices of felon voter participation. Survey respondents were asked the question: "Have you ever registered to vote?" Almost fifty percent (49.1%) of the respondents said that they had registered, while 50.9% said they had not. Fifty percent of the 'yes' respondents had registered to vote prior to having been incarcerated. Twenty-five percent of the 'no' respondents had registered to vote previously, and 75% had not. A second question asked: "Have you ever voted in an election?" Thirty-four percent of the respondent population had voted previously, and 64% had not. Among 'yes' respondents, 35.8% had voted prior to incarceration, and 63.3% had not. None of the 'no' respondents had ever voted in a prior election. A third question was: "Have you ever participated in campaign activities?" Approximately 18% of the respondent population said that they had, and 81.8% said that they had not participated in campaign activities. A total of 18.9% of the 'yes' population had participated in campaign activities, and 81.1% had not. None of the 'no' respondents had participated in campaign activities prior to having been incarcerated.

One can conclude that prior voter participation had a positive impact on the voter attitudes of the respondent groups in this study. Again, consistent with the literature on voter participation in American politics, the greatest level of voter participation among this felon population was voter registration and voting. In addition, although 96% of the respondents may have a 'felt need' to vote in an election, it is more likely that 96% of this felon population would not vote if they could. As indicated by Abramson, Aldrich, and Rohde (1998), people who share social characteristics may share political interests. They further indicated that group similarities in voting behavior also may reflect past political conditions. It is therefore reasonable to assume not only that felon voter participation would be at a significantly lower rate than indicated in the survey, but also that it is most probable that this felon population would have shared political interests with populations having similar socio-political conditions.

Felon voter attitude and awareness is also measured by the degree of knowledge one has regarding state voting requirements and procedures. Insufficient knowledge can fence a population out of the electoral process as effectively as has disenfranchisement. Conversely, as indicated by Abramson, Aldrich, and Rhode, better informed or educated citizens reduce the information costs of voting and are more likely to develop attitudes that contribute to political participation. One question asked of this Virginia felon respondent population was: Do felons in Virginia regain their right to vote, and if so, when or how would this occur? Approximately 26.4% of the respondent population knew that non-violent offenders after 3 years, and violent offenders, drug offenders, and election fraud offenders after 5 years could apply for voter registration through the Circuit Court or Secretary of the Commonwealth, along with the governor's approval or pardon. Seventy-one percent of the respondents had incorrect assumptions about felon disenfranchisement. Twenty-four percent of the respondents indicated that they would lose their right to vote until they completed their sentence and applied for restoration through the governor's approval or pardon. Almost 20% of the respondents thought that felons were disenfranchised for life without any recourse whatsoever. Eleven percent felt that after three years only non-violent offenders could apply for voter restoration through the Circuit Court or Secretary of Commonwealth. And 9.1% thought that they regained their right to vote once they completed their sentence. There was no significant difference between the results of the total population and the 'yes' respondents. Only one 'no' respondent knew the felon disenfranchisement law of Virginia. The shear confusion among respondents regarding disenfranchisement law illustrates the human rights and political problem. The information cost was significant enough to serve as a disincentive for felon voter participation.

Interestingly, felon respondents had much greater knowledge of the voting rights of citizens in the Commonwealth of Virginia than they had of felon voter rights. Fully 79.1% of the respondents knew that one had to be a U.S. citizen, a resident of Virginia, at least 18 years old, mentally competent, and not to have been convicted of a felony without having been restored by the governor and the appropriate authority. The larger portion of "other" responses (9.1%) indicated that one simply had to be a U.S. citizen to vote. Again, there was no significant difference between the responses of the total population and the 'yes' population. Only two 'no' respondents knew the correct answer.

When asked, "How many days before Election Day must you register to vote," 55.5% said they did not know, 21.8% said correctly they had to register at least 30 days prior to election, 13.6% said 7 days, and 8.2% said 15 days. Voter registration is a significant information cost for this population.

It was also important to determine whether respondents had a particular political ideology or party preference. Approximately 19% of the respondents said that they were conservative, 37.3% said they were moderates, and almost 21% said they were liberal. Another 21.8% said they were undecided. As for party preference, 11.8% said they were Republicans, 60.9% said they were Democrats, and 10.9% said that they were Independents. Fifteen percent said that they were undecided. To determine the degree to which respondents understood questions concerning political ideology, two additional questions were asked. "To what degree do you feel childcare funds should be increased?" Approximately 89% of the respondents said that childcare funds should be increased to a moderate or significant degree. The second question was, "Do you approve or disapprove of U.S. involvement in the U.N.?" Fifty-three percent of the survey respondents said they approved; approximately 39% had no opinion. Approximately 58% of the respondents indicated that they were Moderates or Liberals ideologically, with another 22% undecided. Decidedly, the greatest areas of information cost for the respondent population was knowledge of registration requirements and felon voting rights, not political ideology, partisan preference, or citizen voter rights.

A critical standard for measuring voter attitude is political efficacy. In Chapter I, political efficacy was defined as a belief in one's full membership in the body politic; and authorship of the laws, leaders, and policies of the state. It is a definition which implies participant recognition, respect, mutual reciprocity and political influence. Respondent answers to the question as to why they would or would not vote in an election offered explanation as to the human cost and belief in constituent recognition, authorship, and political influence. Strikingly, in New Jersey, Maryland, and Virginia the 'yes' felon survey responses respectively were 90%, 82.1%, and 90% favorable. Eight or nine 'yes' respondents out of ten in each state either felt that their vote could add political recognition and public consideration to felon issues; or that they would vote because it was their right to do so. It should be noted that, Virginia, the state with the most stringent disenfranchisement law, had a belief in constituent political influence equal to New Jersey's.

Because there was such a limited number of 'no' respondents in the Virginia survey, it is not possible to determine any statistical significance among the respondents who indicated that their vote would not matter. Among the 'yes' respondents, 3.6% of the group felt that their vote would not matter. Ninety-three percent of the 'yes' respondents felt that their vote would matter to some degree or more. Almost 51% of this population felt that their vote would matter to a great degree. About 7.3% of this population felt that their vote would matter little to no degree. Not only did the respondents feel that felons should be given the right to vote (98.2% favorable), but the majority of the respondents (63.6%) felt that felons should complete their sentence and their "debt to society" prior to regaining their right to vote.

Political efficacy can be one of the most effective measures of voter attitude. As in chapters IV and V, an abbreviated Sociopolitical Control Scale developed by Marc Zimmerman and James Zahniser was used to measure the degree to which the respondents felt membership, social dignity, empowerment or disempowerment. For purposes of analysis, scales (1-3) have been collapsed into disagree, and scales (4-6) have been collapsed into Agree. This scale measured feelings of leadership, empowerment, community isolation, and policy control for the respondent population. Because the survey results between total respondents and 'yes' respondents were essentially the same in the Sociopolitical Control Scale, comparative analysis was made between 'yes' respondents and 'no' respondents.

[TABLE 17]

YES Respondents Collapsed:	Disagree (1-3)		Agree (4-6)		No Response	
People like me are generally well qualified to participate in the political activity and decision-making in the U.S.	22.6%	(24)	76.5%	(81)	.9%	(01)
I enjoy political participation because I want to have as much say in running government as possible.	17.0%	(18)	83.0%	(88)		(0)
A good many local elections aren't important enough to bother with.	89.6%	(95)	10.4%	(11)		(0)
So many other people are active in local issues and organizations that it doesn't matter much to me whether I participate or not.	90.6%	(96)	9.4%	(10)		(0)
Most public officials wouldn't listen to me no matter what I did.	60.4%	(64)	39.6%	(42)		(0)
Sometimes politics and government seem so complicated that a person like me can't really understand what's going on.	78.3%	(83)	21.7%	(23)		(0)

Total   (106)

[TABLE 18]

NO Respondents Collapsed:	Disagree (1-3)		Agree (4-6)		No Response
People like me are generally well qualified to participate in the political activity and decision-making in the U.S.	50%	(02)	50%	(02)	(0)
I enjoy political participation because I want to have as much say in running government as possible.	75%	(03)	25%	(01)	(0)
A good many local elections aren't important enough to bother with.	75%	(03)	25%	(01)	(0)
So many other people are active in local issues and organizations that it doesn't matter much to me whether I participate or not.	75%	(03)	25%	(01)	(0)
Most public officials wouldn't listen to me no matter what I did.	75%	(03)	25%	(01)	(0)
Sometimes politics and government seem so complicated that a person like me can't really understand what's going on.	100%	(04)		(0)	(0)

Total (04)

Virginia felon respondents offered the highest percentage of positive responses to the Sociopolitical Control Scale of any of the three states (New Jersey, Maryland, and Virginia). Better than seven in ten (76.5%) 'yes' respondents felt that people like themselves were generally well qualified to participate in political activity and decision-making in the U.S. Better than 80% respondents said they enjoy political participation because they want to have as much say in running government as possible. Almost nine in every ten respondents felt that local elections were important; fully nine out of ten respondents felt that it mattered to them as to whether they participated in local issues or not. Three out of five respondents said that public officials would listen to them, and almost eight out of ten respondents felt that politics and government was not too complicated for a person like themselves to understand. These respondents had a strong belief in their right to participate, their knowledge and competence to influence or make policy, and the belief that their vote would matter. 'Yes' respondents believed that their vote could make a difference; and that their participation would represent authorship of the laws, leaders, and policies of the state.

It was significant that the 'no' respondents represented only 3.8% of the Virginia respondents. Fully 96% of the respondents were 'yes' respondents. Still, in comparison to the 'yes' respondents, 'no' respondents disagreed with 'yes' respondents in two areas. They did not want to have as much voice in running government as possible. They were also evenly divided on feeling qualified or unqualified to participate in political activity and decision-making in the U.S. In every other area the 'no' respondents were very positive about themselves. Three out of four 'no' respondents felt that local elections were important enough to bother with. Three out of four 'no' respondents felt that local issues mattered and that it mattered whether they participated. Three out of four 'no' respondents felt that most public officials would listen to them, and none of the 'no' respondents felt that persons like themselves would have any difficulty understanding government or politics because it would be too complicated.

Virginia survey results did not indicate the same degree of political alienation or community isolation as did the 'no' respondents in New Jersey or Maryland. More than one-third of the Virginia felon respondents provided affirmative explanations as to why they would vote if they could. In New Jersey and Maryland, fewer than 20% of the respondents provided explanations as to why they would vote if they could. Better than 50% of the Virginia survey respondents were adamant in their comments: "If I paid my debt, let it go…", "People risked their lives to give me the right to vote…", "I feel by losing my right to vote, it's a life sentence…", and "I do my time, I get out, get a job, obey the laws, pay my taxes – but can't vote. How American is that…?"

Ninety-six percent of the surveyed population said they would vote if they could. Forty-two percent of this population said that they should regain their right to vote when they have completed their prison term, and 39% felt that they should regain their right to vote upon completion of parole or probation. In 2006, there were 31,000 Correction inmates and 47,900 parole and probation felons in Virginia. This felon population represented 1.36% of the 5,800,949 Virginia residents that met Virginia voting requirements, except for disenfranchisement law. The **difference was that they were disqualified from voting for the rest of their lives**. Seventeen percent of this felon population (13,500 persons) came from three cities: Norfolk, Newport News, and Virginia Beach. This disproportionate percentage of felons had been committed from Hampton County and reflected the density, disparate poverty levels, race and ethnicity of cluster neighborhoods in at least two of these cities.

Do Ex-felon Voter Rights Matter in Virginia and Hampton County?

In Virginia and Hampton County, three significant political events potentially impacted on the outcomes of 2005 and 2006: an increase in the total felon disenfranchised population which potentially represented 1.36% of the voter population; voter turnout which resulted in victory margins of .4%, 1.15%, and .02%, respectively, in three separate state elections; and a political climate in which there had been a demographic shift from a largely rural, politically Southern conservative state to a more urbanized, pluralistic, and politically moderate environment.

The three state elections I describe in this chapter were won by margins of 9,329, 23,000, and 323 votes, respectively. The Virginia and Hampton County felon populations had the potential to make a difference in at least one of these elections had they regained the right to vote.

In November, 2006 Jim Webb narrowly defeated Republican incumbent George Allen for the U.S. Senate seat in Virginia. The vote was 1,175,606 to 1,166,277, with Democrat Jim Webb winning by a margin of 9,329 votes (.4%). This victory was compounded by the election of Jim Webb giving his party a majority in the Senate. Both candidates were formidable opponents with outstanding credentials. Allen had previously served as Governor of Virginia; and Webb was a decorated Vietnam War veteran, author and former Secretary of the Navy under Ronald Reagan. Virginia has been a state in political transition. It has been one of the more conservative Southern states, with eight of eleven Congressmen and both Senators belonging to the Republican Party until the 2006 election.[197] At the same time, Democrats had won the last two gubernatorial races in 2001 and 2005. While almost 12% of the respondent group said that they were Republican, approximately 61% of the respondents self-reported that they were Democrats. Assuming that this respondent population would vote as their socio-economic group would, it is reasonable to expect that about 20% of this population would vote if they could. This would mean that approximately 15,800 Virginia felons would vote if they could, and about 2,700 of these felons would have been committed from Hampton County. Adding 61% or 9,638 potential felon votes to Jim Webb's total, and 12% or 1,896 felon votes to George Allen's total would not have altered the outcome of this election, however, their vote would have allowed the felon voice to be heard.

In 2005, a Democrat, Tim Kaine won the gubernatorial race over Republican, Jerry Kilgore by a margin of 5.73%. The margin of victory for Tim Kaine in the respective cities of Norfolk, Newport News, Virginia Beach was: 35.31%, 17.55%, and .67%. The Lt. Governorship was won by a Republican, Tim Bolling over the Democratic candidate Leslie Byrne by 1.15% or 23,000 votes. The total votes were 979,265 (R) to 956,265 (D). Again, the estimated felon voter population of 15,800 potential voters would not have been sufficient to alter the outcome of this election. The margin of victory for Tim Bolling was 23,000 votes. Mathematically even if 90% of the felon population (assuming they had the right to vote) had voted for the Democratic candidate (Leslie Byrne), it would have been insufficient to alter the election outcome. The significance of this election is that it further illustrated that close elections increases the importance of maximizing constituent inclusion, voter turnout, and the consideration of minority interests. In this same election (2005), the Republican Bob McDonnell defeated Democrat Creigh Deeds for State Attorney General by a margin of .02% or 323 votes. The total votes were 970,886 (R) to 970,563 (D).[198] Clearly, the estimated felon voter population of 15,800 potential voters in Virginia as well as the 2,700 potential felon voters in Hampton County would have affected the outcome of this election. Given that these estimates are hypothetical, the real significance of this election was that it illustrated that the felon vote can alter an election or at the very minimum, affect the policy issues and outcomes during an election and within community life. It also teaches that maximizing the inclusion of majority and minority populations in voter participation and voter turnout can be the guarantor of democracy. Fair and equal representation in a democratic state depends on this principle.

CHAPTER 7

Conclusion: Examining the Felon Disenfranchisement Paradigm

African American felon disenfranchisement is a story about intended and unintended social and political exclusion. Globally, groups experiencing social and political exclusion have been described as experiencing a 'rupture in the social bond(s)' or 'social disadvantages'. Dr. Lynn Todman "...suggests that social exclusion refers to processes in which individuals and entire communities of people are systematically blocked from rights, opportunities and resources (e.g., housing, employment, healthcare, civic engagement, democratic participation and due process) that are normally available to members of society and are key to social integration...."[199] Social exclusion takes on the form of political exclusion as a "...multidimensional process of progressive social rupture, detaching groups, and individuals from social relations and institutions and preventing them from full participation in the normal, normatively prescribed activities of the society in which they live...."[200] Felon disenfranchisement makes felons feel this alienation, detachment and social rupture in society. Losing the right to vote has thwarted or blocked felon rights, opportunities, and resources normally available to citizens. It has been described as a civil death which results in weak social networking; limited circulation of information about jobs, political activities, and community events. You know you are experiencing political exclusion when you have poor future prospects, an inability to participate in community activities, inadequate education, housing, and financial precariousness. This story has been a tale about the politics of exclusion for African American felons and their communities. Reasons for such socio-political marginalization include race/ethnicity, gender, religion, economic, and political antagonisms. Political and social exclusion is the experience of building fences in ways that separate us from others. African American felon disenfranchisement is the practice of political exclusion which results in the disproportionate and permanent racial and social exclusion of African American felons and the African American community, especially in urban cluster neighborhoods.

Chapter VII concludes this study of the effect of U.S. felon disenfranchisement policies and practices on a politically marginalized African American population. It is a study of political contradictions. It is a study of racial dominance by a political majority; the effects of permanent political marginalization on a minority population; and the challenge that African American felon disenfranchisement posits not only to the principle of fair and equal representation, but to the essence of democracy. Specifically, I focus on: 1) a theoretical analysis of the impact and intent of felon disenfranchisement law; 2) the legal arguments for and against felon disenfranchisement; 3) and a comparative analysis of case studies of state felon disenfranchisement and its effect on African American communities and the essence of democracy.

A Felon Disenfranchisement Paradigm

Conceptually, state felon disenfranchisement law and practice presents ideological and practical contradictions. Defining principles in American democratic thought include: 1) Voting is a fundamental right through which constituents voice their needs, choices, and interests. A violation of any members right to vote, is a violation of all members right to vote; 2) Fair representation depends on the participation of a whole community in a civil state that encourages unrestricted interest articulation and interest aggregation; 3) Fair and equal representation of groups within the American electoral system requires more than the 'one person, one vote principle,' it requires a principle that allows for 'difference' without permanent political marginalization of any individual or group. Therefore, the challenge has been to learn when and how, in U.S. democratic governance, it is appropriate to treat people differently.

Felon disenfranchisement is an extra-legal system that is dictated by: a political majority; punitive and puritanical beliefs; arbitrarily determined geographic boundaries; and White racial discrimination and political hegemony. Today, for reasons directly related to socio-political disparities based on race, more than one-third of all felons and ex-felons in the U.S. criminal justice system are African American. The figures are both shocking and telling: African Americans represent approximately 13% of the total U.S. population and 37% of the U.S. felon population. The rate of incarceration for African American males is nearly seven times greater than the rate for the total U.S. felon population. The African American felon population represents 25% of the total African American male population with one out of every four African American males involved in the criminal justice system. Felon disenfranchisement therefore inescapably and disproportionately impacts African Americans and their communities.

American society is suffused with racial projects, and the criminal justice system and felon disenfranchisement law are among the political forms which have effectively institutionalized race ideology. Daniel Bell illustrates the power of ideas in society by defining ideology and the ideology of color. Bell states, '... ideology was not simply a cultural worldview, or a mask for interests, but a historically located belief system that fused ideas with passion, sought to convert ideas into social levers, and in transforming ideas, transformed people as well....'[201] Race ideology in a white male dominated society allows a political majority to define both themselves and the 'other,' the political minority as individual citizen and aggregate interest group.

As expressed by Charles Taylor, "identity designates a person's understanding of who they are and their fundamental defining characteristics as a human being, misrecognition allows a person or group to suffer real damage, real distortion."[202] The practice of defining and excluding or restricting felons from the right to vote can only paint what Taylor describes as a 'confining and demeaning picture' of felons.

Because African Americans are a disproportionate number of the felon population, one can understand how much more distorted this 'self-reflection' must become for them. Daniel Bell continues, "... when ideology becomes a striking force, ideology looks at the world with eyes wide shut, a closed system which prefabricates answers to any question that might be asked... which is why ... the ideology of color (race) appeared in the last half century...."[203]

The ideology of race has not only become entrenched in U.S. society, but has effectively and adversely impacted the life chances and political voice of the African American community. White racial dominance and its affect on American culture and the minds, images, and politics of African Americans are real, not imagined. In a February 21, 2009 *New York Times* Op-Ed article, Charles M. Blow writes that: "... in tests taken from 2000 to 2006 (Project Implicit) found that three-quarters of whites have an implicit pro-white/anti-black bias...." Thirty-six percent of Blacks have a pro-white bias, and 40% have a pro-black bias. Latinos have a 69% pro-white bias, and Asians have a 72% pro-white bias. Respectively, Whites, Latinos, and Asians have a 9%, 13%, and 11% pro-black bias. In addition, a recent NYT/CBS News poll (conducted between July 7th and July 14th, 2008) polled almost 1,800 interviewees, 1,530 of whom were registered voters. We live an American culture that teaches race consciousness, (White) racial preference and permeates all racial/ethnic groups. The results of this study indicated that Americans (U.S.) were sharply divided by race heading into the first election that included an African American, major party candidate. Blacks and Whites held markedly different views of Barack Obama, the state of race relations, and how Blacks are treated in America. For example:

1) Black and White Americans agreed that America was ready to elect a Black president, but disagreed on almost every other question.
2) As it was eight years ago, few Americans have regular contact with people of other races.
3) Few say their own workplaces or neighborhoods are integrated.
4) Nearly 70% of Blacks said they had encountered a specific instance of discrimination based on race, compared with 62% in 2000; 26% of Whites said they had been victims of racial discrimination. Over 50% of Latinos said they had been the victim of racial discrimination.

5) Over 40% of Blacks said they believed they had been stopped by the police because of their race, the same figure as eight years ago; 7% of Whites said the same thing.

6) Sixty-four percent of Black respondents felt that Whites had a better chance of getting ahead, a figure slightly higher than the 57% that felt that way in 2000.

7) Fifty-five percent of Whites said race relations were good, almost double the figure for Blacks.

One respondent was quoted as saying "...Basically it's the same old problem, the desire for power. A Black female respondent said, "...people get so obsessed with power and don't want to share it...."[204]

Michael Omi and Howard Winant write that the contemporary state is "... the architect of segregation and chief enforcer of racial difference, and has a tendency to reproduce those patterns of inequality in a new guise."[205] African American felon disenfranchisement and the views reflected in the above NYT/CBS poll both demonstrate how the state has acted and continues to act as the "architect" of institutionalized racism and discrimination. In contrast, we know that in theory and practice, a constitutional democracy cannot allow racial difference to determine the rights of political majorities or minorities without undermining democratic principles.

Equality under the law must be defined with respect for human difference. In Skinner v. Oklahoma (1942), Justice Douglas argued that in cases dealing with fundamental human rights "... courts have to give strict scrutiny to laws which treat people unequally. Such laws have to be justified by very strong arguments...."[206] This is a nation of laws, and not men. As such, the final arbiter of equality in law is the courts. In 1974, Justice Thurgood Marshall argued that "...it is doubtful...whether the state can demonstrate either a compelling or rational policy interest in denying former felons the right to vote...."[207] This study of comparative state felon disenfranchisement tested the extent to which 'democratization was an on-going (progressive) clash, in which some groups strove to overcome subordination while other groups faced threats to the political access they had achieved (Kieser, 1997).'

Felon Enfranchisement: A Legal Argument

The legal argument supporting felon enfranchisement is predicated on
the principle that democracy is a government of laws. The 'rule of law'
exists only so long as it holds true for all citizens, members of political
majorities and minorities. Utilizing judicial review, the courts possess
the power to invalidate laws as unconstitutional, with the Supreme
Court standing as the final authority on matters of constitutional
interpretation. It is the province of the courts to say what the law is. As
held in Marbury v. Marshall, in applying the rule to particular cases, the
court must expound and interpret that rule. Judicial review, then, is the
cornerstone of a 'government of laws' today. Justices must follow it,
rather than any legislative provisions that are inconsistent with the
constitution.

To assure equity in law, where individual rights depend on
established law, remedies must be judicially enforced to protect
discrete and insular minorities. If any law, such as felon
disenfranchisement, is not in conformity with constitutional principles
it cannot become the law of the land. Not only is felon
disenfranchisement a theoretical contradiction, it also contradicts the
14th Amendment equal protection clause. Inconsistencies in state felon
disenfranchisement law have created a crazy quilt of electoral
procedures and practices from state to state. Felons committing the
same crime in New Jersey, Maryland, and Virginia are subject to
different voter restrictions based purely on where they reside, and the
differing moral and political convictions made law in that particular
state. Democracy depends upon the open and free dialogical
relationship of interests groups. Fair representation without the
articulation of political majority and minority interests is a
contradiction in terms. Issacharoff, Karlan, and Pildes cogently made
this point when they wrote, "...those who currently hold power will
deploy that power to try to preserve their control...."[208]

In principle therefore, felon disenfranchisement is inconsistent
with the U.S. constitution, and it is the province of the courts to say so.
As illustrated in Chapter III, the challenge to the courts is to know
when a constitutional interpretation has exceeded the boundaries of
judicial review and become judicial activism. Most recently, the Court
has been criticized as having engaged in liberal judicial activism (i.e.,

Warren and Burger Courts). It was under the Rehnquist Court that conservative judicial activism resulted in the ongoing systematic disenfranchisement of felons (Richardson v. Ramirez, 1974).

The debate over human and political rights is by no means a new phenomenon. Liberty and equality have been ideologically antagonistic throughout the history of the democratic experiment in the U.S. Historically, voter restrictions such as felon disenfranchisement were intended to exclude persons from voting based on their race and class. Felon enfranchisement has been, and continues to be, a critical part of the struggle to achieve democratization in the United States.

Judicial Review or Judicial Activism

In the U.S., judicial review is the cornerstone of 'a government of laws.' And, in Chapter III, I argued that judicial decisions are not always rational when judges rely on ideology rather than the law. As illustrated by this study of felon disenfranchisement, the challenge to the courts has been to know when constitutional interpretation has exceeded the boundaries of judicial review and become judicial activism. U.S. Constitutional Law (Marbury v. Marshall) makes it clear that: the courts must say what the law is; the court is the final authority on matters of constitutional interpretation; and the court must expound and interpret that rule. Contrary to Rehnquist's argument in Richardson v. Ramirez, the constitutional obligation is not to simply give a 'plain reading' of the law, but rather the purpose of judicial review is to read, expound, and interpret the law.

At issue are the boundaries of or limits to constitutional interpretation. Interpretation of the law by any literate human being is inevitable. If one argues that judicial activism is an interpretation of the U.S. Constitution, holding that the spirit of the times and the needs of the nation can and should legitimately influence judicial decisions, then one can say that there is a place for judicial activism in the courts. However, when judges tend to 'look at the world with eyes wide shut' (D. Bell, 2000, p.xi) they go beyond judicial review and their appropriate powers and engage in making law rather than interpreting it. Judicial restraint must be the medium or balance through which judges resist the temptation to influence public policy through their decisions. Judicial activism is not the prisoner of any particular ideological or political viewpoint; it can be conservative or liberal. In most cases, history dictates which definition prevailed over a given period of time.

As previously shown, the legal argument for and against felon disenfranchisement primarily rests with six Supreme Court cases. Principle arguments for fair and equal representation in law for individuals, minority and majority groups, and felons were presented in: Skinner v. Oklahoma, 1942; Baker v. Carr, 1962; Reynolds v. Sims, 1964; Richardson v. Ramirez, 1974; Mobile v. Bolden, 1980; and Hunter v. Underwood, 1985. This study of felon disenfranchisement raised questions concerning the rule of law and consequently, human rights and human dignity. The building blocs through which an argument for and against felon disenfranchisement was constructed emanated primarily through these six Supreme Court decisions. Each case presented another standard of legitimation: strict scrutiny; justiciability; a definition of political equality ('one person, one vote); a standard for an exemption of criminal disenfranchisement law from strict scrutiny; and an argument for restrained judicial activism. As illustrated in at least two or more of the referenced Supreme Court cases, judicial activism (engaged to make law rather than interpret law) proved to be a disservice to U.S. democratization and to African American communities. In part as a result of this illegitimate use of judicial activism, African Americans have experienced a highly disproportionate rate of felon disenfranchisement and voter dilution in their communities.

As summarized in Chapter III, the Supreme Court decision in Richardson v. Ramirez constructed an exemption of criminal disenfranchisement law from strict scrutiny. The court construed the phrase in Section 2 of the 14th Amendment, "... but when the right to vote at any election is denied... except for participation in rebellion, or other crime..."209 as granting states an affirmative sanction to disenfranchise those convicted of criminal offenses. The Supreme Court upheld this decision. Justice Rehnquist argued that the language of Section 2 was intended by Congress to mean what it says. I have argued that the sources upon which the decision was based demonstrate that Section 2 was situational, and was specifically intended as a provision for the readmission of the rebel states beginning in 1867.

How Section 2 became a part of the 14ᵗʰ Amendment had everything to do with what it said and what it meant.

Contrary to Justice Rehnquist's argument that the majority opinion represents a 'plain reading of it,' it is clear that his conclusion was an attempt to restrict the law rather than to interpret the law. To this extent, the majority opinion misrepresented judicial review and constituted judicial activism. Justice Marshall's dissent offered three cogent points in rebuttal:

1) Democratic law is not frozen into immutable form; it is constantly in the process of revision in response to the needs of a changing society;
2) Citizens have a constitutional right to participate in elections on an equal basis, and the judicial role is to protect that right when state statutes selectively distribute the franchise;
3) Fencing out a sector of the population because of the way they would vote is constitutionally impermissible (Carrington v. Rash).

Justice Thurgood Marshall concluded that a "... temporal majority can use...power to preserve inviolate its view of the social order simply by disenfranchising those with different views...."[210] If we are to live by the 'rule of law,' each member of the polity is obligated to manage his or her fear or distrust of political opinion and human rationality. Furthermore, if the rule of law is to prevail, the courts must value judicial review and the restrained use of judicial activism.

Two Supreme Court cases that followed Richardson v. Ramirez represent the illegitimate and legitimate uses of judicial activism. Mobile v. Bolden and Hunter v. Underwood are two Supreme Court decisions that both tested the legality of racially disproportionate representation by intent and impact of racial discrimination (i.e., felon disenfranchisement). In Mobile v. Bolden, 1980, it was alleged that at-large elections of Commissioners "... invidiously discriminated against [African Americans] in violation of the 14ᵗʰ Amendment..."[211] by unfairly diluting the voting strength of African American communities. Upheld by the Court of Appeals, the ruling was reversed by the Supreme Court. The Court held that "...racially discriminating motivation is a necessary ingredient of a 15th Amendment violation...."$_{212}$ Only purposeful discrimination or the denial of the right to vote on account of race would be considered a 14th or 15th Amendment violation. This ruling was not a 'plain reading' of the 14th or 15th Amendments. Discrimination by any definition is purposeful discrimination. This ruling went beyond interpreting the law to making law. The Supreme Court ruling held that the Mobile Commission form government was constitutionally permissible even though the choice may have been of 'mixed motivations,' some of which may have been 'invidious.' A Supreme Court decision is not rational, nor does it meet strict scrutiny standards when it finds a ruling (in its own words) both 'permissible' and 'invidious,' and acknowledges that it is offensive because it is unfairly discriminatory. This majority opinion exceeded the courts judicial authority and demonstrated judicial activism that was in direct violation of the equal protection clause of the 14th Amendment.

In Hunter v. Underwood, 1985, two appellants in Alabama were convicted of misdemeanors. They brought suit and argued that the law was adopted to disenfranchise African Americans in particular, and that this law had the intended effect. After failing in the lower courts, the Court of Appeals reversed the decision, holding that discriminatory intent had been a motivating factor, and there was no finding of a permissible intent. The Supreme Court upheld the decision. The Court of Appeals had ruled that in the face of mixed motives, a violation of the 14th Amendment, and a preponderance of evidence racial discrimination was a substantial or motivating factor in this case. In Hunter v. Underwood, the court affirmed that African American felon disenfranchisement law violated equal protection law, diluted African American political interests, representation, and the voting strength of the African American community. This court ruling exemplifies the legitimate use of judicial review and restrained judicial activism. As demonstrated in these cases, African American felon voter discrimination has had a direct and deleterious impact on the rule of law and democratization in the U.S.

Background to the Study

The literature on felon disenfranchisement supports the hypothesis that race discrimination has a significantly greater political impact within states which permanently disenfranchised some or all African American felons than states which provided for automatic restoration. As illustrated in Chapters IV, V, and VI, there are two underlying and interconnected problems of the sociology of race and race dominance in understanding the impact of felon disenfranchisement on African American empowerment or disempowerment. One of the effects of increasingly more restrictive state felon disenfranchisement law has been an increased demand for the right to vote. In each of the surveyed states, the question was asked: If you were able to vote, would you? In New Jersey, 76% of the respondents said they would; in Maryland, 89% of the respondents said they would; and in Virginia, 96.2% of the respondents said that they would vote if they had the right to. The more restrictive state felon disenfranchisement was, the greater the demand for the right to vote by the survey respondents. Not only did the majority of all respondents see voting as a right, they felt that the right to vote was a measure of social dignity and recognition.

The Sentencing Project (1998) reported that, in comparison to the total adult voting age population, the percentage of disenfranchised felons for 'all' or 'some' permanent disenfranchisement states, and 'automatic restoration' states was 4.3%, 3.14%, and 1.13%, respectively. The more restrictive state felon disenfranchisement law was, the higher the percentage of disenfranchised felons. Among the total African American adult voting age population, the percentage of African American disenfranchised felons for 'all' or 'some' permanent disenfranchisement states, and for 'automatic restoration' states was 23.5%, 17.2%, and 8.3%, respectively. Nationally, the total percentage of disenfranchised felons was 2% while the total percentage of African American disenfranchised felons was 13.1% (Table 1-3). The more restrictive the state felon disenfranchisement law, the higher the percentage of African American felon disenfranchisement. There was also significant disparity between African American felon disenfranchisement and felon disenfranchisement of the total population. African American felon disenfranchisement was seven times greater than the total felon population. African American felon disenfranchisement has a more significant impact in states that had 'all' or 'some' felon disenfranchisement than in automatic restoration states.

By comparison, the percentage of adult felon disenfranchisement in Virginia, Maryland, and New Jersey was 5.3%, 3.6%, and 2.3%. As normative models, these states replicated a similar pattern of felon disenfranchisement as did states nationwide. The more restrictive these states were, the higher the percentage of disenfranchised felons. Among African American felons in Virginia, Maryland, and New Jersey the percentage of adult felon disenfranchisement was 25%, 15.4%, and 17.7%, respectfully. With the exception of rates for African American felon disenfranchisement in New Jersey exceeding those in Maryland, each of these states   represented normative standards for 'permanent' or 'some permanent' disenfranchisement and automatic restoration (see Table 1-2). There was significant disparity between African American felon disenfranchisement and felon disenfranchisement of the total population. While African American felon disenfranchisement had a significant impact in all three states, it was greatest in Virginia and more similar than dissimilar in Maryland and New Jersey.

Quantitatively, as documented by the literature on felon disenfranchisement rates, felon disenfranchisement had a significantly greater impact on permanently disenfranchised African American felons than it had in automatic restoration states. This conclusion was supported by data on state voter restoration rates. Over the past six years in Virginia, of 269,800 ex-felons, only 1.8% of this population was enfranchised. Over the past seven years in Maryland, of 78,800 ex-felons, only .18% of this population was enfranchised. During this same period in New Jersey, of 138,300 ex-felons the right to vote was automatically restored to this population once they completed their sentences (see Table 1-4). This statement does not mean to imply that ex-felons in New Jersey, Maryland, or Virginia that could vote did actually register to vote. What it demonstrates is that at least on an individual basis, the right to vote, social dignity, equal and fair representation was not denied enfranchised ex-felons. These facts also underscore the political inequity of this crazy quilt of state felon disenfranchisement law.

State felon disenfranchisement law in the New Jersey, Maryland, and Virginia reflect varying and inconsistent voting restoration and restriction policies that range from automatic restoration to 'some' (partial) or permanent (and full) disenfranchisement.

- In New Jersey, ex-felons could vote if they were not in jail, on probation, or parole because of a felony conviction.
- In Maryland, felons who had completed the court-ordered sentence of a first offense, restitution and fines could have their right to vote automatically restored. Felons who committed more than one conviction had to wait at least three years before achieving automatic restoration.
- In Virginia, no person who had been convicted of a felony was qualified to vote unless their civil rights had been restored by the Governor or other appropriate authority.

The only significant distinction in voting rights law between the states was felon disenfranchisement. Generally, citizens in each state could vote so long as they were U.S. citizens, at least 18 years old by election day, a resident of the state in which they wished to vote (for approximately 30 days or less), mentally competent, and registered to vote at least 21 to 30 days before election. There has been a trend toward reducing the registration requirement in some states, with the assumption that this would stimulate voter participation and reduce an unnecessary obstacle. It is therefore fair to conclude that felon disenfranchisement was singularly purposeful inasmuch as it had an exclusionary intent.

In studying the impact of felon disenfranchisement law in each of the model states, three specific questions were asked. What were the voting rights and practices of citizens and felons in each state? What was the affect of state felon disenfranchisement on felon voter participation, efficacy, knowledge, and attitudes? And, does state felon disenfranchisement have a disproportionate impact on African American felons and the political representation of the African American community? This examination included an analysis of the impact of African American political empowerment on local elections.

To review, the study groups were violent, non-violent/CDS, or property offenders who were within one year of their parole eligibility or max-out date. Sex offenders and arsonist were not included in this study. By definition, the 'offender' was an incarcerated inmate in a correctional complex, major institution or satellite housing unit under the jurisdiction of the Department of Corrections. By identifying the study group as felons who are within one year of parole eligibility or release date, I defined the study group as a population that would be ex-felons once having completed their sentence. A Felon Voter Participation Survey was used to ascertain felon voter attitudes and whether felons would vote if they could.

Comparative Case Studies of Felon Disenfranchisement

The Felon Voter Participation Survey results documented the affect of state felon disenfranchisement on felon voter participation, knowledge, attitudes, and efficacy. This survey was not a random sampling, but rather a sample determined by accessibility to the specified felon population in each of the targeted states. The central question asked in the survey was: If you were able to vote in an election, would you? Not only did the total 'yes' felon voter survey responses exceed, by far, the voter participatory interest rate among U.S. citizens, but the self-reported reasons as to why respondents would vote were informed, impassioned, consistent with democratic principles, and demonstrated a compelling need for recognition, human dignity and rights. Examples from the surveys exemplify this and follow below:

New Jersey:
> "...I would vote because everyone has the right to voice their choices..."
> "...I would vote because I feel my vote would make a difference..."

Maryland:
> "...I have made a mistake in my life. My vote may be the one to help change things in my children's life..."
> "...I am 22 years old, African American. Through the history I have studied, I have been mislead and miseducated about myself... and... life events. I would vote..."

Virginia:
> "...The only way for change is a heard voice and a stated opinion...."
> "...People risked their lives to give me the right to vote..."
> "...It's a constitutional right that I may have lost forever..."
> "...I feel by losing my right to vote, it's a life sentence...."

As these statements demonstrate, the right to vote mattered to this felon population.

The surveyed population was also asked, 'If you indicated that you would vote in an election, why would you vote?'

[TABLE 19]

Why would you vote in an Election?			
	New Jersey	Maryland	Virginia
My vote would not matter.	15.2%	10.3%	3.6%
My vote could add political recognition and public consideration to felon issues.	16.8%	20%	28.2%
It is too much time and trouble to vote, so I would not vote.	5.7%	3.7%	9%
I would vote because it is my right to do so once I have paid my debt to society.	61.8%	55.3%	61.8%
No response	.5%	10.7%	5.5%

Respectively, 78%, 75.3%, and 90% of the respondents who said they would vote if they could in New Jersey, Maryland, and Virginia, said that the two major reasons they would vote were either: 1) "their vote could add political recognition and public consideration to felon issues"; or 2) "they would vote because it was their right to do so once they paid their debt to society".

The majority of the respondents felt that acquiring the right to vote was empowering. Their responses were equal to or slightly lower than the surveyed population response to the question "would you vote in an election?" The larger proportion of affirmative responses in New Jersey (61.8%), Maryland (55.3%), and Virginia (61.8%) claimed that they would vote because 'it was their right to do so once they had paid their debt to society.'

In New Jersey, Maryland, and Virginia, 20.9%, 14%, and 12.6%, respectively of the 'yes' respondents said the reasons they would not vote were that: "their vote would not matter," or that it was "too much time and trouble to vote." These findings from the case study surveys suggested that fewer survey respondents would vote than said they would. This tendency to overstate voter participation was consistent with the literature on voter behavior in the U.S. Additionally, the information costs of voter participation for low income, undereducated citizens were greater than higher income, better educated citizens. Whether and why felons chose to vote or not was an indication of how important participation in governance and representation was to them.

Demographically, the felon survey population was described by race, legal status, age, education, and income.

[TABLE 20]

Felon Survey Population Demographics by %			
	New Jersey	Maryland	Virginia
Race			
Black	75%	75%	70%
Latino	12.7%	6%	1%
White	8.3%	13%	22.7%
Legal Status			
Violence	20%	51%	14.5%
CDS	66%	43%	66.4%
Property	14%	4%	13.6%
Age			
18+	99+%	99+%	99+%
22-40	83%	70%	58.2%
Education			
< High School	38%	50+%	25%
High School/GED	45%	36%	52%
Income			
Low	51%	52%	51%
Middle	40%	40%	44%
Upper			2.7%

There were a disproportionate number of African Americans in each of the Correction systems of the surveyed states. African Americans made up 14% of the New Jersey population; 29% of the Maryland population, and 20% of the Virginia population; however, they comprised 64%, 76%, and 58% of these states felon population, respectively. Of the survey populations, African Americans consisted of 75% (NJ), 75% (MD), and 70% (VA) of the respondents. This survey population was predominantly from urban cluster neighborhoods, low to moderate income, poorly educated, and mostly 'minority', population. This population was a 'discrete and insular minority' which met the standard for measuring equity under law, compelling clarity in law whenever courts consider legislation that treats one group differently than another.

Voter attitude and voter participation among the surveyed population was measured by voter registration rates, voter participation rates, and participation in campaign activities.

[TABLE 21]

Felon Survey Voter Participation				
		New Jersey (auto)	Maryland (some)	Virginia (all)
Registration				
	Yes %	35%	32%	49.1%
	No %	64%	68%	50.9%
Voter Participation				
	Yes %	24%	19%	34%
	No %	75%	80%	64%
Campaign Activities				
	Yes %	17%	11%	18.2%
	No %	81%	89%	81.8%

Respectively, 35%, 32%, and 49.1% of the surveyed populations of New Jersey, Maryland, and Virginia self-reported that they had registered to vote at some point during their adult life prior to being incarcerated. Again, 24%, 19%, and 34%, respectively of the surveyed populations from New Jersey, Maryland, and Virginia said that they had voted in an election prior to having been incarcerated. And, 17%, 11%, and 18.2% of the surveyed populations from New Jersey, Maryland, and Virginia indicated that they had participated in campaign activities prior to incarceration. Most of the surveyed felon population indicated they had never participated in any aspect of the electoral process. Not unlike voting patterns among the general population, the highest level of voter participation among surveyed felons in all three states was voter registration, followed by voting in an election. Interestingly, Virginia – the one state that practices permanent felon disenfranchisement – reported having had the highest rate of felon voter participation among the three surveyed states.

In addition to felon voter participation, felon voter attitudes were measured by political knowledge and political efficacy. The Felon Voter Survey measured specific knowledge and information as it related to felon voter rights, citizen voter rights, registration laws, political ideology, and political preference.

[TABLE 22]

Felon Voter Knowledge and Information (Percentages represent respondents correct responses)			
	New Jersey	Maryland	Virginia
State Felon Voting Rights	65%	68.3%	26.4%
State Voting Requirements	66%	22.7%	80.2%
State Registration Requirements	9.3%	25.3%	21.7%

Sixty-five percent of the New Jersey felon respondents, 68.3% of the Maryland respondents, and 26.4% of the Virginia respondents knew the felon voting rights law of their particular state. Sixty-six percent of the New Jersey respondent group, 27.7% of the Maryland group, and 80.2% of the Virginia group knew the voting requirements in their particular state. State registration requirement law had the lowest response rate of all three measures in each of the three states. Only 9.3%, 25.3%, and 21.7% of the respondents in New Jersey, Maryland, and Virginia knew the registration requirements in their particular state. In all three states, respondents indicated limited knowledge of the meaning of party preference and political ideology. It is not possible to determine from the survey data whether there was any correlation between state disenfranchisement law and the various levels of felon voter knowledge, however, the survey response did indicate a need to institute a voter education program for felons in each of the State Correctional systems.

Political efficacy was an effective measure of voter attitude and political participation. External political efficacy was defined as the belief that political authorities respond to constituent attempts to influence them. Political efficacy implied that there was an atmosphere of mutual reciprocity and that one could trust that one would be heard and responded to by their political representatives. A survey question was asked, "To what degree do you feel your vote matters."

[TABLE 23]

To What Degree Does Your Vote Matter?			
	New Jersey	Maryland	Virginia
Degree	64.2%	70.7%	92.7%
No Degree	32%	26%	7.3%

In New Jersey, Maryland, and Virginia 63.2%, 70.7% and 92.7%, respectively, of the respondents felt that their vote mattered to a degree or great degree. In New Jersey, Maryland, and Virginia, 32%, 26%, and 7.3% of the respondents did not feel that their vote mattered. The demand for felon voter participation was clearly greatest in the permanently disenfranchised state of Virginia. The greater the restriction on felon voter rights, the more the right to vote mattered to the survey respondents. This suggested that increased restrictions in felon disenfranchisement law could adversely impact external political efficacy among felons. As stated by Charles Taylor (1994, p. 25), there was a human cost to political non-recognition. "If a (polity) mirrors back a confining or demeaning picture of (felons), they will suffer real damage or distortion imprisoning them in a false, distorted, and reduced mode of being."

An abbreviated Sociopolitical Control Scale was used in the felon survey to measure the degree to which the surveyed population felt external political efficacy, a sense of social dignity, autonomy, policy control, community isolation, leadership competence, empowerment or disempowerment.

[TABLE 24]

Sociopolitical Control Scale

Measures: Political efficacy, policy control, community isolation, leadership competence, and empowerment or disempowerment)

Yes Respondents Collapsed:	New Jersey % agree		Maryland % agree		Virginia % agree	
People like me are generally well qualified to participate in the political activity and decision-making in the U.S.	65.2%		67.7%		75.5%	
I enjoy political participation because I want to have as much say in running government as possible.	61.1%		52.7%		80.9%	
A good many local elections aren't important enough to bother with.	21%	(73.3)	20%	(75.3)	10.9%	(89.1)
So many other people are active in local issues and organizations that it doesn't matter much to me whether I participate or not.	19.3%	(76.2)	19.7%	(76.3)	10%	(90)
Most public officials wouldn't listen to me no matter what I did.	38.6%	(57.5)	38.6%	(57.7)	39.1%	(60.9)
Sometimes politics and government seem so complicated that a person like me can't really understand what's going on.	29.2%	(66.3)	27.7%	(68.3)	20.9%	(79.1)

The majority of respondents in all three states felt that they were qualified to participate in political activities, that they wanted to have a say in running government, that local elections were important enough to bother with, that it mattered to them that they participate in local issues and organizations, that most politicians would listen to them, and that government was not too complicated for them to understand. A majority of the surveyed population had a strong belief in their right to participate, in their knowledge or competence to influence or make policy; and a relative trust that they would be heard and responded to. Respondents not only felt that their vote mattered, but that exercising their right to vote would be empowering. Two significant points are noteworthy: this perception was not unanimous, and felon respondents in the state that had the most restrictive felon laws (Virginia) were the most adamant with regard to their right to vote.

This study elucidates a challenge in U.S. democratization, as well as highlights a human rights dilemma. In this study, the percentage of state disenfranchised felons ranged from least to most from automatic restoration state, to 'some' permanent disenfranchisement state, to permanent felon disenfranchisement state. Among the three surveyed states, the percentage of disenfranchised felons was least in New Jersey and greatest in Virginia. African American felons were clearly disproportionately represented in each of the states featured in this study. Race discrimination has had a significantly greater political impact within states which permanently disenfranchise some or all African American felons than states which provide automatic restoration. As indicated in the Sociopolitical Control Scale, Virginia felon respondents also had the greatest belief in political efficacy, policy control, leadership competence, and empowerment. In New Jersey, Maryland, and Virginia, one out of five, one out of seven, and one out of eight respondents who said they would vote if they could felt that their vote would not matter, or that it took too much time or trouble to vote. If a 'specific class' of politically marginalized African American felons felt qualified to participate in political activities and wanted to have a say in running government, but were denied this constitutional right (while others were afforded this same right), their sense of political efficacy, policy control, and empowerment would diminish; and their sense of community isolation and disempowerment would increase. Permanent political marginalization resulted in the debasement of the human character and the human condition, as well as the dilution of voter participation and equal representation. The more restrictive state felon disenfranchisement is, the greater the debasement and socio-political impact on African American felons.

The Impact of Felon Disenfranchisement on the African American Community

To conclude this chapter, I want to address the ways in which felon disenfranchisement can and does impact African American communities. Fair representation is measured not only by who could and would vote, but also whether the African American felon vote could make a difference in an election. In each of the states I identified an urban cluster neighborhood from which a significant proportion of the African American felon population had been arrested and incarcerated. Prisoners returned disproportionately to these cluster neighborhoods within these respective urban counties. They returned to high density localities more commonly defined by race, ethnicity, class, and the accompanying SES. Nancy LaVigne (2007) indicates that these communities lack strong social mechanisms that reinforce pro-social behavior, feature low levels of social cohesion, and are without strong norms, social trust, or support systems.

This definition of cluster neighborhoods not only describes communities from which it is most likely felons will be arrested and incarcerated, but this description also correlates with felon criminogenic behaviors and high risk indices for recidivism. Where one lives matters. Life chances and voter attitudes affect, and are affected by where one resides. As previously noted, it is not the African American, but the African American condition that results in strong correlations between race/ethnicity and arrests and incarceration.

The urban cluster neighborhoods in this study were Essex County, New Jersey, Baltimore City, Maryland, and Hampton Roads (Norfolk), Virginia, MSA. Each of these high density localities were defined by race/ethnicity, median household income, education, poverty levels, and other demographics.

[TABLE 25]

African American and Felon Populations by State and Cluster Neighborhood (2006)					
	New Jersey	Essex	Maryland	Baltimore City	Virginia	Norfolk
Black	14%	37.1%	29.5%	65%	20%	44%
Black Felon	64%	18%	76.5%	67.5%	60%	17%

* 18% represents all felons from Essex County

* * 17% includes three Hampton Roads Cities: Norfolk, Newport News, and
Virginia Beach

Each of these high density urban localities had greater than twice the percentage of African Americans living within their community than lived in the respective state. One out of seven residents of New Jersey was African American; almost two out five residents of Essex County were African American. Almost three out of ten residents of Maryland were African American; and almost two-thirds of Baltimore City was African American. One out of five residents in Virginia was African American; and more than two out five residents of Norfolk was African American.

In comparison to the percentage of African Americans living in each of the surveyed states, all three states had a disproportionate percentage of African American felons incarcerated in their state prisons (New Jersey, 64%; Maryland, 76.5%; and Virginia, 60%). A disproportionately high percentage of African American felons in New Jersey, Maryland, and Virginia were arrested and incarcerated from each of these urban cluster localities. Almost one-fifth of the felon population in New Jersey came from Essex County; two-thirds of the felon population of Maryland came from Baltimore City; and almost one out of six of the felons in Virginia came from the Norfolk area.

The criminal justice system has had a disproportionate impact on the African American community. One of the effects of the inequities of this social justice system has been the political marginalization of the voting strength of the African American community.

[TABLE 26]

Comparative Demographics State and Felon Cluster Neighborhoods (2006)						
	New Jersey	Essex	Maryland	Baltimore City	Virginia	Norfolk
Density (per 100,000)	1,134.5	6,285.4	541.9	8,038.9	178.8	4,362.8
Median H/H Income (in thousands)	64.5	34.5	57.0	29.7	51.1	31.8
Poverty	8.7%	24.5%	9.2%	21.5%	9.5%	19.4%

Four social indicators that defined populations that would most likely be at high risk for arrests and incarceration in these communities were density, median household incomes, poverty levels, and education. Population density for Essex County was almost six times greater than the overall density for the state of New Jersey; population density in Baltimore City was almost 15 times greater than in Maryland; and population density in Norfolk was 24 times greater than in Virginia. In each state the median income was 40% to 50% lower in the respective cities than the state. Essex County, Baltimore City, and Norfolk had greater numbers of persons living below the poverty level by a ratio of almost three to one. The average reading level among the felon population was a sixth grade reading level, and the average math proficiency level was fifth grade. These urban demographic indices combined to describe localities in which it was most likely that high risk criminogenic behaviors might occur. This type of demographic data defined urban localities and this population as a 'special class' of persons who satisfy the legal standard requiring equity under the law. This law mandated strong, compelling justification whenever the court considered issues which treated discrete and insular minorities differently than others (Skinner v. Oklahoma).

Could an African American felon population, living in these localities make a difference in an election? What follows are four case summaries that tested whether or not the felon vote could have affected electoral outcomes. The first case was argued in the courts of justice and the court of public opinion. The 2000 Presidential Election was a political lockup that threatened the essence of U.S. democracy. During the 2000 Presidential Election almost 4,700,000 felons, more than 2% of the voting age population, were disqualified from voting. Of the 436,000 Florida ex-felons included in this number, 204,000 or 31% of this number were African American. G.W. Bush won the state of Florida by 537 votes. If Florida had had automatic restoration at that time, the felon vote could have made a difference in Florida, and in history.

In Essex County, the New Jersey State Senatorial primary election for Legislative District #28 was held in June, 2001. There were almost 101,000 registered voters in the primary election. Thirteen percent of the Democratic voters turned out for this election. The party line candidate, Willie Brown received 5,238 votes and the incumbent, Ron Rice, received 6,224 votes. The margin of victory was only 986 votes. Between 2000 and 2001, approximately 26,000 and 30,000 ex-felons returned to Essex County. If 17-24% of this ex-felon population had participated in the election as a voting bloc, they could have had an impact on the election. It should be noted, that based on the candidate records it was more likely that ex-felons would have supported the incumbent, Ron Rice.

In the 2002 Maryland gubernatorial race, 55% of the voters were registered Democrats and 29% were registered Republican. Almost 80% were registered Democrats in Baltimore City and 9.5% were registered Republican. The Republican (Ehrlich) won the gubernatorial seat over the Democrat (Townsend) by 51% to 48%. The margin of victory was 56,677 votes. In Baltimore City, Townsend won over Ehrlich by 75% to 24%, a margin of almost 80,000 votes. With an ex-felon population of approximately 79,000 and 17-24% of this population (if enfranchised) voting, the ex-felon population could not have altered this election outcome. This case does, however, underscore the importance of maximizing voter inclusion and voter turnout.

In Virginia in 2005 the Republican Bob McDonnell defeated Democrat Creigh Deeds for State Attorney General by a margin of .02%, or 323 votes. The total votes were 970,886 (R), and 970,563 (D). If Virginia allowed automatic restoration, the estimated potential felon voter population of 15,800 voters in Virginia as well as the 2,700 estimated felon voters in Hampton County could have had an impact on this election outcome.

Summary

African American voter dilution and the debasement of the African American community was not an accident. It is a condition that is the result of racial and class antagonisms, greed, and it reflects the worst in humankind rather than the best. It tells us why 'we built fences that separated us from others,' and who we are as a people. We must now answer the question, what do we, as a polity, wish to become?

We can create systems to end political marginalization and racial domination, assure the rights of political minorities, fulfill the promise of fair and equal representation (allowing for difference), or we can do none of these things. In part, the problem lies within the human character. Democracy calls upon each of its members to have the courage to face the fear or threat of personal and intimate want and deprivation and to strive toward a condition wherein no one suffers from this deprivation.

This study underscores the fact that the U.S. began as an imperfect union. Having begun nation building with an ambitious ideal and the promise that democracy is a government of laws and not men, it required the inclusion of several constitutional amendments over two hundred years to forge an effective language and definition of constituent democracy and the right to vote. I argue that democracy only exists as long as it exists for all citizens no matter what their station or definition in life may be. In the U.S., it was through a series of Supreme Court cases that a measure for voter eligibility and equity in law was defined. As a representative government, the U.S. relied on practical definitions of justiciability, judicial review, judicial activism, strict scrutiny, judicial restraint, equal rights and protections under the law to frame a constitutional democracy. The arguments for and against felon voter rights were best represented by Supreme Court Justices Rehnquist and Thurgood Marshall (Richardson v. Ramirez, 1980). Although the majority opinion was upheld, the affirmative sanction for felon disenfranchisement should have been disallowed because 'democratic law is constantly in the process of revision in response to the needs of a changing society (T. Marshall)'. The argument for felon enfranchisement is consistent with the ruling held in Hunter v. Underwood (1985). In law, felon disenfranchisement of African Americans was not only irrational, but it was also purposefully discriminatory and met the legal standard of racial discrimination by both intent and impact on the African American community.

Comparative analysis of state felon disenfranchisement case studies documents the discriminatory impact of racially motivated violations of the 14th Amendment equal protection clause. Research and survey data illustrated: first, that there was a greater impact of African American felon disenfranchisement in states that permanently disenfranchised some or all felons than existed in states that provided automatic restoration; and secondly, that the impacted felon populations were most commonly from urban cluster neighborhoods reflective of the racial/ethnic and socio-economic profiles described by the courts as 'discrete and insular minorities, unable to use the ordinary political process to overcome discrimination. In spite of the social and political circumstances described, this study demonstrates that the surveyed felon population felt that they were qualified to vote; if given an opportunity, that they would vote; and that the right to vote mattered to them. Because the overwhelming majority of the surveyed felon population felt this way, it is reasonable to conclude that denying the right to vote to persons knowledgeable of their right to vote and its importance is disempowering.

There is a correlation between the right to vote, how one sees themselves in the polity, and the life chances of members of the African American community. The African American community will not achieve socio-economic parity with the general population until there is equity in voter rights and fair representation. Power concedes nothing without a demand. The purpose of felon disenfranchisement was to silence the political voice of the African American community. The inclusion of African American felons in the electoral process is not only their lawful right, it is a way to make the voice of the African American community demonstrably more audible.

CHAPTER 8
Epilogue

"...A community may build its fences in many places and in many ways. Only by examining where and how [and why] we build the fences that separate us from others can we discover who we are as a community, and only after doing so can we seek to become who we would like to be...."[213]

I remember how the lessons began. My brother and I had gone to visit our grandparents for a week of our school summer vacation. One day Granddad, my brother, and I were walking down the street, on a very public block of "downtown". Granddad said, I'm going to teach you boys how to deal with white folks, so you can get along later in life. Do as I do. As a white man came toward us from the opposite direction, my grandfather hurried toward him while we stood some twenty paces or so behind. As he approached this man he (Granddad) bowed slightly, tipped his hat, stepped to the side (off of the sidewalk, into the dirt), kept his head down, and made comment as to how nice a day, this day was. He waited for us to follow him. I remember this feeling of confusion, disappointment, and finally rage in my very small body. I could not understand why my grandfather was in the dirt, not looking at the man he was speaking to, holding his hat and smiling. Wasn't he somebody? The Reverend? The community leader? A man? My grandfather? Nor could I understand the "peacock" like stance of the "dominant" character, his smile and acceptance (reward) for this ignominious gesture. This same man turned and walked toward my brother and me. Because I could no longer see (through my rage) I don't remember my brother's actions, just my own.

I remember walking purposefully toward this man holding my ground on this sidewalk as though I owned the cement blocks streaming past my feet as I walked. By the time this man and I met, I had built up such a head of steam, the man was forced to move to the opposite side of this walkway to avoid colliding in a manner which would most probably have injured both of us. I could not help myself. I could not get off the sidewalk. And, I could not explain. And, I knew I was in trouble. This man looked at my grandfather with the look of "you better teach this boy something", and my grandfather apologized on my behalf.

Suffice it to say that I was not my grandfather's favorite anything. Not only was I the "dark" one (who reminded too many of my father), disallowing the family to affirm their "Cherokee Indian" heritage, but now I was also insolent and unresponsive to the "social etiquettes" of interracial interactions: race dominance.

(Author)

I began this study with a hypothesis: The loss of the right to vote, equal protection and fair representation for African American felons dilutes the political interests, efficacy, and representation of African American felons and politically marginalizes the voting strength of the African American community. Race discrimination has a significantly greater political impact within states which permanently disenfranchise all or some African American felons than states which provide for automatic restoration.

I also began with a theoretical premise. The right to vote is the essence of a democratic society. Voting is a fundamental right through which all members of the body politic are able to voice their needs, choices and interests. To the extent that the democratic state does not secure this right, or does so for some but not others, human potential is minimized and we relegate the state to the worst in humankind rather than the best. This study of African American felon disenfranchisement has been an examination of deferred minority rights controlled by a political majority. It is a relationship that is best understood from the 'minority' perspective. As illustrated in this study, the problem of race and race dominance is intimate and yet permeates political institutions and social relationships within the U.S. As a result, this study is an examination of political antagonism between a political majority and minority, and how each saw themselves and one another.

This inter-group antagonism is best described by Charles Taylor (1994):

> "Our identity is partly shaped by recognition or its absence...Non-recognition or misrecognition can be harmful or a form of oppression, imprisoning someone in a false, distorted, and reduced mode of being..."[214]

Thus, the human rights struggle has historically been an intensely personal one. Just so, the examination of African American felon disenfranchisement is a study of human need, human rights, and human capacity vis-à-vis the democratic state.

Chapter VIII concludes this study of the effect of U.S. felon disenfranchisement policies and practices on a politically marginalized African American population. It has been a study about racial dominance and the political majority; the rights of a political minority and the effects of permanent political marginalization; and the challenge African American felon disenfranchisement presents to the principle of fair and equal representation in a constitutional democracy.

The Lessons of African American Felon Disenfranchisement

I have learned in life that there are only two kinds of people. Those people who live their experiences and those who live the lessons of their experiences. Those who live their experiences tend to repeat them. And those who live the lessons of their experiences are able to live life's possibilities. This is not only true of our individual lives, but it is also true of our collective lives, as citizens of a polity. The point is, there are valuable lessons we can learn from the study of African American felon disenfranchisement.

The reason I became a Political Scientist is foundational to the lessons we can learn from this work. I learned early in life, in order to make it in life on the "streets" as an unguarded urban youth, I had to learn what to expect of people. I learned to expect people to satisfy their needs. Sometimes by any means necessary, sometimes not. I therefore learned that no one is safe or secure until everyone is. This lesson, learned at an early age, is supported by antagonisms demonstrated by political majorities and minorities and the conclusions reached in this study. These lessons became fundamental to my definition of political science.

Political Science functions to harmonize the human experience with human nature, the human condition, and the human spirit. I am committed to using the ordinary political process to assist discrete and insular minorities overcome discrimination, human debasement, social and political disparities. Hannah Arendt has defined poverty as the social question; not only does it represent constant deprivation and want, acute misery, and act as a dehumanizing force, it is also "... abject because it puts (people) under the absolute dictate of their bodies, that is, under the absolute dictate of (human need) as all (people) know it from their most intimate experience...."[215]. This definition of poverty illustrates that the threat of abject poverty, as an intimate experience, is the source of most social and political antagonisms. It is a human condition that all people seek to avoid. Felons are a discrete and insular minority clustered in environments of abject poverty, acute misery, constant want and deprivation. Just as poverty is best understood as a human condition, felons are best understood as a political condition that is the direct result of socio-political antagonisms and deprivations.

The problem of political inequalities by race begins with social disparities based on race. Disparities in at least four social indicators define the populations that are most likely to be at high risk for arrests, sentencing, and incarceration: density, median household income, education, and poverty. A disproportionately high number of African Americans live in these urban cluster neighborhoods. It is not the African American, but the African American condition that has resulted in strong correlations between race/ethnicity and arrests and incarceration. Urban sociology has intimately linked this African American with who is most likely to be arrested and incarcerated, and

therefore disenfranchised.   It is what I describe as a "Felon
Criminogenic Paradigm" in which disparate life chances results in
disparate arrests and incarceration rates for specific 'urban cluster'
populations. These processes are systemically reinforced by collateral
effects such as felon disenfranchisement. This paradigm suggests an
urgency for practical interventions such as life chance parity, social
rights (the right to work, vote, and learn/knowledge), and felon
enfranchisement.

[FIGURE 1]

Felon Criminogenic Paradigm

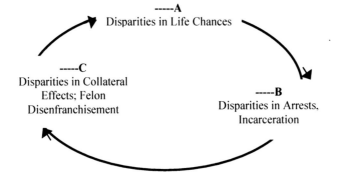

Interventions:
   A.   Life Chance Parity
   B.   Parity in Social Rights (right to: work, vote, learn [educate])
   C.   Felon Enfranchisement

So, what does all of this mean? What are the lessons?

•   As illustrated by this "Felon Criminogenic paradigm," the
     study of African American felon disenfranchisement makes
     the problem of political marginalization more comprehensible.
     Felon disenfranchisement is an extra-legal system dictated by

permanent political majorities, in the interests of political majorities. It is based on moralistic beliefs, modern racism, and stereotypes about human difference.

- The disenfranchisement of felons was not about 'purity at the ballot box' but rather it is about the exercise of power, privilege, and racism.

- As long as a political majority is able to permanently control or determine who can vote, no person or minority's rights are guaranteed or secure.

- Felon disenfranchisement law disproportionately impacted on the African American's right to equal protection as specified in the 14th Amendment. This disproportional impact on African American felons was directly related to disparate life chances, the criminal justice system, and the sociology of race.

- The criminal justice system has had a disproportionately debilitating impact on urban cluster neighborhoods and the African American community.

- One of the effects of the inequities of this social justice system has been the political marginalization of the African American community.

- Race discrimination has a significantly greater political impact within states that permanently disenfranchise African American felons than it does in automatic restoration states.

- Permanent political marginalization results in the debasement of the human character and the human condition, as well as the dilution of voter participation and equal representation for African Americans.

- Politically marginalized African American felons feel both willing and qualified to participate in the electoral process, but are denied this constitutional right.

- The issue of felon disenfranchisement is a human rights issue and a challenge to U.S. democratization.

The human cost of political mis- or non-recognition is measured in terms of losses to social dignity, autonomy, policy control, empowerment, leadership competence, disparate life chances, and civility in the polity.

Postscript

> *"Better to build schoolrooms for the 'boy',*
> *Than cells and gibbets for the 'man'..."*
>   (Eliza Cook, 1818-1889)

Frederick Douglass once said, "...You have seen how a man was made a slave; you shall see how a slave becomes a man...".[216] This admonition applies to the African American felon in much the same way. The history of the struggle for human rights and universal suffrage in the U.S. has been a progressive history, having passed from a nation in which only white male, propertied citizens could vote, slowly growing to encompass the inclusion of: non-propertied white males; African American males; women; and finally, persons 18 years and older. At no time has this struggle been achieved without a demand. The lesson is that 'power will concede nothing without a demand.' It never has, and it never will. The struggle to achieve the right to vote for ex-felons has, and will continue to follow the lessons of this history. African American felon enfranchisement is the next inevitable struggle for U.S. democratization. By 'rejecting prevailing orthodoxy in describing the ways in which race and racial power are constructed and represented in American culture', and more particularly in the U.S. criminal justice system, it is intended that this research will contribute to full, fair and equal representation in American democracy.

The lessons of African American felon disenfranchisement can be divided into two parts. African American felon disenfranchisement had a disproportionate impact on the political representation of the African American community, and it diluted the political interests, efficacy, and representation of African American felons; and we can describe how or what is required for ex-felons to have an impact on an election.

African American felon disenfranchisement was effective; it achieved its goal. African American felon disenfranchisement politically marginalized the voting strength of the African American community. Here is the evidence: As illustrated in New Jersey, Maryland, and Virginia the African American felon vote did not make a difference in who got elected or served. Perhaps the greatest evidence, however, is that the African American urban condition, or quality of life and life chances either did not change or, overtime, worsened. Data indicates that density was six, fifteen, or twenty-four times greater in the urban core of each state than the density in each of the respective states; the median household income for urban cities was 40% to 50% lower than the average household income in the respective states; and by a ratio of two or three to one, the urban cities of the respective states had a greater number of persons living below poverty level.

Political minorities are not politically viable until they are able to effectuate change and improve the quality of life for themselves and their children through representation, policy formation and implementation. Based on the foregoing African American community profiles, the interests and needs of the African American community were not served. This research indicates that, if the African American felon population were able to vote, the African American community could affect who their representation would be and what the outcome or life chances for themselves and their children could become. Social disparities in cluster neighborhoods (i.e., density, median household incomes, health, education, poverty levels) and even who gets arrested and incarcerated based on race, are issues determined by the ways race and racial power are constructed and represented in American culture.

We can conclude from this research that African American ex-felons can have an impact on elections in one or more of the following ways: 1) bloc voting in a close local election where there is a limited voting margin of between 1 or 2%; 2) in collaboration with other minority interest groups and in response to a contested, single-issue campaign; 3) and, through the institution of a felon voter education drive, increased felon voter knowledge, registration, and participation (voter mobilization and turnout). These options have limited feasibility until draconian felon disenfranchisement law is ruled unconstitutional. Maximizing the political inclusion of minority populations (and their interests) through issue formation, voter participation and voter turnout is the only guarantor of constituent democracy. Fair and equal representation depends on this principle.

Appendix

A. Signed consent form
B. New Jersey survey of felons pending release
C. Maryland survey of felons pending release
D. Virginia survey of felons pending release

Center for Urban Education, Inc.

INFORMED CONSENT FOR PARTICIPATION IN RESEARCH

I, (print name) _____, State #_____

- have fully read, or had read to me, the research proposal which describes the research for which I wish to volunteer.
- have had an opportunity to ask questions of the person, or persons, conducting the research.
- have no reservations about participating in this project. I further agree to hold the Center for Urban Education, Inc., its affiliates, representatives or associates safe and harmless with regard to this research and its outcomes.

_____
Resident Signature
    Date

_____
Witness Signature
    Date

NEW JERSEY
VOTER PARTICIPATION SURVEY
CENTER FOR URBAN EDUCATION, INC.
JOHN E. PINKARD SR., PH.D. CANDIDATE

Directions:

The following questions are designed to survey RCRP and DRC resident attitudes toward voter participation in local and general elections in the U.S. **Your participation in this survey is completely optional and voluntary.** The survey is intended to assist providers to better understand voter participation attitudes and expectations and hopefully enhance the ways RCRP/DRC's can best serve you. We estimate that it would take no more than 15-20 minutes of your time to complete this survey. Please put a check [✓] in the appropriate space. Thank you.

I. **Background Information**

1. Are you: 1) Male [   ]   2) Female [   ]

2. Are you a citizen of the U.S.A.?   1) Yes [   ]   2) No [   ]

3. Are you foreign born?   1) Yes [   ]   2) No [   ]

4. If foreign born, of which country are you a citizen? _____

5. What is your race/ethnicity?
   - [   ] 1. African American or Black
   - [   ] 2. Latino or Hispanic
   - [   ] 3. Non-Latino White
   - [   ] 4. Asian
   - [   ] 5. Other: please specify _____

6. How old are you?

    1) 17 and below [   ]   6) 36-40   [   ]
    2) 18-21   [   ]   7) 41-45   [   ]
    3) 22-24   [   ]   8) 46-50   [   ]
    4) 25-29   [   ]   9) 51 and over   [   ]
    5) 30-35   [   ]

7. What is the highest educational level you have achieved?

    1) 6th or less   [   ]
    2) 7th, 8th   [   ]
    3) 9th, 10th   [   ]
    4) 11th, 12th   [   ]
    5) H.S. graduate   [   ]
    6) G.E.D.   [   ]
    7) College or Voc. Ed.   [   ]

8. What is your legal status?

    1) Violent offense   [   ]
    2) CDS, nonviolent   [   ]
    3) Property offense   [   ]

9. How many times have you been convicted of a felony?

    1) once   [   ]   2) two times   [   ]
    3) three times   [   ]   4) four or five times [   ]
    5) more than five times [   ]

10. How would you classify your household income?

    1) low income   [   ]   2) middle income [   ]
    3) upper income   [   ]

11. Have you ever registered to vote:

    1) Yes [   ]   2) No [   ]

12. Have you ever voted in an election in the U.S.?

    1) Yes [   ]   2) No [   ]

13. Have you ever participated in campaign activities for any local, state, or national candidate?
      1) Yes [   ]   2) No [   ]

14. If you were able to vote, would you vote in an election?
      1) Yes [   ]   2) No [   ]

II. **Please use the 6-point scale below to indicate how strongly you agree or disagree with each of the following statements as they apply to you. Place the number from 1-6 in the blank to the left of each statement.**

```
1           2           3           4           5           6
├───────────┬───────────┬───────────┬───────────┬───────────┤
Strongly                                            Strongly
disagree                                               agree
```

[   ] 15. People like me are generally well qualified to participate in the political activity and decision making in the U.S.

[   ] 16. I enjoy political participation because I want to have as much say in running government as possible.

[   ] 17. A good many local elections aren't important enough to bother with.

[   ] 18. So many other people are active in local issues and organizations that it doesn't matter much to me whether I participate or not.

[   ] 19. Most public officials wouldn't listen to me no matter what I did.

[   ] 20. Sometimes politics and government seem so complicated that a person like me can't really understand what's going on.

III. Please check [✓] the one that you think is the correct answer.

21. In N.J., U.S. citizens who have been convicted of a felon crime:

    [   ] 1) Lose their right to vote for life?

    [   ] 2) Until they are released from prison?

    [   ] 3) Until they are released from probation?

    [   ] 4) Until they have completed parole?

    [   ] 5) Until they have completed prison, probation, and parole?

22. In N.J., U.S. citizens have the right to vote if:

    [   ] 1) You are a U.S. citizen?

    [   ] 2) You are least 18 years old by the time of the next election?

    [   ] 3) you have been residing at your present address for at least 30 days?

    [   ] 4) You are not in prison or on probation or on parole?

    [   ] 5) All of the above

23. To what degree would you consider yourself a political liberal or conservative?

1) very conservative	[ ]	2) conservative	[ ]
3) moderate	[ ]	4) liberal	[ ]
5) very liberal	[ ]	6) undecided	[ ]

24. If you are a U.S. citizen, politically would you consider yourself:

    1) Republican   [ ]

    2) Democrat   [ ]

    3) Independent   [ ]

    4) Independent Democrat [ ]

    5) Independent Republican [ ]

    6) Third Party preference [ ]

    7) Undecided   [ ]

25. To cast a vote in New Jersey, how many days before Election Day must you register?
    [   ] 1) At least 7 days before
    [   ] 2) At least 15 days before
    [   ] 3) At least 22 days before
    [   ] 4) At least 29 days before
    [   ] 5) I do not know

26. Do you feel felons should be given the right to vote?
    1) Yes [ ]   2) No [ ]

IV. Please check (✓| one in each of the following questions:

27. To what degree do you feel your vote would matter in the overall electoral system?
    1) no degree   [ ]   2) very little degree   [ ]
    3) a degree   [ ]   4) good degree   [ ]
    5) great degree   [ ]

28. Should felons be given the right to vote when they have completed:
    1) Prison   [ ]   2) Probation   [ ]
    3) Parole   [ ]   4) all of the above [ ]
    5) none of the above [ ]

29. To what degree do you feel child care funds for the poor should be increased?
    1) none   [ ]   2) very little   [ ]
    3) moderately   [ ]   4) significantly   [ ]

30. Do you approve or disapprove of U.S. involvement in the United Nations?
    1) approve [ ]   2) disapprove [ ]   3) no opinion [ ]

V. **Fill-ins**

31. If you answered yes or no to question number 14, please explain why you would or would not vote in an election.
    - [   ] 1) My vote would not matter.
    - [   ] 2) My vote could add political recognition and public consideration to felon issues.
    - [   ] 3) It is too much time and trouble to vote, so I would not vote.
    - [   ] 4) I would vote because it is my right to do so once I have paid my "debt" to society.

    Please explain your answer: _____
    _____
    _____

32. Felons should not be given the right to vote because: (Please check [✓] one)
    - [   ] 1) The views of felons would not be respected.
    - [   ] 2) Felons would not vote anyway.
    - [   ] 3) Once you have committed a felony, you should not be given this privilege again.
    - [   ] 4) Felons do not understand the issues well enough to make good electoral decisions or judgments.
    - [   ] 5) None of the above.

    Please explain your answer: _____
    _____
    _____

33. If you think felons should be given the right to vote, in your opinion, when should they be given this right? (Please check [✓] only one answer.)
    - [   ] 1) While serving their time in prison.
    - [   ] 2) Upon completion of their prison term.
    - [   ] 3) Upon completion of parole or probation.

    Please explain your answer: _____
    _____
    _____

MARYLAND
VOTER PARTICIPATION SURVEY
CENTER FOR URBAN EDUCATION, INC.
JOHN E. PINKARD SR., PH.D. CANDIDATE

Directions:

The following questions are designed to survey your attitude toward voter participation in local and general elections in the U.S. **Your participation in this survey is completely optional and voluntary.** The results of this survey will be used as part of a Ph.D. Dissertation. It is intended that the results of this study will also be used to enhance ways Community Corrections Programs can best serve you. We estimate that it would take no more than 15-20 minutes of your time to complete this survey. Please put a check [✓] in the appropriate space. Thank you.

I. Background Information

1. Are you: 1) Male [   ]   2) Female [   ]

2. Are you a citizen of the U.S.A.?   1) Yes [   ]   2) No [   ]

3. Are you foreign born?   1) Yes [   ]   2) No [   ]

4. If foreign born, of which country are you a citizen? _____

5. What is your race/ethnicity?
    [   ] 1. African American or Black
    [   ] 2. Latino or Hispanic
    [   ] 3. Non-Latino White
    [   ] 4. Asian
    [   ] 5. Other: please specify _____

6. How old are you?

1) 17 and below [ ]	6) 36-40 [ ]
2) 18-21 [ ]	7) 41-45 [ ]
3) 22-24 [ ]	8) 46-50 [ ]
4) 25-29 [ ]	9) 51 and over [ ]
5) 30-35 [ ]	

7. What is the highest educational level you have achieved?

1) 6th or less   [ ]
2) 7th, 8th   [ ]
3) 9th, 10th   [ ]
4) 11th, 12th   [ ]
5) H.S. graduate   [ ]
6) G.E.D.   [ ]
7) College or Voc. Ed.   [ ]

8. What is your legal status?

1) Violent offense   [ ]
2) CDS, nonviolent   [ ]
3) Property offense   [ ]

9. How many times have you been convicted of a felony?

1) once   [ ]   2) two times   [ ]
3) three times   [ ]   4) four or five times [ ]
5) more than five times [ ]

10. How would you classify your household income?

1) low income   [ ]   2) middle income [ ]
3) upper income   [ ]

11. Have you ever registered to vote:

1) Yes [ ]   2) No [ ]

12. Have you ever voted in an election in the U.S.?

1) Yes [ ]   2) No [ ]

13. Have you ever participated in campaign activities for any local, state, or national candidate?
    1) Yes [   ]   2) No [   ]

14. If you were able to vote, would you vote in an election?
    1) Yes [   ]   2) No [   ]

II. **Please use the 6-point scale below to indicate how strongly you agree or disagree with each of the following statements as they apply to you. Place the number from 1-6 in the blank to the left of each statement.**

```
1        2        3        4        5        6
├────────┼────────┼────────┼────────┼────────┤
Strongly                                  Strongly
disagree                                     agree
```

[   ] 15. People like me are generally well qualified to participate in the political activity and decision making in the U.S.

[   ] 16. I enjoy political participation because I want to have as much say in running government as possible.

[   ] 17. A good many local elections aren't important enough to bother with.

[   ] 18. So many other people are active in local issues and organizations that it doesn't matter much to me whether I participate or not.

[   ] 19. Most public officials wouldn't listen to me no matter what I did.

[   ] 20. Sometimes politics and government seem so complicated that a person like me can't really understand what's going on.

III. Please check [✓] the one that you think is the correct answer.

21. Consistent with Maryland's State Constitution (amended 1972 and 1977/8), citizens who have been convicted of a felon crime could regain the right to vote:

    A. If you have only one prior felony conviction or infamous crime, you may qualify to register to vote if you have completed:

        [   ] 1) Prison
        [   ] 2) Probation
        [   ] 3) Parole
        [   ] 4) Community Service, restitution, and fines
        [   ] 5) All of the above
        [   ] 6) None of the above

    B. If you have been convicted more than once of a felony or other infamous crime, you will have to complete:

        [   ] 1) Prison
        [   ] 2) Probation
        [   ] 3) Parole
        [   ] 4) Community Service, restitution, and fines
        [   ] 5) A three year waiting period
        [   ] 6) All of the above
        [   ] 7) None of the above

    C. In the State of Maryland, the law concerning convicted felons right to vote changed effective:

        [   ] 1) July, 2007
        [   ] 2) July, 2008
        [   ] 3) July, 2009
        [   ] 4) July, 2010

    D. The New Maryland State law concerning convicted felons right to vote restores this right:

        [   ] 1)When felons are released from prison?
        [   ] 2)When felons complete probation?
        [   ] 3)When felons complete parole?

[   ] 4)When felons complete prison, probation, and
parole?
[   ] 5)At no time will felons be allowed to regain their
right to vote?

22. In Maryland, U.S. citizens have the right to vote if:
[   ] 1) You are a U.S. citizen?
[   ] 2) You are a resident of Maryland?
[   ] 3) You are at least 18 years of age by the time of the
next election?
[   ] 4) You are not under guardianship for mental
disability?
[   ] 5) You have not been convicted of buying or selling
votes?
[   ] 6) You have not been convicted more than once of a
crime of violence?
[   ] 7) You have not been convicted of an infamous crime
unless you have been pardoned; you have
completed your sentence; or at least three years
has passed since you completed your sentence(s)?
[   ] 8) If you qualify for items 1–4?
[   ] 9) All of the above?
[   ] 10) None of the above?

23. How would you classify your political values?
1) very conservative   [   ]   2) conservative   [   ]
3) moderate   [   ]   4) liberal   [   ]
5) very liberal   [   ]   6) undecided   [   ]

24. Which political party best represents your party preference?
1) Republican   [   ]
2) Democrat   [   ]
3) Independent   [   ]
4) Independent Democrat   [   ]
5) Independent Republican [   ]
6) Third Party preference [   ]
7) Undecided   [   ]

25. To cast a vote in Maryland, how many days before Election
    Day must you register?
    [   ] 1) At least 7 days before
    [   ] 2) At least 15 days before
    [   ] 3) At least 22 days before
    [   ] 4) At least 30 days before
    [   ] 5) I do not know

26. Do you feel felons should be given the right to vote?
        1) Yes [   ]   2) No [   ]

IV. **Please check (✓| one in each of the following questions:**
27. To what degree do you feel your vote would matter in the
    overall electoral system?
    1) no degree   [   ]   2) very little degree   [   ]
    3) a degree   [   ]   4) good degree   [   ]
    5) great degree   [   ]

28. Should felons be given the right to vote when they have
    completed:
    1) Prison   [   ]   2) Probation   [   ]
    3) Parole   [   ]   4) all of the above [   ]
    5) none of the above [   ]

29. To what degree do you feel child care funds for the poor
    should be increased?
    1) none   [   ]   2) very little   [   ]
    3) moderately   [   ]   4) significantly   [   ]

30. Do you approve or disapprove of U.S. involvement in the
    United Nations?
    1) approve [   ]   2) disapprove [   ]   3) no opinion [   ]

V. **Fill-ins**
31. On question number 14 you were asked if you were able to
    vote, would you? If you answered yes or no to question
    number 14, please explain why you would or would not vote
    in an election.

[　] 1) My vote would not matter.
[　] 2) My vote could add political recognition and public consideration to felon issues.
[　] 3) It is too much time and trouble to vote, so I would not vote.
[　] 4) I would vote because it is my right to do so once I have paid my "debt" to society.

Please explain your answer: _____

_____
_____
_____

32. Felons should not be given the right to vote because: (Please check [✓] one)
[　] 1) The views of felons would not be respected.
[　] 2) Felons would not vote anyway.
[　] 3) Once you have committed a felony, you should not be given this privilege again.
[　] 4) Felons do not understand the issues well enough to make good electoral decisions or judgments.
[　] 5) None of the above.

Please explain your answer: _____

_____
_____
_____

33. If you think felons should be given the right to vote, in your opinion, when should they be given this right? (Please check [✓] only one answer.)
[　] 1) While serving their time in prison.
[　] 2) Upon completion of their prison term.
[　] 3) Upon completion of parole or probation.

Please explain your answer: _____

_____
_____
_____

VIRGINIA
VOTER PARTICIPATION SURVEY
CENTER FOR URBAN EDUCATION, INC.
JOHN E. PINKARD SR., PH.D. CANDIDATE

Directions:
    The following questions are designed to survey your attitude
toward voter participation in local and general elections in the U.S.
Your participation in this survey is completely optional and
voluntary. The results of this survey will be used as part of a Ph.D.
Dissertation. It is intended that the results of this study will also be
used to enhance ways Community Corrections Programs can best serve
offender populations. We estimate that it would take no more than 15-
20 minutes of your time to complete this survey. Please put a check
[✓] in the appropriate space. Thank you.

I. **Background Information**
    1. Are you: 1) Male [   ]   2) Female [   ]

    2. Are you a citizen of the U.S.A.?   1) Yes [   ]   2) No [   ]

    3. Are you foreign born?   1) Yes [   ]   2) No [   ]

    4. If foreign born, of which country are you a citizen? _____

    5. What is your race/ethnicity?
        [   ] 1. African American or Black
        [   ] 2. Latino or Hispanic
        [   ] 3. Non-Latino White
        [   ] 4. Asian
        [   ] 5. Other: please specify _____

6. How old are you?
         1) 17 and below [   ]   6) 36-40 [   ]
         2) 18-21   [   ]   7) 41-45 [   ]
         3) 22-24   [   ]   8) 46-50 [   ]
         4) 25-29   [   ]   9) 51 and over [   ]
         5) 30-35   [   ]

7. What is the highest educational level you have achieved?
         1) 6th or less   [   ]
         2) 7th, 8th   [   ]
         3) 9th, 10th   [   ]
         4) 11th, 12th   [   ]
         5) H.S. graduate   [   ]
         6) G.E.D.   [   ]
         7) College or Voc. Ed. [   ]

8. What is your legal status?
         1) Violent offense   [   ]
         2) CDS, nonviolent   [   ]
         3) Property offense   [   ]

9. How many times have you been convicted of a felony?
         1) once   [   ]   2) two times   [   ]
         3) three times [   ]   4) four or five times [   ]
         5) more than five times [   ]

10. How would you classify your household income?
         1) low income [   ]   2) middle income [   ]
         3) upper income [   ]

11. Have you ever registered to vote:
         1) Yes [   ]   2) No [   ]

12. Have you ever voted in an election in the U.S.?
         1) Yes [   ]   2) No [   ]

13. Have you ever participated in campaign activities for any
local, state, or national candidate?
       1) Yes [   ]   2) No [   ]

14. If you were able to vote, would you vote in an election?
       1) Yes [   ]   2) No [   ]

II. Please use the 6-point scale below to indicate how strongly you agree or disagree with each of the following statements as they apply to you. Place the number from 1-6 in the blank to the left of each statement.

1	2	3	4	5	6

Strongly   Strongly
disagree   agree

[   ] 15. People like me are generally well qualified to participate in the political activity and decision making in the U.S.

[   ] 16. I enjoy political participation because I want to have as much say in running government as possible.

[   ] 17. A good many local elections aren't important enough to bother with.

[   ] 18. So many other people are active in local issues and organizations that it doesn't matter much to me whether I participate or not.

[   ] 19. Most public officials wouldn't listen to me no matter what I did.

[   ] 20. Sometimes politics and government seem so complicated that a person like me can't really understand what's going on.

III. Please check [✓] the one that you think is the correct answer.

  21. In Virginia, U.S. citizens who have been convicted of a felon crime:

    [   ] 1) Regain their right to vote once having completed their full sentence including incarceration, parole, or probation?

    [   ] 2) Lose their right to vote for life?

    [   ] 3) Lose their right to vote until they complete their sentence and apply for restoration through the local Circuit Court or Secretary of Commonwealth?

    [   ] 4) Lose their right to vote until they complete their sentence and apply for restoration through the Governor's approval or pardon?

    [   ] 5) Non-violent offenders after 3 years, and violent offenders, drug offenders, and election fraud offenders after 5 years can apply for voter restoration through the local Circuit Court or Secretary of the Commonwealth, along with the Governor's approval or pardon?

    [   ] 6) After three years of having completed their sentence, only non-violent offenders can apply for voter restoration through the local Circuit Court or Secretary of the Commonwealth?

  22. In Virginia, U.S. citizens have the right to vote if:

    [   ] 1) You are a U.S. citizen?

    [   ] 2) You are a resident of Virginia?

    [   ] 3) You are at least 18 years of age by the time of the next election?

    [   ] 4) You have not been adjudicated to be mentally incompetent without competency having been re-established?

    [   ] 5) You have not been convicted of a felony, without having been restored by the Governor or an appropriate authority?

    [   ] 6) All of the above?

[   ] 7) None of the above?

23. How would you classify your political values?
           1) very conservative [   ]   2) conservative [   ]
           3) moderate   [   ]   4) liberal   [   ]
           5) very liberal   [   ]   6) undecided [   ]

24. Which political party best represents your party preference?
           1) Republican   [   ]
           2) Democrat   [   ]
           3) Independent [   ]
           4) Independent Democrat [   ]
           5) Independent Republican [   ]
           6) Third Party preference [   ]
           7) Undecided   [   ]

25. To cast a vote in Virginia, how many days before Election Day must you register?
           [   ] 1) At least 7 days before
           [   ] 2) At least 15 days before
           [   ] 3) At least 22 days before
           [   ] 4) At least 30 days before
           [   ] 5) I do not know

26. Do you feel felons should be given the right to vote?
           1) Yes [   ]   2) No [   ]

IV. Please check (✓| one in each of the following questions:
27. To what degree do you feel your vote would matter in the overall electoral system?
           1) no degree   [   ]   2) very little degree [   ]
           3) a degree   [   ]   4) good degree   [   ]
           5) great degree [   ]

28. Should felons be given the right to vote when they have completed:

   1) Prison   [   ]   2) Probation   [   ]
   3) Parole   [   ]   4) all of the above   [   ]
   5) none of the above [   ]

29. To what degree do you feel child care funds for the poor should be increased?

   1) none   [   ]   2) very little   [   ]
   3) moderately   [   ]   4) significantly   [   ]

30. Do you approve or disapprove of U.S. involvement in the United Nations?

   1) approve [   ]   2) disapprove [   ]   3) no opinion [   ]

V.   Fill-ins

31. On question number 14 you were asked if you were able to vote, would you? If you answered yes or no to question number 14, please explain why you would or would not vote in an election. (Please check [✔] only one answer.)

   [   ] 1) My vote would not matter.
   [   ] 2) My vote could add political recognition and public consideration to felon issues.
   [   ] 3) It is too much time and trouble to vote, so I would not vote.
   [   ] 4) I would vote because it is my right to do so once I have paid my "debt" to society.

   Please explain your answer: _____

   _____
   _____
   _____

32. Felons should not be given the right to vote because: (Please check [✔] only one answer.)

   [   ] 1) The views of felons would not be respected.
   [   ] 2) Felons would not vote anyway.

[   ] 3) Once you have committed a felony, you should not
         be given this privilege again.
[   ] 4) Felons do not understand the issues well enough to
         make good electoral decisions or judgments.
[   ] 5) None of the above.

Please explain your answer: _____

_____

_____

_____

33. If you think felons should be given the right to vote, in your
    opinion, when should they be given this right? (Please check
    |✓| only one answer.)
    [   ] 1) While serving their time in prison.
    [   ] 2) Upon completion of their prison term.
    [   ] 3) Upon completion of parole or probation.

    Please explain your answer: _____

    _____

    _____

    _____

Endnotes

1. M. Williams, *Voice, Trust, and Memory, marginalized groups and the failings of liberal representation*, Princeton U. Press (Princeton, N.J., 1998) P. 3.
2. P. Green, *Retrieving Democracy, In Search of Civic Equality*, Rowman and Allenheld Publishers (Totowa, N.J., 1985) P. 175.
3. Ibid., P. 172, P. Green, *Retrieving Democracy*.
4. K. Crenshaw, N. Gotanda, G. Peller, K. Thomas, *Critical Race Theory, the key writing that formed the movement*, The New Press (N.Y., N.Y., 1995) P. xi, xiii.
5. Ibid., P. 174, P. Green, *Retrieving Democracy*.
6. Reynolds v. Sims, 377 U.S. 533 (1964)
7. J. Shklar, *American Citizenship, the Quest for Inclusion*, Harvard University Press (Cambridge, Mass., 1995) P. 2.
8. Ibid., P. 1, J. Shklar, *American Citizenship*.
9. Ibid., P. 3, J. Shklar, *American Citizenship*.
10. S. Nagy Hesse-Biber, P. Leavy, *Approaches to Qualitative Research, A Reader on Theory and Practice*, Oxford University Press (New York, N.U., 2004) P. 1.
11. Ibid., P. 1; S.N. Hesse-Biber and P. Leavy, *Approaches to Qualitative Research*.
12. K. Crenshaw, N. Golanda, G. Peller, K. Thomas, *Critical Race Theory*, The New Press (N.Y., N.Y., 1995) P. xiii.
13. Ibid., P. xiii; Crenshaw, Golanda, Peller, *Critical Race Theory*.
14. Ibid., P. iii; Crenshaw, Golanda, Peller, *Critical Race Theory*.

15. Ibid., P. 6; S.N. Hesse-Biber and P. Leavy, *Approaches to Qualitative Research*.

16. Ibid., P. 26; S.N. Hesse-Biber and P. Leavy, *Approaches to Qualitative Research*.

17. Lani Guinier, *The Tyranny of the Majority*, The Free Press (New York, N.U., 1994) P. viii – Stephen Carter.

18. Peter Veniero, Paul Zoubeck, *Interim Report of the State Police Review Team Regarding Allegations of Racial Profiling*, (State of N.J., 1999) P. Summary, 26, 27, 29.

19. Michael Omi, Howard Winant, *Racial Formation in the United States*, Rutledge Press (New York, N.Y., 1994) P. 59.

20. D.R. Kinder, L.M. Sanders, *Divided by Color – Racial Politics and Democratic Ideals*, (University of Chicago Press, 1996) P. 291.

21. Ibid., P. 292, D. Kinder, L. Sanders, *Divided by Color*.

22. Ibid., P. 292, D. Kinder, L. Sanders, *Divided by Color*.

23. Harrison, Paige M., Karberg J., *Bureau of Justice Statistics – Prison and Jail Inmates at Midyear 2002* (Washington, D.C.: U.S. Department of Justice 4/03) P. 2 Table 14, p. 13.

24. Hannah Arendt, *On Revolution*, 1990 (Penguin Books) P. 60.

25. Ibid., P. 1, M. Omi, H. Winant, *Racial Formation in the U.S.*.

26. M. Tustinet, *Making Constitutional Law* (Oxford U. Press, N.Y., N.Y.., 1997) P. 94.

27. Ibid., P. 95, M. Tustinet, *Making Constitutional Law*.

28. Ibid., P. 95, M. Tustinet, *Making Constitutional Law*.

29. Ibid., P. 96, M. Tustinet, *Making Constitutional Law*.

30. Ibid., P. 100, M. Tustinet, *Making Constitutional Law*.

31. M. Mauer, M. Chesney-Lind, *Invisible Punishment*, (New Press, N.Y., 2003) P. 1.

32. *New York Times*, May 6, 2008.

33. *New York Times*, Department of Justice, May 6, 2008, 2009.

34. Substance Abuse and Mental Health Services Administration (1999).

35. Beck, Allen, Mumola, Christopher, *Bureau of Statistics, Sourcebook of Criminal Justice Statistics* (Washington, D.C., 1999) P. 435, 10, 11, Table 16.

36. Key Recommendations from Punishment and Prejudice: Racial Disparities in the War on Drugs (Washington, D.C.: Human Rights Watch).

37. Neuspiel, D.R., *Racism and Perinatal Addiction"*, Ethnicity and Disease 6:47-55 [also *New England Journal of Medicine* 322:1202-1206].

38. Durose, Matthew, Langon, *Bureau of Justice Statistics, State Court Sentencing of Convicted Felons, 1998* (Washington, D.C.: Department of Justice, 2001). Table 25.

39. Ibid., P. 1, M. Mauer, M. Chesney-Lind, *Invisible Punishment.*

40. Andrew Shapiro, *Challenging Criminal Disenfranchisement. Under the Voting Rights Act: A New Strategy"* (Yale Law Journal – Vol. 103, No. 2, December 1993) P. 537; [Also, (*Losing the Vote*, 1998, P. 5)].

41. Anthony C. Thompson, *Releasing Prisoners, Redeeming. Communities* (New York University Press, 2008) P. 122.

42. James McGuire, *Defining Correctional Programs*, Compendium 2000 on Effective Correctional Programming, Chapter I, P. 1.

43. Ibid., P. 1, M. Mauer, M. Chesney-Lind, *Invisible Punishment.*

44. Ibid., P. 63, H. Arendt, *On Revolution.*

45. U.S. Constitution, X Amendment, P. 14.

46. A. Keyssar, *The Right to Vote*, The Contested History of Democracy in the U.S., Basic Books Publishers (N.Y., N.Y., 2000) P. 1.

47. Ibid., P. 2, A. Keyssar, *The Right to Vote.*

48. Ibid., P. 3, A. Keysser, *The Right to Vote.*

49. Ibid., P. 15, U.S. Constitution,, XIV Amendment, Section I.

50. Ibid., P. 15, U.S. Constitution,, XIV Amendment, Section I.

51. Ibid., P. 16, U.S. Constitution,, XV Amendment.

52. Ibid., P. 17, U.S. Constitution, XIX Amendment.

53. Ibid., P. 18, U.S. Constitution, XXIV Amendment.

54. Ibid., P. 19, U.S. Constitution, XXXVI Amendment.

55. E.A. Hull, *The Disenfranchisement of Ex-felons*, Temple U. Press (Philadelphia, Pa., 1992) P. 1.

56. Sentencing Project, *Losing the Vote*, Human Rights Watch.

57. J. Fellner, M. Mauer, *Losing the Vote*, Human Rights Watch and the Sentencing Project (Washington D.C. and New York, N.Y., 1998) Table II, P. 9.

58. H. Stanley and R. Niemi, *Vital Statistics on American Politics, 2001-2002*, CQ Press (Washington, D.C., 2001) P. 34.

59. Ibid., P. 25, E.A. Hull, *The Disenfranchisement of Ex-felons*.

60. Bureau of Justice Statistics (Department of Justice) Key Facts at a Glance (chart), 2008, P. 1.

61. H. Stanley and R. Niemi, *Vital Statistics on American Politics, 2005-2006*, CQ Press (Washington, D.C., 2006) P. 34.

62. S. Platt, *Respectfully Quoted, A Dictionary of Quotations*, Barnes & Noble, Inc. (N.Y., N.Y., 1993) P. 88.

63. R.A. Keiser, *Subordination or Empowerment?*, Oxford University Press (N.Y., N.Y., 1997) P. 3.

64. Ibid., P. 3, R.A. Keiser, *Subordination or Empowerment*.

65. Ibid., preface, xi, A. Keyssar, *The Right to Vote*.

66. Ibid., P. 340-7, A. Keyssar, *The Right to Vote*.

67. Ibid., P. 350-53, A. Keyssar, *The Right to Vote*.

68. Ibid., P. 353, A. Keyssar, *The Right to Vote*.

69. Ibid., P. 352, A. Keyssar, *The Right to Vote*.

70. Ibid., P. 358-9, A. Keyssar, *The Right to Vote*.

71. Ibid., P. 359-61, A. Keyssar, *The Right to Vote*.

72. A.L. Shapiro, *"Challenging Criminal Disenfranchisement Under the Voting Rights Act: A New Strategy"*, The Yale Law Journal, Vol. 103, November, 1993 No. 2, P. 537.

73. Ibid., P. 538, A.L. Shapiro, *"Challenging Criminal Disenfranchisement Under the Voting Rights Act*.

74. Ibid., P. 538, A.L. Shapiro, *"Challenging Criminal Disenfranchisement Under the Voting Rights Act*.

75. Ibid., P. 540, A.L. Shapiro, *"Challenging Criminal Disenfranchisement Under the Voting Rights Act*.

76. Ibid., P. 541, A.L. Shapiro, *"Challenging Criminal Disenfranchisement Under the Voting Rights Act*.

77. Ibid., P. 363, A. Keyssar, *The Right to Vote*.

78. Ibid., P. 393-6, A. Keyssar, *The Right to Vote*.

79. _____, Constitution of Maryland, Article I, Section 4, http://aomol.net/msa/mdmanual, P.1.

80. _____, New Jersey State Constitution 1947 (amendments adopted through 2006), Article II, Section I:7, http://www.njleg.state.nj.us/lawsconstitution, P. 4,5.

81. _____, Constitution of Virginia, Article II, Section I, http://legis.state.va.us/laws/search/Constitution.htm, P. 3,4.

82. Ibid., P. 29; J. Fellner, M. Mauer, Losing the Vote; M. Colgate Love, *Relief from the Collateral Consequences of a Criminal Conviction: A State-by-State Resource Guide*, Williams S. Hein and Co., Inc. (Buffalo, N.Y., 2006) P. 135-139.

83. P. McKernan, President CCCPNJ, Voadv.org, 2007.

84. J. Petersilia, *When Prisoners Come Home: Parole and Prisoner Re-entry*, Oxford University Press (N.Y., N.Y., 2003) P. 17.

85. _____, Voting Rights Act of 1965: An Act http://www.smpcollege:com/smpgovt/documents/doc.16, p. 1.

86. S. Issacharoff, P. Karlan, R. Pildes, *The Law of Democracy: Legal Structure of the Political Process*, the Foundation Press, Inc. (Westbury, N.Y., 1998) P. 2.

87. Ibid., P. 2, Issacharoff, Karlan, Pildes, *The Law of Democracy*.

88. J. Nowak, R. Rotunda, *Constitutional Law, fifth edition*, West Publishing Co. (St. Paul, MN., 1995) P. 1.

89. Ibid., P. 2, Issacharoff, Karlan, Pildes, *The Law of Democracy*.

90. Ibid., P. 5, Nowak, Rotunda, *Constitutional Law*.

91. Ibid., P. 4, Nowak, Rotunda, *Constitutional Law*.

92. Ibid., P. 2, Issacharoff, Karlan, and Pildes, *The Law of Democracy*.

93. _____, *Reynolds v. Sims* (1964), .http://usinfo.state.gov/usa/infousa/facts/democrac/68.htm, P. 2.

94. Ibid., P. 9, *Reynolds v. Sims* (1964).

95. Ibid., P. 12, *Reynolds v. Sims* (1964).

96. Ibid., P. 12, *Reynolds v. Sims* (1964).

97. Ibid., P. 13, *Reynolds v. Sims* (1964).

98. Ibid., P. 13, *Reynolds v. Sims* (1964).

99. Ibid., P. 14, *Reynolds v. Sims* (1964).

100. Ibid., P. 15, *Reynolds v. Sims* (1964).
101. Ibid., P. 15, *Reynolds v. Sims* (1964).
102. Ibid., P. 16, *Reynolds v. Sims* (1964).
103. Ibid., P. 17, *Reynolds v. Sims* (1964).
104. _____ *Richardson v. Ramirez* (1974),
      http://www.hrw.org/reports98/vote/usvot98, P. 8.
105. _____ *Richardson v. Ramirez* (1974),
      http://www.hrw.org/reports98/vote/usvot98, P. 8.
106. Ibid., P. 8, *Richardson v. Ramirez* (1974).
107. Ibid., P. 9, *Richardson v. Ramirez* (1974).
108. Ibid., P. 9, *Richardson v. Ramirez* (1974).
109. Ibid., P. 11, *Richardson v. Ramirez* (1974).
110. Ibid., P. 11, *Richardson v. Ramirez* (1974).
111. Ibid., P. 12, *Richardson v. Ramirez* (1974).
112. Ibid., P. 13, *Richardson v. Ramirez* (1974).
113. Ibid., P. 14, *Richardson v. Ramirez* (1974).
114. Ibid., P. 14, *Richardson v. Ramirez* (1974).
115. Ibid., P. 26, *Richardson v. Ramirez* (1974).
116. Ibid., P. 26, *Richardson v. Ramirez* (1974).
117. Ibid., P. 26, *Richardson v. Ramirez* (1974).
118. Ibid., P. 26, *Richardson v. Ramirez* (1974).
119. Ibid., P. 27, *Richardson v. Ramirez* (1974).
120. Ibid., P. 28, *Richardson v. Ramirez* (1974).
121. Ibid., P. 28, *Richardson v. Ramirez* (1974).
122. Ibid., P. 29, *Richardson v. Ramirez* (1974).
123. Ibid., P. 30, *Richardson v. Ramirez* (1974).
124. Ibid., P. 31, *Richardson v. Ramirez* (1974).
125. _____, Mobile v. Bolden, 446 U.S. 55 (1980),
      http://supreme.justia.com/us/446/55, P. 1.
126. Ibid., P. 1, *Mobile v. Bolden*, (1980).
127. Ibid., P. 1, *Mobile v. Bolden*, (1980).
128. Ibid., P. 2, *Mobile v. Bolden*, (1980).
129. Ibid., P. 2, *Mobile v. Bolden*, (1980).
130. Ibid., P. 2, *Mobile v. Bolden*, (1980).
131. Ibid., P. 3, *Mobile v. Bolden*, (1980).

132. _____ Hunter v. Underwood, 471 U.S. 222 (1985) http://caselaw,lp.findlaw.com/scripts/getcase.pl?court, P. 4.

133. Ibid., P. 4, *Hunter v. Underwood* (1985).

134. Ibid., P. 5, *Hunter v. Underwood* (1985).

135. Ibid., P. 5, *Hunter v. Underwood* (1985).

136. Ibid., P. 6, *Hunter v. Underwood* (1985) .

137. CERD Report: International Convention on the Elimination of all Forms of Racial Discrimination (CERD / C / USA / CO / 6) Feb., 2008, P. 2.

138. Liles, Alabama Law Review [Vol. 58:3:615], Feb., 2007, P. 622.

139. _____, "The Disenfranchisement of Ex-felons: Citizenship, Criminality, and The Purity of the Ballot Box", *The Harvard Law Review*, Vol. 102, April, 1989 No. 6, P. 1317.

140. J. Shklar, *American Citizenship, the Quest for Inclusion*, Harvard University Press (Cambridge, Mass., 1995) P. 1.

141. M. Mauer, R. King, *Uneven Justice: State Rates of Incarceration by Race and Ethnicity*, The Sentencing Project, 2007, P. 3.

142. Ibid., P. 1, M. Mauer, R. King, *Uneven Justice.*

143. Ibid., P. 1, M. Mauer, R. King, *Uneven Justice.*

144. Ibid., P. 1, M. Mauer, R. King, *Uneven Justice.*

145. H.W. Stanley, R.G. Niemi, *Vital Statistics on American Politics 2007-2008*, CQ Press, 2008 (Washington D.C.), Pg. 14.

146. S. Verba, K.L. Schlozman, H.E. Brady, *Voice and Equality*, Harvard U. Press, 1995 (Cambridge, Mass.) P. 50.

147. Ibid., P. 54, Verba, Schlozman, Brady, *Voice and Equality.*

148. P. Abramson, J. Aldrich, D. Rohde, *Change and Continuity in the 1996 and 1998 Elections.* CQ Press, 1999 (Washington, D.C.) P. 91.

149. G.M. Pomper, *The Election of 2000*, Chatham House Publishers, 2001 (N.Y., N.Y.) P. 138.

150. U.S. Elections Project: 2008 General Election Turnout Rates, P. 1 and 2 (last update 3/31/12).

151. Ibid., P. 78-9, Abramson, Aldrich, Rohde, *Change and Continuity in the 1996 and 1998 Elections.*

152. Ibid., P. 138, Pomper, *The Election of 2000*.

153. Ibid., P. 138, Pomper, *The Election of 2000*.

154. N. LaVigne, *Mapping for Community Based Prisoner Reentry Efforts, 2007* – Community Oriented Prisoner Reentry Services (Washington., D.C.) P. 7.

155. Ibid., P. 7, LaVigne, *Mapping for Community Based Prisoner Reentry Efforts, 2007*.

156. Ibid, Introduction, LaVigne, *Mapping for Community Based Prisoner Reentry Efforts, 2007*.

157. Ibid., P. 123, Anthony Thompson, *Releasing Prisoners, Redeeming Communities*.

158. U.S. Census Bureau (Maryland) 2006, http://quickfacts.census.gov.

159. U.S. Census Bureau, Baltimore City (2006), http://quickfacts.census.gov/qfd/states.

160. Maryland Division of Correction Annual Report 2004, www.dpscs.state.md.us/doc , P. 44; P. 39.

161. Maryland State Board of Elections, http://www.elections.state.md.us/voter .

162. Baltimore.sun.com, http://www.Baltimoresun.com/news/local, 5/22/07.

163. Chapter 159, Senate Bill 488 – Martin O'Malley, Governor, "Voter Registration Protection Act", P. 2.

164. U.S. Presidential Election, 2008, http://en.wikipedia.org/wiki/2008, P. 15.

165. U.S. Census Bureau Quickfacts, http://quickfacts.census.gov/qfd/states and Maryland State Board of Elections Voter Registration Activity – Yearly Report 2006 (by County and Total).

166. Pomper, G., *The Election of 2000* (Chatham House Publishers) © 2001 (P. 137).

167. New York Times "After the Vote", November 6, 2008, P. 8.

168. Ibid, P. 19-21, U.S. Presidential Election, 2008.

169. Ibid, P. 1-2, U.S. Census Bureau, 2006.

170. Ibid., P. 1-2, U.S. Census Bureau, Baltimore City.

171. Maryland Division of Corrections Annual Report 2004, www.dpscs.state.md.us/doc, P. 39 and; Maryland Department of Public Safety and Correctional Services, 2007, @ www.dpscs.state.md.us, P. 2.

172. Ibid., P. 40, The Maryland Division of Corrections Annual Report, 2004.

173. Ibid., P. 42, The Maryland Division of Corrections Annual Report, 2004.

174. Ibid., P. 44, The Maryland Division of Corrections Annual Report, 2004.

175. Bell, G., *The End of Ideology* (Harvard University Press) © 2000, P. 17.

176. U.S. Presidential Election, 2008, http://wikipedia.org/wiki/2008; Official 2008 Presidential General Elections results (Baltimore City) http://www.elections.state.md.us/elections/2008.

177. CNN.com Election 2002, P.4. http://www.cnn.com/Election/2002 (State Results); Ibid P.1, County Results: Maryland Governor.

178. Van Smith, Siegel F., City Journal "Can Mayor O'Malley Save Ailing Baltimore", Winter 2001, http://www.city-journal.org/html; 1999 Baltimore City Election, http://www.elections.state.md.us/elections/baltimore/1999.html.

179. ____, "The Disenfranchisement of Ex-felons: Citizenship, Criminality, and the Purity of the Ballot Box", The Harvard Law Review, Vol. 102, April 1989 No. 6, P. 1317.

180. Virginia, http://en.wikipedia.org/wiki/Virginia.

181. Virginia, http://quickfacts.census.gov/qfd/States/51000.html.

182. Hampton Roads, http://en.wikipedia.org/wiki/HamptonRoads.

183. http://en.wikipedia.org/wiki/Norfolk,_Virginia.

184. http://en.wikipedia.org/wiki/Newport_News_Virginia.

185. http://en.wikipedia.org/wiki/Virginia_Beach_Virginia.

186. Statistical Summary FY 2004, Va. Dept. of Corrections, www.vadoc.state.va.us., P.2.

187. Prisoner Reentry in Virginia, Keegan S., Solomon A., Urban Institute Justice Policy Center, 2004, P.32.

188. http://legis.state.va.us/Laws/search/constitution.htm.

189. http://en.wikipedia.org/wike/Constitution_of_Virginia.

190. http://en.wikipedia.org/wiki/Constitution_of_Virginia.

191. http://en.wikipedia.org/wiki/Constitution_of_Virginia.

192. http://quickfacts.census.gov/qfd/states/5100, http://www.sbe.virginia.gov/Statistics_Polling_Places/Registration_Statistics/voting and http://en.wikipedia.org/wiki/Virginia.

193. http://en.wikipedia.org/wiki/2008_United_States_Presidential_Election.

194. Virginia, http://quickfacts.census.gov/qfd/states/51000.html.

195. http://en.wikipedia.org/Virignia-Beach-Virginia, http://en.wikipedia.org/Norfolk-Virginia, and http://en.wikipedia.org/Newport-News-Virginia.

196. Virginia Department of Corrections, Statistical Summary FY 2004 and 2007, Research and Management Services Unit, www.vadoc.virginia.gov.

197. http://en.wikipedia.org/wiki/Virginia_United_States_Senate_Election_2006.

198. http://uselectionatlas.org/RESULTS/compare.php?year_2005 and http://www.dkosopedia.com/wike/Virginia_2005_Election_results.

199. Lynn Todman, Institute on Social Exclusion @ the Adler School of Professional Psychology, 2007.

200. The Salvation Army: The Seeds of Exclusion, 2008 Social Exclusion – Wikipedia.

201. Daniel Bell, *The End of Ideology*, Harvard U. Press (2001), pg. xi.

202. Charles Taylor, *Multiculturalism: The Politics of Recognition*, Princeton U. Press (Princeton, N.J., 1994) P. 25.

203. Ibid., Pg xi, *The End of Ideology*.

204. New York Times/CBS News Poll, July 7 – July 14, 2008.

205. Michael Omi, Howard Winant, *Racial Formation in the United States*, Rutledge Press (New York, N.Y., 1994) P. 59.

206. Ibid., P. 96, M. Tustinet, *Making Constitutional Law.*
207. Ibid., P. 15, J. Fellner, M. Mauer, *Losing the Vote.*
208. Ibid., P. 2, Issacharoff, Karlan, Pildes, *The Law of Democracy.*
209. Ibid., P. 8, *Richardson v. Ramirez* (1974).
210. Ibid., P. 31, *Richardson v. Ramirez* (1974).
211. ____, Mobile v. Bolden, 446 U.S. 55 (1980), http://supreme.justia.com/us/446/55, P. 1.
212. Ibid., P. 1, *Mobile v. Bolden*, (1980).
213. Ibid., P. 1317 ____, The Disenfranchisement of Ex-felons: Citizenship, Criminality, and the Purity of the Ballot Box.
214. Ibid., P. 25, Charles Taylor, *Multiculturalism.*
215. Ibid., P. 60, Hannah Arendt, *On Revolution.*
216. John Bartlett, Bartlett's Familiar Quotations, Little, Brown and Co., (New York, 2002)   P. 509.

Bibliography

Abramson, P., Aldrich, J., Rohde, D., *Change and Continuity in the 1996 and 1998 Elections*, Washington, D.C.

Arendt, Hannah, *On Revolution*, New York, N.Y.

_____, Baker v. Carr, http://en.wikipedia.org/wiki/baker_v._Carr, 1962.

Bartlett, J., *Bartlett's Familiar Quotations*, N.Y., 2002.

_____, Baltimore.sun.com, http://Baltimore.sun.com/news/local, 2007.

Beck, Allen, Mumola, Christopher, *Bureau of Statistics, Sourcebook of Criminal Justice Statistics*. Washington, D.C., 1991.

Bell, D., *The End of Ideology*, Harvard University Press, 2000.

Bonczar, T.P., *Prevalence of Imprisonment in the U.S. Population*, 1974-2001, Bureau of Justice Statistics, 2003.

Bureau of Justice Statistics Key Facts at a Glance, 2008.

CCCPNJ, *The Coalition of Community Corrections Providers of New Jersey Newsletter*, Trenton, N.J., CCCPNJ Publication, 2006.

CERD Report: International Convention on the Eliminations of All Forms of Racial Discrimination, 2008.

Civil Rights Act, 1965, Document 16, Section 4.

Colgate Love, M., *Relief from the Collateral Consequences of a Criminal Conviction: A State-by-State Resource Guide*, Buffalo, N.Y., Williams S. Hein and Co., Inc., 2006.

_____, CNN.com, http://www.cnn.com/election/2002.

_____, Constitution of Maryland, http://aomol.net/msa/mdmanual, 1978.

_____, Constitution of Virginia, http://legis.state.va.us/law/search/constitution.htm, ©1972.

Crenshaw, K. Gotanda, N., Peller, G., Thomas, K., *Critical Race Theory*: N.Y., N.Y., 1995.

Disenfranchisement of Ex-felons: Citizenship, Criminality, and the Purity of the Ballot Box

Durose, Matthew, Langon, *Bureau of Justice Statistics: State Court Sentencing of Convicted Felons*. Washington D.C.: Department of Justice, 1998.

Fellner, J., Mauer, M., *Losing the Vote*, Washington D.C., Human Rights Watch and the Sentencing Project, 1998.

Green, P., *Retrieving Democracy*: Totowa, N.J., 1985.

Guinier, L., *The Tyranny of the Majority*. New York, N.Y.: The Free Press, 1994.

Harrison, P., Karberg J., *Bureau of Justice Statistics – Prison and Jail Inmates at Midyear 2002*. Washington, D.C.: Bureau of Justice, 2002.

Hesse-Biber, Leavy P., *Approaches to Qualitative Research*, New York, N.Y.: Oxford University Press, 2004.

Hull, E.A., *The Disenfranchisement of Ex-Felons*, Philadelphia, Pa., Temple University Press, 1992.

Human Rights Watch. *Key Recommendations from Punishment and Prejudice: Racial Disparities in the War on Drugs*. Washington, D.C.: Human Rights Watch,

_____, Hunter v. Underwood, http://caselaw.lp.findlaw.com/scripts/getcase.pl?court, 1985.

Issacharoff, S., Karlan, P., Pildes, R., *The Law of Democracy: Legal Structure of the Political Process*, Westbury, N.Y., Foundation Press, Inc., 1998.

Keegan S., Solomon A., *Prisoner Reentry in Virginia*, 2004.

Keiser, R.A., *Subordination or Empowerment?*, N.Y., N.Y., Oxford University Press, 1997.

Keyssar, A., *The Right to Vote*, N.Y., N.Y., Book Publishers, 2000.

Kinder, D., Sanders, L., *Divided by Color-Racial Politics and Democratic Ideas*. Chicago, Illinois: U. Chicago Press, 1996.

King, R.; Mauer, M.; Young, M., *Incarceration and Crime: A Complex Relationship*, The Sentencing Project, 2005.

LaVigne, N., *Mapping for Community Based Prisoner Reentry Efforts, 2007*, Washington, D.C.: Community Oriented Prisoner Reentry Services.

Liles, <u>Alabama Review</u>, 2007.

Maryland State Board of Elections Yearly Report, Voter Registration Activity, 2006.

_____, Maryland Department of Public Safety and Correctional Services, www.dpscs.state.md.us, 2007.

_____, Maryland Division of Correction Annual Report, www.dpscs.state.md.us/doc, 2004.

_____, Maryland State Board of Elections, http://www.elections.state.md.us/voter.

Mauer, M., Chesney-Lind, M., *Invisible Punishment.* Washington, D.C.: Reed Business Information, Inc., 2002.

Mauer, M.; King, R., *Uneven Justice: State Rates of Incarceration by Race and Ethnicity*, The Sentencing Project, 2007.

McGuire, J., *Defining Correctional Programs Compendium 2000.*

_____, Mobile v. Bolden, http://supreme.justia.com/us/446/55, 1980.

Neuspiel, D., "Racism and Perinatal Addiction". Ethnicity and Disease 6:47-55 [Also *New England Journal of Medicine* 322:1202-1206].

_____, <u>New Jersey State Constitution</u>, http://www.njleg.state.nj.us/lawconstitution, 1947 (updated 2006).

New York Times, Department of Justice, May 6, 2009.

New York Times, *"After the Vote"*, 11/06/08.

New York Times, CBS Poll, 7/14/08.

Nowak, J., Rotunda, R., *Constitutional Law, fifth edition*, St. Paul, MN., West Publishing Co,, 1995.

Omi, M., Winant, H., *Racial Formation in the United States.* New York, N.Y.: Rutledge Press, 1994.

Petersilia, J., *When Prisoners Come Home: Parole and Prison Re-entry*, N.Y., N.Y., Oxford University Press, 2003.

PEW Center on the States. *One in 100: Behind Bars in America.* 2008.

Platt, S., *Respectfully Quoted, A Dictionary of Quotations*, N.Y., N.Y., Barnes and Noble Inc. 1993.

Pomper, G, *The Election of 2000*, Chatham House Publishers, 2001.

Reynolds v. Sims 377 U.S. 533 (1964).

_____, Reynolds v. Sims,
http://usinfo.state.gov/usa/infousa/facts/democrac/68.htm,
1964.

_____, Richardson v. Ramirez,
http://www.hrw.org/reports98/vote/usvot98, 1974.

Shapiro, A., "Challenging Criminal Disenfranchisement under the
Voting Rights Act: A New Strategy". Connecticut: *Yale Law
Journal* – Vol. 103, No. 2, 1993).

Shklar, J., *"American Citizenship, the Quest for Inclusion.* Cambridge,
Mass., Harvard University Press, 1995.

Stanley, H., Niemi, R., *Vital Statistics on American Politics, 2001-
2002,* Washington D.C., CQ Press, 2002.

Stanley, H., Niemi, R. *Vital Statistics on American Politics, 2006-2006,*
Washington D.C., CQ Press, 2006.

Stanley, H.W., Niemi, R.G., *Vital Statistics on American Politics 2007-
2008,* Washington, D.C., CQ Press, 2008.

Statistical Summary, Virginia Department of Corrections, 2004.

Substance Abuse and Mental Health Services, Administration Report,
1999.

_____, "The Disenfranchisement of Ex-Felons: Citizenship,
Criminality, and the Purity of the Ballot Box", Vol. 102, April,
1989 No. 6, *The Harvard Law Review,* 1989.

Taylor, C, *Multiculturalism,*

Thompson, A., *Releasing Prisons, Redeeming Communities*

Tustinet, M.V., *Making Constitutional Law,* New York, N.Y.: Oxford
University Press, 1997.

U.S. Constitution, X Amendment.

_____, U.S. Census Bureau (Maryland), http://quickfacts.census.gov.,
2006.

_____, U.S. Census Bureau (Baltimore City),
http://quickfacts.census.gov/qfd/states, 2006.

_____, U.S. Presidential Election, http://wikipedia.org/wiki/2008.

Van Smith, S., City Journal, Winter 2001, http://www.city-journal.org.

Veniero, P., Zoubeck, P., *Interim Report of the State Police Review
Team Regarding Allegations of Racial Profiling.* New Jersey:
State of N.J., 1999.

Verba, S., Schlozman, K.L., Brady, H.E., *Voice and Equality,*
Cambridge, Mass., Harvard U. Press, 1995.

Virginia Department of Corrections, *Statistical Summary*, 2004.
Voter Registration Protection Act, Senate Bill 488, Chapter 159, P. 2.
_____, *Voting Rights Act of 1965*,
     http://www.smpcollege:com/smpgovt/documents/doc16, 1965.
Williams, M., *Voice, Trust, and Memory*: Princeton, N.J., 1998.

Index